# Islams and Modernities

# Islams and Modernities

## Third Edition

### AZIZ AL-AZMEH

**VERSO**

London • New York

First published by Verso 1993
Second edition published by Verso 1996
This edition published by Verso 2009
© Aziz Al-Azmeh 1993, 1996, 2009
New material © Al-Azmeh 2009

1 3 5 7 9 10 8 6 4 2

**Verso**
UK: 6 Meard Street, London W1F 0EG
US: 20 Jay Street, Suite 1010, Brooklyn, NY 11201
www.versobooks.com

Verso is the imprint of New Left Books

ISBN-13: 978-1-84467-384-1 (hbk)
ISBN-13: 978-1-84467-385-8 (pbk)

**British Library Cataloguing in Publication Data**
A catalogue record for this book is available from the British Library

**Library of Congress Cataloging-in-Publication Data**
A catalog record for this book is available from the Library of Congress

Typeset by Hewer Text UK Ltd, Edinburgh
Printed in the US by Maple Vail

# Contents

# Acknowledgements

The Prologue was delivered at the conference on *L'Islam en Europe – L'Islam vue d'Europe*, held in Aix-en-Provence in November 1992.

Chapter 1 was delivered to a conference held at the Institute of Cultural Studies, University of Århus, in May 1993. It was subsequently discussed with the Race Relations Seminar at the University of Oxford, and at the Institute for Advanced Studies, Berlin. It was revised and expanded for publication.

Different versions and portions of Chapter 2 were delivered at the State Library, Berlin (in association with the Einstein Forum); Jawaharlal Nehru University, New Delhi; the Brecht Forum, New York; and the Humanities Center at the State University of New York, Stony Brook. This article first appeared in *International Sociology*, 16:1, 2001, pp. 75–93.

Chapter 3 is a translation by John Howe of a lecture delivered at the Institut du Monde Arabe, Paris, in February 1993. It was published in *Dirāsāt 'Arabiyya*, 205–6, 1993; the French version is in *Revue d'Etudes Palestiniennes*, 49, 1993.

Chapter 4 is an edited amalgam of two texts: 'Universalism, Democracy, Islam and the Arabs' was presented to a conference at the Collège Internationale de Philosophie in Paris; 'Islam as a Political Category' was prepared for the 15th World Congress of the International Political Science Association in Buenos Aires, July 1991. Parts of it were later discussed at the Near Eastern Studies Department, Princeton University, and in the journal *Esprit*, Paris. I am particularly grateful for comments from Jean Leca, Richard Rorty, Olivier Mongin and from interested audiences.

Chapter 5 was originally a paper delivered to the East–West Philosophers' Conference, Honolulu, Hawaii, in 1989. It was published in Eliot Deutsch, ed., *Culture and Modernity*, University of Hawaii Press 1991. Copyright permission is gratefully acknowledged.

Chapter 6 was, in part, delivered at a conference of the International Institute of Islamic Thought and Civilization, Kuala Lumpur, in August 1994.

Chapter 7 is the text of a public lecture delivered at the Free University, Berlin, in 1988. It was published in *History of Political Thought*, XI, 1990. Copyright permission is gratefully acknowledged.

Chapter 8 was published in Ian R. Netton, ed., *Arabia and the Gulf*, London 1988. Copyright permission is gratefully acknowledged.

Chapter 9 was delivered as an inaugural lecture at the University of Exeter. It was published as a pamphlet by the Department of Arabic and Islamic Studies, University of Exeter.

Parts of Chapter 10 were delivered in a variety of forms over recent years as lectures in a variety of different forums. It has benefited much from keen and diverse audiences at the universities of Georgetown, Columbia, Harvard, California (Berkeley) and Lund; at the Central European University, Budapest, the Nehru Memorial Museum and Library, New Delhi, and the Institutes of Advanced Study in Berlin and Uppsala. An early version was published as a pamphlet under the title *Reconstituting Islam* by the Center for Muslim–Christian Understanding, Georgetown University, in 1995 (a Swedish translation appeared as 'Att rekonstituera islam', in *Tidskrift för mellanösternstudier*, 2, 1998, pp. 4–21). I borrow the term 'postmodern obscurantism' from a conversation in Beirut with Aijaz Ahmad, to whom this article is dedicated. This article first appeared in the *Journal for the Study of Religions and Ideologies*, 5, 2003, pp. 21–47.

قال ابن المقفّع : إياكَ والتتبُّعَ لوحشيِّ الكلام طَمَعاً
في نَيْل البلاغة

Beware of pursuing savage speech in
your quest for eloquence.

Ibn al-Muqaffa‘
(d. 759)

# Preface to the Third Edition

The essays included in this book were written in the late 1980s and early 1990s, largely in response to what I argue are correlative phenomena which mirror each other in many ways that, when I first published these texts, appeared rather incongruous. One of these phenomena was political and social identitarianism, particularly but by no means exclusively Islamic, whose tenor was in increasing degrees, without mincing words, savagely narcissistic. The other consists in claims for post-modernism and post-coloniality, whose temper was one of triumphalist abandon to postures of omniscience. Three years after the publication of the book in 1993, a second, expanded edition appeared, by which time the phenomena discussed in it had already taken on a markedly accentuated and clearer aspect, not least as Islam itself was moving from the margins to the centre of global preoccupations, long before September 2001.

Events subsequent to these editions have in many ways validated the analyses of cultural, social and political conditions and developments offered in this book. If anything, identitarian reclamations have become manifest on a far larger scale, and have indeed become crucial for the workings and for the understanding of the present. Redactions of 'Difference' have been translated into international relations, and 'Culture' has become a geo-strategic disposition. The insistent global salience of culturalism, of political irrationalism and romanticism, of socio-political and cognitive claims for indigenism, of social and political involution east and west, have increasingly taken on the character of indisputable common sense, a *doxa* so insistent and prevalent as to preclude self-reflexivity and to disparage critical reflection. The sense of incongruity gave way progressively to a more robust cognitive certitude, attended by a political vexation that, for all the certitude, was almost incredulous.

xi

Altogether, this and the demand for and discussions around this book justify a third edition, to which two more recent essays are included: one (Chapter 9) charts the global conditions that lend firmer consistency and broader intelligibility to the once seemingly incongruous phenomena discussed, and another (Chapter 2) treats in part the most radical and primitivist form of Islamism, that associated with Osama Bin Laden, who had yet to become a household name, in a more extensive, global ideological and historical context. It is hoped that these extensions of the book's thematic and analytical range will bind its various elements into a firmer texture, with a more deliberate integration of its themes, and account for matters that have become clearer since it was written.

Peculiarly evocative of the common sense–precluding self-reflexivity mentioned above are some incongruous comments with which the appearance of the book was met, and the thrust of some subsequent discussions around it. The book's anti-essentialism was widely welcomed, and, among other things, much was made of the plural forms in its title. *Islams and Modernities* is a book that, with the use of the plural forms, intended both a certain irony – which seems to have escaped some readers – and sought to reinstate and encourage a critical, properly historical analysis of the themes treated. Contrary to much comment, the plural form was not intended to dissolve the categories of Islam and of Modernity into a skittish revelry of Difference, or a ponderous or otherwise distempered redemption of Authenticity. The two are cognitively and politically nihilistic in equal measure, and wholly inconsistent with both the letter and the overall thrust of the book.

*Islams and Modernities* was intended, in contrast, to reaffirm the nominal character of the category 'Islam', and to argue against its use as an explanatory or causal concept. What is most explicitly and clearly intended is not the effacement of general concepts, but the reinstatement of history against culturalist claims for abidance: the dissolution of essentialist categories is intended as the initial condition of historical enquiry, not the terminal datum of an unbounded constructivism. The book argued against transfiguring societies and histories into 'cultures' forever captive to supposedly homogeneous initial conditions. Yet many of the book's readers thought that, with its anti-essentialism, it was postmodernist and post-colonialist, despite the explicit criticism and clear abjuration of these political, cognitive and cultural styles.

Among other things, the analyses proffered indicated that the element of cognitive novelty claimed by postmodernism and post-coloniality is in fact a bundle of themes that are, in historical fact, old and stale yet now luridly reconditioned, and it is as if we see one opaque and sombre doctrine obscured by the garishness of another. They are, true to their actual heritage, far more consequentially deployed by the Right, whose staple they always were, than by the Left. What was once a tragedy is repeated as a grim travesty.

It is in effect precisely culturalism and its correlative postmodernist and postcolonialist cant that betokens the ideological and conceptual hegemony of the Right over the Left, and the domestication of the latter by the former, most especially in Europe and North America since 1989: this date, after all, emblematically marked the resolution of the Cold War in which much of the Left, with its anti-Sovietism, had been often an active if unwitting auxiliary, and signalled concretely a new and vigorous global historical itinerary of capitalism to which the Left has capitulated ideologically. It is unsurprising that post-colonialist and postmodernist triumphalism, and the reduction of Left platforms to *bien pensant* platitudes, came to the fore as an international phenomenon following the crest of US vainglory after 1989, and that it was best elaborated in the United States.

Personal sentiments apart, what we have is clearly an objective complicity, in which postures of correctness, highly mannered or unmannerly as the case might be – and ultimately apolitical – are substituted for political ideology in the strong sense, now dismissed as 'grand narratives'. In many ways, it seems fair to say that persons such as Bernard-Henri Lévy or Christopher Hitchens represent the more consequent and consistent representatives of the European Left, which has always had a strong seam of anti-Communism, the more *zeitgemäss*; they are the more consequently political as they draw concrete conclusions from correct postures in terms of the present balance of power, reduced to the capacity for brute force. In the South, the effortless drift of the Left, individuals, organized groups, and even states, towards populism and communalism, towards neo-liberalism, or a combination of both, seems unstoppable.

What *Islams and Modernities* sought to approach was logico-historical concreteness, on the assumption that Difference is not boundless, and that it is primarily an element in a structured relation: political by nature, not a metaphysical substance. Difference, the book claims, is performative, not substantive. It forms part of a process of combined and uneven development, whose governing parameters are those of modernity regarded as an objective historical dynamic, a dynamic that is cognitively accessible. Modernities do not and cannot free any modern history from bondage to Modernity.

Finally, the book now being reissued seeks to appeal not to Muslim subjectivities or voices, but critically to inracinate these in their real conditions, thus, it is hoped, removing claims to exceptionalism and incommensurability that are now regularly witnessed in the almost self-parodic patterning of some Muslims by themselves, and their almost caricatural patterning by outsiders. The word 'modernities' that appears in the title is not intended to remove the structured, integrative historical process that modernity is, as might be suggested by the pragmatic thrust, under present conditions, of the notion of 'multiple modernities'. In effect, this notion seems to remove the categorical salience of modernity, in a mood of anti-modernism with egalitarian postures, some of which are disingenuous. It seems that this multiplication is in effect a profound homage to culturalism, in a move that can imply an unqualified devolution, effacing a concept by rhetorical deflation.

In this book, by contrast, modernity is rather, in a modernist mode, intended to reaffirm both the historicity and universality of phenomena discussed, including aspects of the histories of Islam, all the while, unlike the latter, retaining its explanatory force as the overall description of a global historical dynamic now more than two centuries old. This book is offered yet again in order to recalibrate the terms of debate in an environment stiflingly anti-modernist, often in the name of modernism; it seeks to rehabilitate critical thought besieged by the tenebrous solemnities of one or other magus of postmodernism – a Heidegger or a Gadamer. It betokens a refusal to capitulate to incongruity, to yield on reason and public responsibility in favour of reticence, however translucent, or to give way to silence, however lucid.

The tradition of the dead generations weighs like a nightmare on the minds of the living. And, just when they appear to be engaged in the revolutionary transformation of themselves and their material surroundings, in the creation of something that does not yet exist, precisely in such epochs of revolutionary crisis they timidly conjure up the spirits of the past to help them; they borrow their names, slogans and costumes so as to stage the new world-historical scene in this venerable disguise and borrowed language. Luther put on the mask of the apostle Paul; the Revolution of 1789–1814 draped itself alternately as the Roman republic and the Roman empire . . . Cromwell and the English people had borrowed for their bourgeois revolution the language, passions and illusions of the Old Testament. When the actual goal had been reached . . . Locke drove out Habakkuk.

Thus wrote Karl Marx on historical necromancy in an age earlier than ours and with different concerns, motifs and tropes which, their tragic historical consequences notwithstanding, are being repeated in today's culturalism.

The contrast between Locke and Habakkuk is as alive today as it was in centuries past, although the past two decades have seen the latter being ferried ahead of the former. The legacy of Marx, not least the forensic historical and cultural criticism it exemplarily renders possible, beyond the flippancies of deconstruction, transcends the one and the other conceptually, and assimilates their later history. Being beyond both Islams and modernities, and being the most accomplished manifestation of modernity itself, it subordinates them both – history and mystification alike – to historical reason, and makes a book such as this possible.

One final comment is in order, in view of the systemic crisis of neoliberal capitalism at the time of writing (mid-October 2008). I think it will be clear from this book that post-colonial discourse, and postmodernism in general, mirror the regimes of deregulation in place since 1989, extending them to the deregulation of culture and the deregulation of state functions; 'hybridity', which more authentic voices, much praised in post-colonial discourse, would take for the evil of miscegenation, devolves into consumer choice for those capable of choice and of consumption, much as does fusion cuisine. The deregulation of culture is clearly designed to free society, especially the arcadia of authenticity, of the presumptions of 'grand narratives' of development and advancement, of cultural development and advancement, of Jacobin pertness. Given this raging crisis, it would be interesting to see how these modes of discourse would fare once their material base has been shaken, and once it becomes clear that *The Communist Manifesto* is not so much a spectral presence haunting the minds of recalcitrants, but rather a source of enlightenment. Post-colonialist theorists, even the *recherché fakirs* among them, may choose to be so enlightened.

# PROLOGUE

# Muslim 'Culture' and the European Tribe

Un Parisien est tout surpris quand on lui dit que les Hottentots font couper à leurs enfants mâles un testicule. Les Hottentots sont peut-être surpris que les Parisiens en gardent les deux.

Voltaire

The essays assembled in this book derive from the contention that there are as many Islams as there are situations that sustain it. European Islam in its various forms and places is no exception. It is perhaps a measure of the potency of the imaginary Islam as it is conceived in mediatic representation and according to the spontaneous philosophy of 'experts', academics included, that this elementary contention needs to be defended at a time like ours. We can surely assume that among the permanent acquisitions of the social and human sciences is the realization that ideological and other forms of collective representation are unthinkable without internal change and structural bearing. And it is a fact that this acquisition is almost invariably put to use in the study of contemporary ideologies, mass movements and other phenomena of European histories and realities. But it is not generally put to use regarding *phenomena islamica*, which are regarded as generically closed, utterly exotic, repellently mysterious, utterly exceptionalist.

I do not wish to elaborate much on this pervasive and unflinching misrecognition, although I suggest, in this and in subsequent essays, many factors that make it prevalent. For now, I am commenting on the recent transition, most specifically in Britain, from structural considerations of immigration to a culturalist notion of ethnic diversity which has come to predominate in the past two decades and which was consecrated by the Rushdie affair. There are definite structural foundations for this transition in the demotic consciousness, and there is little mystery in this that cannot be unravelled with reference to elementary notions of

1

ideology, in which relations of subordination and domination are sublimated,[1] so that a fetishism of 'culture' becomes a part of the social imaginary of advanced capitalism and its new divisions of labour on the international scale. Thus, and in the first instance, primary importance must be attributed to the impossibility of socio-economic assimilation experienced by second-generation immigrants born in situations of urban degradation and into marginal, declining and unskilled industry, at a time of increasing state indifference and hostility coupled with racism in the very capillaries of the 'host society'.[2] Added to this are pressures that push Asian Muslim (and other) shopkeepers to cater for the poorest, as slum landlords and purveyors of cheap goods, and thus take on the classic features of a middleman minority confronted with racist reactions.[3] The work of the ethnic entrepreneur, operating through kinship networks which provide the basis for domestic commodity production as well as for the sweatshop, is a classic condition conducive to social involution,[4] and the formation of social as well as geographical ghettos. Finally, modern communications have enhanced the sense of immigrant deracination by facilitating the illusion of truth to the realities of the country of origin, a sense reinforced by the reality, made possible by increasing globalization, of transnational economic and social networks which form a central part of immigrant life.

Thus structural and spatial segregation and social involution and ghetto formation lie at the basis of the culturalism that is now becoming the prevalent mode of discourse as the non-European presence in Europe, most particularly of Muslims who, for a host of reasons not connected with historical or social reality, are assumed to form a community by virtue of sharing a religion which, peculiarly, has been dubbed a 'culture'. The reader will note that concrete material adduced in support of my arguments here concerns exclusively British Muslims of Pakistani origin, and it is indeed with them that the following paragraphs are chiefly concerned. Like other groups, British Muslims of Pakistani origin constitute a specific configuration of socio-economic locations. Yet generalizations about social groups in terms of religion in order to describe their specificities and to underpin factors that overdetermine their socio-economic and ideological positions have become habitual, although they are irresponsible, for the forces that make for social involution are not religious;[5] religious difference underwrites and does not overdetermine social exclusivism. The hyper-Islamization of collectivities of Muslim origin has accompanied hardening tendencies to social involution premised on structural features of communities of Muslim origin. This representation, which assumes a homogeneity overriding differences between those of rural and of urban origin, rich and poor, educated and illiterate, is by no means a reflection of social reality, which is one of stunning diversity.

Some Britons of Pakistani origin, like the Kashmiris of Mirpuri origin, who predominate in Bradford, are of rural origin with hardly any social awareness of city life even in Pakistan itself. Their culture is above all rural, with Muslim religious elements incorporated within this primary determination – but Muslim religious elements of a mystical and magical character, unconnected to the legalism of the puritanical Islam of their advocates and spokesmen. Their rural origin explains the tendency to be far more socially conservative on matters such as girls' education than Indian Muslims, for instance, who belong to a different 'culture' born of different geographical, social and educational imperatives.[6] Facts such as the reasonable integration of wealthier Pakistanis within their class in Britain, the regional conditions of origin and socio-economic diversities among the Pakistanis of Britain (not to speak of British Muslims generally – certainly not a corporate group)[7] are often overlooked. Also habitually ignored are the facts of class division among Pakistanis, with the religious authorities leading the representation of the poorer sections as far back as the late 1970s,[8] and the fact that there were forces for integration as well as for involution among British citizens of Pakistani origin before the Rushdie affair, including generous openness to knowledge, no matter how reserved, of Christianity and of the ambient society.[9] In the same vein of mystification, the considerable alienation of young Pakistanis, especially girls, from their background is ignored.[10] Instead, emphasis is exclusively laid on the undeniable forces for involution and ghettoization. Features observable and ascendant since 1989 are projected back into an indistinct, though very proximate past.

Of these features one might cite many indices. Some are connected with kinship networks,[11] which, among Pakistanis as others, are increasingly international and encourage life in a fantasy of rootedness. Others are newer. An interview with a marriage bureau owner who serves the British Pakistani community indicates a growing tendency for men in Britain to seek wives from Pakistan rather than from British-bred Pakistani women, and of the former they are choosing increasingly younger and more cloistered girls of more conservative outlook.[12] Other features are the proliferation of exclusivist Muslim organizations, like Young Muslims' annual fairs, Muslim fun-fairs, Muslim medical advisory services, not to speak of an unelected Muslim parliament. With the Rushdie affair, a number of Muslim internationalist infrastructures of an educational, welfare and propaganda nature (beholden to networks controlled by Iran, Saudi Arabia and the Pakistani *jamaat-i islam-i*) were put into high gear and conjured up the notion of an 'Islamic community' as a distinctive and identifiable entity. But it must not be assumed that these and cognate phenomena are in any sort of continuity, direct or indirect, with the Muslim 'culture' of origin, for there is no such culture of origin, and the trans-Islamism we witness is highly recherché, and specific to the present and the very recent past, as well as to Britain and to political interests articulated here in the name of Islam.

Thus the presumptions of Muslim cultural homogeneity and continuity do not correspond to social reality. Muslim reality in Britain is, rather, composed of many realities, some structural, some organizational and institutional, but which are overall highly fragmentary.[13] Nevertheless, abstracted from its socio-economic bearings, European Islam, and Islam *tout court*, has been represented as a cohesive, homogeneous and invariant force, indeed an otherness so radical that it is possible to speak of it as a historical enemy, much in the same way as communism was addressed in some circles.[14] It is represented as a repellent exoticism by mass psychological mechanisms very like those involved in anti-Semitism.[15] Yet the median discourse on Islam in Britain as in Europe is not predominantly or always overtly racist or quasi-racist. What we have is a culturalist differentialism; we are presented with supposed differences of 'culture' within a discourse which can be either xenophile or xenophobic:[16] both are premised on irreducible and impermeable difference.

Now culture, like nature, is one of the most difficult notions to use in the social sciences. This difficulty is compounded by the fact that its increasingly pervasive and irresponsible use has come to indicate little beyond an aesthetic of otherness, and more generally a negative aesthetic of otherness, which invigilates ideological processes that oversee the constitution of specific identities under specific conditions of socio-economic confinement, buttressed by what is known, in the 'host' society, as multiculturalism.

The origins of this exclusivist and differentialist notion of culture are quite straightforward. A culturalist relativism *avant la lettre* was available in the repertory of European social thought from the time of Romanticism in the late eighteenth and early nineteenth centuries and was counterposed to the universalist notions of civilization – 'Politically, as

4

so often in this period, it veered between radicalism and reaction and very often, in the confusion of major social change, fused elements of both'.[17] Thus differentialist culturalism comprehends both a libertarian streak and a segregationism, today as well as in its places of origin, as mirror images, with anti-racist xenophilia mirroring racist xenophobia, or indeed like racist xenophobia which wants 'cultures' to coexist in mere spatiality without interpenetrating. The trajectory of this notion of 'culture', in the nineteenth century, was one in the course of which it was elaborated as racism along biologistic lines,[18] and the irrationalist vitalism of this notion is still its most active constituent. In the course of the past two decades, three displacements affected this notion: race became ethnicity, then culture; normative hierarchy and inequality gave way to representation in terms of difference; and xenophobia was in many circles replaced by xenophilia.[19] Thus we find fused in racist and anti-racist discourse alike the concept of non-transmissible lifestyles, a concept garnered by the race relations industry, the Labour Party and professional ethnology deriving from the heritage of the German Romantic historical school and from British functionalist anthropology alike.[20]

It is irrelevant to the force of this differentialist culturalism that it is tied to a specific vantage point in both time and place. This is a cosmopolite post-imperial (but not necessarily post-imperialist) North with a particular grid of misrecognition to which is commonly applied the cliché 'postmodernism'.[21] This is a fictitious sense of novelty and of radical diversity primed to become automatically operational as a means of ideological and representational uniformization whenever collective representations of global and local social and political conflict are called forth.[22] It is a shibboleth which reduces realities to Reality, expressed in bytes, and therefore amenable to manipulation; in other words, a recent from of the ideological production which had previously been termed 'the end of ideology'.

Culturalist differentialism is born equally in a situation of a radical notion of ascriptive individualism, a social condition which is projected on to a metaphysical screen describing universal conditions. And finally, in Britain, this condition is equally engendered by a tradition, become a knee-jerk policy of husbanding internal and external affairs, of politico-ethnic and politico-cultural categorization which, in the past, resulted in the catastrophic divisions of India, Palestine and Ireland, and which today results in regarding as natural – therefore not worth the effort of resistance – both the ghettoization of Britain and 'ethnic cleansing' in the Balkans.

This culturalist differentialism nevertheless, and despite the individualistic liberalism of its proponents, exists in 'a vicious circle of complicity' with xenophobic racism.[23] It has in Britain completely internalized the Powellite notions about nations or other collectivities being predetermined boundaries of sympathy, over-determined by an instinctivism[24] which does not need to present itself necessarily in terms of racial hatred: all it requires is a 'discursive deracialization' underpinned by exclusivism and 'arguments from genuine fears' premised on the supposed authority of 'common sense'.[25]

Like racism, culturalist differentialism is an essentialist perceptive system premised on a notion of a pregiven 'culture' which, like race, has no sociological definition. Culture is here an obscure term coined to schematize without precision an indeterminate reality.[26] Indeed, it is the enormous advantage of this notion that it is put forward to indicate sheer difference, for in this sense it can not be disproved because it is tautological: chicken tandoori is not roast chicken; a black headscarf is not a fashion accessory; Muslim prayer is not a High Church Christmas mass.[27] In all, tokens of a banal nature are taken up and affirmed as tokens – or stigmata – of difference, and differences elevated to Difference based in an absolutization of heritage which, although cultural, is attributed to a state of nature in which cultures subsist, according to this discourse.[28]

In the chapters that follow, the reader will find ample elements of a discourse on 'cultures' of an Islamic name that contextualizes them into the flow of historical and social forces, and thus deculturalizes and demystifies them. What remains to be done here is symptomatically and briefly to examine some aspects of another actor in this 'vicious circle of complicity', namely, the British Muslim advocates of culturalist Islamism.

There is no doubt that British Muslims, most particularly those of Pakistani and, to a somewhat lesser extent, of Bengali origin, are witnessing a heightened sense of religiosity, albeit against a background of Bengali adherence to secular nationalist rather than to religious political advocacy.[29] Until recently, religiosity was connected with upward social mobility among the poorest elements, and correlated to intra-communal competition.[30] The Rushdie affair accelerated this tendency and made public a number of sentiments and stigmata which have become part of public mythology and hence have taken on autonomous trajectories[31] in the construction of inter-communalist myths, and thus in the generation of putative identities. Initially disembodied from social practice, religious vision and ritual observance under conditions of migration to Europe takes on a certain autonomy from social processes and prescribes an autonomist notion of the religious ego and a body of allied prescriptions.[32] It also proffers a fetishism of the collective self as a socio-political imperative.

Thus Islamic 'culture' takes on the aspect of a psychodrama, and the serious business of inventing a culture begins, primarily by the conjuration and proclamation of tokens (stigmata to others) of exoticism, particularly ones which give a pronounced visual edge to the boundaries of exclusion/inclusion. Basic and most plastic among these are dressing up, and exhibitionistic piety, with dramaturgical direction provided by such political or quasi-political organizations as are poised to take over this new political constituency, with the full complicity of the xenophile/xenophobic 'host culture', the one in the name of 'multiculturalism', the other with an apartheitic intent closer in spirit to the advocates of this exclusivism themselves. A past is invented, sensibilities discovered. It therefore becomes possible to assert, for instance, that Rushdie's use of the now infamous 'Mahound' is provocative,[33] although there is no tradition of awareness of this name in either medieval or modern Islam, and knowledge of this name was, until 1989, the preserve of a handful of Western antiquarians, who might well and justifiably object that it is far more complex than opponents of Rushdie imagine. Yet 'Mahound' is given the status of 'popular' knowledge quite artificially. Suddenly, we hear of 'an authentically Islamic temper' and of what constitutes a 'real Muslim'.[34] We hear of 'cultural treason' against Muslims[35] and opponents of this phantasmagoric trend, like the present author, are dismissed as 'Christian' because they dispute the conjurations of the Islamist party. We also encounter positions of sanctimonious sentimentalism as 'Muslim sensibility' without further qualification, and are told of arcadian scenes of spring cleaning in Damascus by 'Muslim housewives',[36] although Christian Damascene households are by no means less fastidious about cleanliness – and indeed Damascene Muslim micro-sociological lore, to which I can testify at first hand, regards Christian housewives as rather more fastidious than Muslims, and their houses and streets somewhat neater. An ethnographic account tells of women in Pakistani households in Oxford supervising children reading in the back room – reading the Koran only is mentioned, not homework.[37] It also tells of Mughal families taking pride in their descent from Muslim conquerors, with too much accent on religion and too little on nobility[38] – the proper Muslim nobility consists of *sayyids*,

7

not Mughals, whose title to nobility is conquest and statehood. Thus blanks in personal sanctimoniousness or naïve research are filled with fanciful material weighted towards misrecognizing reality as a constituent in the Islamist psychodrama. And the primary victim, Salman Rushdie himself, edging towards compromise at a particular moment, recast his intellectual genealogy in such a way that the Arabian Nights, the influence of which he professes, became 'Islamic' literature.[39]

A sentimentalist view of a spurious, unsullied reality prior to the corruption of the present, or of such a fantastic reality continuing in the present, is then made into the main constituent of a political and social programme, as subsequent chapters of this book will indicate in some detail. This spurious prior reality is termed 'culture'. It is neither 'real' nor old, but is a *recherché* cluster of modes of visible behaviour which are said by certain Islamist authorities to represent the 'true prior reality' – one that British Pakistani Muslims had never known until recently, for it is not only traditions that are invented, but also collective memories. The most notable title under which this politics of nostalgia for an imagined past is officiated is of course the 'application' of Islamic law: a law which was never a code that could be 'applied', as the Appendix to this chapter indicates. This 'law' is supposed to distinguish a *genre de vie* which is as impermeable as it is intransitive, and therefore deserving of the title 'culture'. It is thus that the politics of nostalgia imagines a past, or a prior reality, conjures an affection for a past that never was, and turns this sentimentalist imperative into a programme to be imposed on the social and political realities of today.

All in all, therefore, we have, in the play of this psychodrama, an efflorescence of fantastic genealogies and explanations, all premised on xenophobic/xenophile differentialism, from the flirtations of the willing Beauty and the eager Beast (such as the contributions of John Berger and David Caute to the Rushdie affair), through to the shrill xenophobia of a Fay Weldon or Anthony Burgess, across to the platitudinous liberalism of the median discourse of differentialism.

But there is more than psychodrama, self-parody and caricature in this explosion of the fantasy. For we have the steady accumulation of pressure points on the education system (with a view to creating Muslim schools where girls could be properly socialized) and elsewhere with a view to detaching British Muslims, especially Asians and most particularly Pakistanis, from the mainstream of modern life, and their resocialization within a new culture of exclusivism and xenophobia. This is the impact of the calls for Muslim communalist institutions,[40] with a subculture in the process of invention. Such, for instance, is the case of the Yummies (young, upwardly mobile Muslims), who stand against non-liberal liberalism, who dress sharply in clothes to pray and play in, who cloister together in home-centred communities, immune from the vices of the ambient society, but nevertheless sharing house-work.[41]

But British Muslims are perhaps no more than a case in point in the Europe of the Lombard League, of Jean-Marie Le Pen, of minuscule regionalism. Muslim differentialist discourse, a counter-racism or a racism in reverse, would seem appropriate in a Britain where cultural-ist differentialism has, as mentioned, fully internalized the Powellite conception of history as the savage play of ascriptive sympathies and antipathies, in which the 'natural' condition of groups of different ori-gins is one in which they are wholly apart, and in which any attempt to mix them would render conflict inevitable. Such is perhaps natural in a Europe that regards itself as tribal territory with precise border controls, in which nations (for some sections of their members) regard themselves as tribes, all ranged above one another according to a tribu-tary model of subalternity. Such, in an age of dubious postmodernity, is the consequence of 'the new Cartesianism of the irrational'.[42] And such is the natural outcome of a situation in Croatia and Serbia succinctly described by an outstanding columnist, a situation which is not alien to Western Europe except in sheer density and extent – but intensity is by definition shifting and conjunctural, and it is not clear to what extent the West European body politic is systemically immune to this:

> Miraculous Virgins make their scheduled appearance. Lurid posters show shafts of light touching the pommels of mysterious swords, or blazoning the talons of absurd but vicious two-headed eagles. More than a million Serbs attend a frenzied rally, on the battle site of Kos-ovo, where their forebears were humiliated *in 1389*, and hear former Communists rave in accents of wounded tribalism. Ancient insignias, totems, feudal coats of arms, talismans, oaths, rituals, icons and rega-lia jostle to take the field. A society long sunk in political stagnation, but nevertheless across the threshold of modernity, is convulsed: puk-ing up great rancid chunks of undigested barbarism.[43]

Tribalism, xenophilia, xenophobia and Islamist exclusivism alike are premised on a very classical trope of modern European irrationalist political and social thought (hence its attractiveness to postmodernism)

– right-wing Romanticism,[44] with the attendant organicism of its notions of history, the corporatism of its notion of society, and the voluntarism of its notion of political action. These matters will be discussed in chapters 1 and 3.

## Appendix: Blasphemy and the Character of Islamic Law

When in 1608, King James asked the jurist and parliamentarian Sir Edward Coke why it was that law could not be interpreted by any intelligent man in the light of reason, Sir Edward resorted to an argument for the technical nature of legal reason:

> True it is that God has endowed Your Majesty with excellent science, and great endowments of nature; but Your Majesty is not learned in the law of this your realm of England, and causes which concern the life, or inheritance, or goods, of fortune of your subjects, are not to be decided by natural reason, but by the artificial reason and judgement of the law, which law is an art which requires long study and experience before that a man can attain to the cognizance of it.

A response of the same nature could be given by any jurist with technical competence in the field of Islamic law to the claims made for this law by advocates of Islamist political ideologies. These advocates claim to speak for a univocal body of legislation which is not grounded in the vast historical experience of Muslims. They also speak in terms of explicit and demonstrable commands deriving from scriptural statements without the mediation of legal reason. Finally, they give the impression, and sometimes make the utopian presumption, of a universal extraterritoriality which has no grounds in Islamic scriptures or in the historical experience of Muslims.

This may not be surprising. This advocacy is made by ideologues with at best a rudimentary knowledge of Muslim scriptures. In the case of divines with undisputed knowledge of Islamic scripture and legal texts, it arises from the suspension of such knowledge in favour of immediate ideological and political purposes. It is unfortunate that an impression of ferocious crudity and simplicity is being given of Islamic law, an impression which is certainly undeserved by the vast corpus of writings on law and legal methodology (deontic logic, analogical connections, rhetorical methods, philological and lexical procedures) stretching over centuries and vast expanses of territory, the ensemble of which is Islamic law.

The first characteristic feature of Islamic law which ought to be indicated as a corrective concerns its technical nature. Islamic law is highly technical, indeed arcane, to those who have not sought properly to tackle its vast body of literature. Some of the great jurists such as Sarakhsī, the greatest figure in the Hanafite school to which the vast majority of Indian Subcontinent Muslims adhere (along with Afghans, Turks and the Arabs of Syria and Iraq), went to great lengths to demonstrate that his notions and procedures are so technical that they have none but a most tangential connection with ethical or dogmatic considerations.[45] The divine origin of some of the utterances which enter the conveyor belt of legal reason – that is, the text of the Koran – is technically irrelevant to their legal aspect. Infractions of law are punishable in this world, infractions of divine purpose in the next. This must be the first matter to bear in mind today, when ignorance and politics are wilfully confusing Islamic law with the requirements of Islamist ideology.

The second point concerns legal innovation. Contrary to political and ideological pretensions, the historical reality of the practice of Islamic law has been one of wide latitude in opinions over specific points of law (the *ikhtilāf*). The corollary of this, quite naturally, is the mutability of this law in the context of changing circumstances, a mutability which does not accord with the utopian archaism of Islamist politics. And indeed, the reform of Islamic law over the past century has instituted a condition of 'absolute discretion' (*ijtihād mu laq*) based on the reinterpretation of scriptural and other foundation texts, in addition to what Islamic legal theory designates as the 'auxiliary' sources of law: custom, public interest and equity. The prevalent trend in Muslim law reform in the present century has indeed been an attempt to generalize the classical precepts in such a manner as to have them merge with a notion of natural law; such has been the achievement of the great reformer Mu ammad Abduh. In theoretical terms, Muslim jurists (though not the Shi'a) have always adopted a highly sceptical view of the finality of their judgements; hence the readiness mutually to recognize views that may be contradictory. It is recognized – though this recognition is not shared by Islamist ideologues – that it is against natural justice and natural law (which accords with divine will) to foist ordinances of relevance to the seventh century upon the twentieth.

Moreover, Islamic law is not a code. This is why the frequently heard call for its 'application' is meaningless, most particularly when calls are made for the application of *sharīa* – this last term does not designate law, but is a general term designating good order, much like *nomos* or *dharma.* Islamic law is a repertoire of precedents, cases and general principles, along with a body of well-developed hermeneutical and paralogical techniques. In certain respects, it resembles English law quite strongly; one can study these connections (as with Germanic law) in the seminal work of the Arab world's premier jurist of this century, A. Sanhury,[46] and of his French associates, Edouard Lambert, Linant de Bellefonds and others. This characteristic nature of Islamic law reinforces its legal latitudinarianism, a fact which explains how it emerged and reigned successfully as one of the great legal systems of the world over more than twelve centuries in very different parts of the globe. Little wonder, then, that Islamic law has a predominantly objectivist character, as Sanhury and his associates have shown. This (in marked contrast to French law) reinforces its technical nature and further accentuates its being the preserve of fully trained jurists.

One final point must be mentioned. Islamic law as a corpus is predominantly private: it treats of obligation, contract, personal status (including succession) and other aspects of secular life. These are termed by Islamic jurists *uqūq al-'ibād*, the rights of persons. A much smaller corpus of public law exists under the rubric *uqūq Allāh*, the rights of God. These concern the obligations incumbent upon properly constituted Islamic polities; they are redundant in the absence of such a polity and have no extraterritorial competence, and a Muslim *in partibus infidelium is a musta'min* 'under safe conduct', obliged to follow the laws of his or her country of residence. Substantively, the rights of God concern protecting and maintaining the Muslim body politic through international relations both martial and pacific, and through invigilating its internal integrity by the creation of a *Rechtsstaat* and the suppression of ideological sedition – that is, unbelief, apostasy and the very difficult notion of blasphemy.

Apostasy as a legal notion was questioned in the Middle Ages, abolished in Ottoman territories before the middle of the nineteenth century, and regarded by the famous Muslim reformer of the present century, Mu ammad Rashīd Ri ā, as a political matter concerning the seventh century and, as such, of no consequence to the present age; indeed, the Koran states quite unequivocally that there should be no compulsion in matters of religion (*la ikrāha fid-dīn*). Unbelief and blasphemy have had different meanings and accents over the historical experience of Muslims, although there does exist a hard core of dogmas which are universally held, regardless of their historical justification; all traditions harden in this manner. Additionally, all traditions vary, over time and place, in the severity and in the systematic character with which unbelief and dogmatic deviance are pursued. Likewise, most traditions reach a point where doctrinal purity and univocality become redundant. Such is the case with those parts of the world with Muslim majorities, especially in the Arab world, except for subcultural pockets and among political minorities which espouse a fundamentalist primitivism entirely inattentive to the historical experience of Muslims and to the historical character of their law. Islam has, moreover, never had a central authority which determines rectitude and which has exclusive title to the legitimacy which renders its territories the Abode of Islam, and thus the location of the practice of the Islamic legal system. This is especially so in modern times, when the Rights of Persons have been partly incorporated into the civil codes of such countries as Egypt, Syria and Iraq (all the achievements of Sanhury), but according to modern legal principles. What was not thus incorporated has been forgotten – and even such as was codified has lost its 'Islamic' and taken on an entirely civil character. The Rights of God, on the other hand, though rarely abolished in any explicit manner, have been left in abeyance and relegated for exaction in the next world.

Thus any consideration of the question of blasphemy or of heresy, be it that of Mr Rushdie or of others, must first face the historical irrelevance of his task, and must also be cognizant of its technical impossibility in the very terms of the Islamic legal corpus and system themselves. Calls for the 'application of Islamic law' have no connection with the Muslim legal tradition built upon multivocality, technical competence and the existence of an executive political authority which controls the legal system. It is a political slogan, not a return to a past reality.

## Notes

1. Veronique de Rudder, 'L'Obstacle culturel: la différence et la distance', *L'Homme et la société*, January 1986, pp. 39, 45. Gerd Baumann's *Contesting Culture. Discourses of Identity in Multi-ethnic London* (Cambridge, 1996) alas came to my attention too late for me to make use of its excellent detailed ethnography and general considerations on the current conceptions of 'culture'.

2. See, among many others, ibid., p. 29; Verity Saifullah Khan, 'The Pakistanis: Mirpuri Villagers at Home and in Bradford', in James L. Watson, ed., *Between Two Cultures: Migrants and Minorities in Britain*, Oxford 1977, pp. 75–6, 80, 86 and passim; Tariq Modood, 'British Asian Muslims and the Rushdie affair', *The Political Quarterly*, 6/1–2, 1990, pp. 145 and passim.

3. Pnina Werbner, 'Shattered Bridges: The Dialectics of Progress and Alienation among British Muslims', *New Community*, 17, 1991, pp. 342–3.

4. Haleh Afshar, 'Gender Roles and the "Moral Economy of Kin" among Pakistani Women in West Yorkshire', *New Community*, 15, 1989, pp.211–26.

5. Saifullah Khan, 'The Pakistanis', pp. 58, 74, 80, 86.

6. Daniele Joly, 'The Opinions of Mirpuri Parents in Saltley, Birmingham, about their Children's Schooling', Centre for the Study of Islam and Muslim–Christian Relations, Birmingham, *Research Papers – Muslims in Europe*, no. 23, September 1984, pp. 20–21.

7. For instance, Werbner, 'Shattered Bridges', pp. 342–3.

8. Pnina Werbner, 'Ritual and Social Networks. A Study of Pakistani Immigrants in Manchester', unpublished PhD thesis, Manchester University, 1979, pp. 338–9.

9. Werbner, 'Shattered Bridges', pp. 339 and passim; Paul Bhai, 'Image of Christian Life among Muslim Residents – A Study of Birmingham', unpublished dissertation for the Certificate in the Study of Islam, Centre for the Study of Islam and Muslim–Christian Relations, Birmingham, 1979, passim.

10. R. Sharif, 'Interviews with Young Muslim Women of Pakistani Origin', Centre for the Study of Islam and Muslim–Christian Relations, Birmingham, *Research Papers – Muslims in Europe*, no. 27, 1985, pp. 11, 14 and passim.

11. Saifullah Khan, 'The Pakistanis', pp. 58, 74 and passim.

12. *Muslim News*, 23 March 1990; Modood, 'British Asian Muslims', p.147.

13. Modood, 'British Asian Muslims'; Jørgen Nielsen, 'A Muslim Agenda for Britain: Some Reflections', *New Community*, 17, 1991, especially p. 472.

14. An example of this vulgar discourse is Daniel Pipes, *The Rushdie Affair. The Novel, the Ayatollah, and the West*, New York 1990, pp. 214ff.; and see Aziz Al-Azmeh, 'The Middle East and Islam: A Ventriloquial Terrorism', in *Third World Affairs, 1988*, London 1988, pp. 23ff.

15. T. Adorno in Theodor Adorno et al., *The Authoritarian Personality*, New York 1950, ch. XIX.

16. On differentialism, see in general Pierre-André Taguieff, *La Force du préjugé. Essai sur le racisme et ses doubles*, Paris 1987.

17. Raymond Williams, *Keywords*, London 1976, s.v. 'Culture'.

18. Colette Guillaumin, *L'Idéologie raciste. Genèse et langage actuelle*, Paris and The Hague 1972, ch. 1.

19. Taguieff, *La Force du préjugé*, p. 14.

20. Claude Lévi-Strauss, *A View from Afar*, transl. J. Neugroschel and P. Hoss, Harmondsworth 1987, p. 26.

21. On this phenomenon, the reader is referred to Alex Callinicos, *Against Postmodernism*, Cambridge 1989; David Harvey, *The Condition of Postmodernity*, Oxford 1989; and Fredric Jameson, *Postmodernism, or, the Cultural Logic of Late Capitalism*, London 1991.

22. See Christopher Norris, *Uncritical Theory. Postmodernism, Intellectuals, and the Gulf War*, London 1992.

23. Taguieff, *La Force du préjugé*, pp. 16, 43, 416.

24. Martin Barker, *The New Racism: Conservatives and the Ideology of the Tribe*, London 1981, pp. 14ff., 97, and chs 3 and 4 passim.

25. Frank Reeves, *British Racial Discourse: A Study of British Political Discourse about Race and Race-Related Matters*, Cambridge 1983.

26. Guillaumin, *L'Idéologie raciste*, pp. 2, 13; Taguieff, *La Force du préjugé*, pp. 19ff.

27. Cf. de Rudder, 'L'Obstacle culturel', pp. 32–3.

28. Cf. Taguieff, *La Force du préjugé*, pp. 15–16; Etienne Balibar in E. Balibar and E. Wallerstein, *Race, Nation, Class: Ambiguous Identities*, London 1991, pp. 17–18, 21–2, 57.

29. See especially, Stephen William Barton, *The Bengali Muslims of Bradford*, Leeds 1986, pp. 184–5.

30. Werbner, 'Ritual and Social Networks', pp. xxv, 60ff, 357.

31. Werbner, 'Shattered Bridges', pp 344–5.

32. Werner Schiffauer, 'Migration and Religiousness', in T. Gerholm and Y.G. Lithman, eds, *The New Islamic Presence in Western Europe*, London and New York 1988, pp. 151–2,155.

33. Malise Ruthven, *The Satanic Affair*, London 1990, p. 36.

34. For instance Shabbir Akhtar, *Be Careful with Muhammad*, London 1989, p. 7 and passim.

35. Ali Mazrui, in L. Appignanesi and S. Maitland, eds, *The Rushdie File*, London 1989, pp. 221–2.

36. Rana Kabbani, *Letter to Christendom*, London 1989, pp. ix, 19–20, 35, 37 and passim.

37. Alison Shaw, *A Pakistani Community in Britain*, Oxford 1988, p. 64.

38. Ibid., p. 93.

39. Interview in *The Guardian*, 17 January 1991.

40. See particularly the sweet reasonableness of Modood, 'British Asian Muslims', passim.

41. *Muslim Wise*, January 1990, pp. 14–15.

42. Umberto Eco, *Travels in Hyperreality*, transl. W. Weaver, London 1987, p. 129.

43. Christopher Hitchens, 'Appointment in Sarajevo', *The Nation*, 14 September 1992, p. 236.

44. Romanticism was a central feature of Western political discourse in the past 200 years, but is very little recognized and imperfectly known, and is usually and quite erroneously regarded as marginal in studies of Western political thought. See the recent overview of Michael Löwy and Robert Sayre, *Révolte et méloncholie. Le romantisme à contre-courant de la modernité*, Paris 1992, chs 1 and 2. The authors of this rather traditional history of ideas are, without justification, keen to save Romanticism from fascism and the religious right, which they classify as 'reactionary modernism' (pp. 93ff, 237). This gloss is contrary to interpretations made in this book, particularly in ch. 3.

Tzvetan Todorov's *On Human Diversity: Nationalism, Racism, and Exoticism in French Thought* (transl. C. Porter, Cambridge, MA, 1993) alas only came to my attention after this book had gone to press. But I should like to signal the meticulous detail with which Todorov treats the possible transformations of essentialist relativism (chs 2 and 3 passim, especially pp. 219ff) and the ease with which racism can give way to culturalism (pp. 156–7).

45. See Baber Johansen, 'Die Sündige, gesunde Amme. Moral und gesetzliche Bestimmung ( ukm) im islamischen Recht', *Die Welt des Islams*, 28, 1988, pp. 264–82.

46. See Enid Hill, 'Islamic Law as a Source for the Development of a Comparative Jurisprudence: Theory and Practice in the Life and Work of Sanhuri', in A. Al-Azmeh, ed., *Islamic Law: Social and Historical Contexts*, London 1988, pp. 146–97; and Aziz Al-Azmeh, *Al-'Ilmaniya* [Secularism], Beirut 1992, pp. 211ff.

# 1

# Culturalism, Grand Narrative of Capitalism Exultant

Nous les pouvons donc bien appeler barbares eu égard aux règles de
la raison, mais non pas eu égard à nous, qui les sur-passons en toute
sorte de barbarité.

Montaigne

I should like to question, and radically to question, the theme of cross-
cultural conversations.[1] This is not because I wish there to be eternal
incomprehensibility between peoples, or because I wish to promote
xenophobia, and encourage ethnic cleansing and correlative acts of barbarity. It is, rather, because I believe that the notion of cross-cultural
conversations rests upon an unreflected assumption of the fixity and
finality of the interlocutors in this conversation which, even at the hands
of serious philosophical authors, tends to cause reason to degenerate to
the tritest statements on common maxims of etiquette.[2] It is this very
same assumption of fixity and irreducibility underlying the etiquette
of inter-culturalism, of multiculturalism as a form of conservative etiquette, that I see as the apparently paradoxical correlative of the sorts
of assumptions about others – other *ethnoi*, other religious groups – that
prepare the grounds, in the realms of conception and imagination, for
the entire range of possibilities, extending from the rapturous fascination with the exotic at one extremity, to bellicose dehumanization of the
Other and genocidal demonization on the other.

The other consideration that leads me to question the theme of cross-
cultural conversations is the culturalism it subtends. By culturalism I
understand the view that regards an entity termed 'culture' to be the
determining moment in the history and present condition of a historical
mass. A historical mass, in this sense, is one whose imputed distinctiveness, individuality, and indeed whose very name – the West, Islam and
so on – is taken to subtend a culture so singular and irreducible as to be

in itself constitutive of both the history and the present condition of this mass, or at the very least the element that overdetermines its elements and totalizes them as mere manifestations. Culturalism is consequently the view that regards conceptual and imaginary representations as the ultimate and irreducible constraints at work in the life of the historical mass in question, despite the fact that social and historical life demonstrates to us daily that not all social and historical constraints are conceptual, and that although cultures are in a certain sense genetically transmitted and do indeed use genetic traits – ethnographic detail, real or imagined, encoded in a genealogy and in a pseudo-history of uniqueness and continuity, of the West or of Islam, for instance – as symbols and markers, yet this is not sufficient ground for asserting that societies, or historical masses, are perpetuated by cultures.[3] It is still less legitimate to assert that what are imprecisely known as cultures have an absolutely determinant role in setting the constitution of this mass, or that culture is in itself a sufficient defining element in this mass, or that culture overdetermines a given history to such an extent that it is in itself not only the chief iconic marker of this mass, but is also substantively representative of an inner nature ascribed to it.[4] While much historical and sociological writing that conceives itself as postmodern or post-structuralist protests, sometimes legitimately, that culture is not merely that which is remaindered after accounting for society and the economy, the crude transition to culturalist determinism is normally seen somewhat naturally to flow as a corollary of this protest.[5]

That which invariably comes to pass in this connection is that, both for native votives of the cult of authenticity and for foreign priests of the cult of Difference, visible tokens of ethnographic distinctiveness, of dubious reality, pervasiness and consequence are taken for iconic markers not only of a totalizing ethnographic description, but also of ethnological typification, that is, of insertion into a genealogical and taxonomic lore used by the protagonists of culturalism. Ethnography is thus replaced by ethnology, and this latter is ever captive to the *topoi* of what I should, following a recent precedent, designate by the name 'culturalist differentialism'.[6] Most salient in the enunciations of this differentialism are stigmata of otherness, of iconic character, that purport visibly to represent the culture in question in its entirety: examples of this are the head scarf, the saffron string or the repudiation of grand narratives. Far from being treated with the appropriate circumspect fascination, this coquette of the spirit, referred to as culture, is a term rather thoughtlessly applied to objects poorly apprehended and regarded with the eyes of sheer exoticism. The perspective which today renders culturalism an epistemological and normative imperative is an aesthetic of difference and of otherness, in which matters of otherness are perceived as either the objects of enthusiastic fascination or the occasions of disagreeable sensation of varying degrees of intensity.

This trope of radical otherness sustains two complementary practical positions, the one xenophobe and the other xenophile. These are both possible variants of the differentialist stance: the former affords the sustenance of a policy of distanciation with regard to others, the latter renders possible a libertarian communalism claiming roots in sympathy rather than in the antipathy and xenophobia that animate the exclusivist position. In both cases we are supposed to use this culturalism to 'correct asymmetries', to stem 'the suppression of diversity'.[7] Xenophiles emphatically add that this perspective guards against the 'arrogant, intolerant, self-aggrandizing rational subject of modernity' by 'resurrect[ing] the virtues of the fragmentary, the local, and the subjugated in order to unmask the will to power that lies at the very heart of modern rationality and to decenter its epistemological and moral subject'.[8]

This position, with its legion of representatives, is linked to more than anti-imperialist revindication. It embodies what is perceived, and not for the first time, as a crisis in the supposed excess of Cartesian reason, and encompasses a correlative shift from the innocent naturalness of reason to reclaiming an innocent naturalness of desire, need, locality, fragmentariness. In order to describe this position I shall borrow from Umberto Eco the delightful expression 'new Cartesianism of the irrational'.[9] Thus, for example, from the motto 'different cultures, different rationalities' is derived the possibility of dissolving reason by its dismissal as 'hyper-rationality', and the ridiculous construal of myth as 'so-called myth'.[10] We shall see later that this celebration of sheer otherness in the context of an undisciplined liberal discourse is really the result of the political domestication of 'post-colonial' discourse.[11] To the same discursive and ideological universe belongs nature romanticism, the reiteration of notions of ecological and environmental integralism, including the adulation or adoption of exotic religions with varying degrees of New Age tropes. Very much like the weariness of reason and of modernity, forms of romantic rusticism were prevalent in European and non-European thought in other periods of crisis, namely in the 1920s and 1930s in the wake of the Bolshevik Revolution, and previously in the wake of the French Revolution. Now, as then, notions of a return to natural innocence, to the recovery of immediacy and of subjectivity, and disenchantment with abstraction in thought have always come together as a bundle, and it is as such that they will be treated in what follows.

There is not very much need to dwell at length on the xenophobe variety of culturalist differentialism, but I do nevertheless propose briefly to highlight some of its major features before I get on to the sympathetic differentialism with which I should like to take issue, and before I examine the common bases shared by these two positions and indicate the precise historical, conceptual and political concordances and genealogies they share. Xenophobe differentialism is an essentialist system of social perception premised on a notion of a pre-given culture which, although like race it lacks a sociological definition, is yet coined to schematize without precision an indeterminate reality,[12] and to regard this object of the imagination as a predetermined boundary of natural sympathy. Overdetermined by a social instinctivism, this position, so prevalent in public discourse in Western Europe today and the mainstay of anti-immigration arguments, does not present itself in terms of racialism or of racial hatred. It has in the last two decades modified its terms, deployed a discursive deracialization and underpinned its position and its socio-political consequences of exclusivism with 'arguments from genuine fears' premised on the supposed authority of 'common sense'.[13] By arguments stemming from considerations such as these, xenophobia is not only legitimized but also naturalized on a par with Fate itself.

I need only add briefly that arguments from 'predetermined boundaries of sympathy' appear in the public mind to be sustained by recent socio-biological thinking, with its genetic engineering associations. Although eugenics is very much out of fashion, molecular biology has engendered a renewed confidence in physicalist interpretations.[14] Socio-biological notions of gene-culture, coevolutionary circuits and the sweeping links between gene pools and cultures envisioned by very widely read socio-biologists like Richard Dawkins and E. O. Wilson are reviving associations between human collectivities and the notion of stocks with predetermined characteristics – and indeed, qualities and deficiencies – and naturally correlative boundaries of natural sympathy. Thus cultures become natures, and the history of human masses becomes a natural history. This is a point to which I will return.

I now come to the celebration and positive valorization of difference. This is taking place at the confluence of many discourses and their correlative social and political positions. There is on the one hand the communalist social philosophy, or the philosophy of communal democracy, associated with various tendencies ranging from the medievalism of Alisdair Macintyre to thinkers of the postmodernist era like Richard Walzer. There is also the perfunctory postmodernism of ethnicist, religious and gender communalism, and the self-conscious nihilism of demotic postmodernism one encounters in mediatic and even in high-minded presentations of this term. These represent a curious blend of radically conservative social philosophies with the remnants of a left-wing libertarianism disassociated and disoriented, and with an anti-communism consolidated by the demise of 'actual existing socialism' as a viable global contestation. They subsist in an international scene marked by the revival everywhere of right-wing ideologies, racism and bigotry, associated with the resuscitation of reactionary philosophies of the not-too-distant past, and paraded as beacons of enlightenment, here regarded as the destroyers of the supposed illusions that communism made possible. Thus the resuscitation, not only by the right, and the central positioning of Ernst Jünger in Germany, of Emmanuel Levinas and others in France, and of Nietzsche and Heidegger throughout the world – Heidegger is here not only the high priest of Being and of its revelations, of the will to will, of *Verworfenheit*, but also as the philosophical mate of the Earth with the blood and soil it immediately produces: the pursuer of idyllic milestones in the Black Forest, the rustic speaking in philosophical tongues. All these are considered bereft of any regard for the non-textual parameters of their work; this regard will have revealed even the most complex philosophical speculation to be overdetermined and will have radically deprived these speculations of the innocent illumination attributed to them.[15]

This celebration of difference and rediscovery of the wholesome also bespeaks conditions of post-Keynesian social fragmentation and involution. This was again, in its turn, a consequence of the disappearance of the Soviet bloc and the waning, most particularly in the United States, of notions of citizenship in favour of those of ascriptive and savage identities, ethnic and religious origin, and gender. There is also – and this is germane to our discussion – the treatment of countries of the South as if they were recoverable according to North American notions: a treatment which describes societies of the South in terms of the communalist democratic tropes used by self-constituting pressure groups arising from North American conditions, and using the same politically correct vocabularies of empowerment, recovering local and regional histories, and so forth. The net effect of these vocabularies and tendencies, again of North American origin, duly globalized by the intelligentsia as by Non-Governmental Organizations, is to assist the process of upward social mobility at the top of these groups, and confirm systemic disadvantage at the lower end. They have now devolved to naively-adopted shibboleths that accrue from a systemic conformism that recalls notions of repressive tolerance put forward by Herbert Marcuse three decades ago, and carried further into arguments of mediatic manipulation of consent by Noam Chomsky. Thus arguments from North American conditions are universalized by the setting of universal agendas according to North American perceptions. These matters are associated with certain forms of appropriating (and I think frequently misappropriating) the antiorientalist theses of Edward Said and the historical theses of Martin Bernal: in this way, orientals, most particularly those who describe themselves as post-colonial, re-orientalize themselves radically when they speak of regaining their authenticity and singularity. Thus arises a traffic in mirror images between re-orientalized orientals speaking for authenticity and postmodernists speaking for Difference.

I will try to show that, despite libertarian pronouncements, this is profoundly detrimental both to the perception and to the actualization of projects for liberation and self-empowerment. All of these, in their different ways, base their presumptions on what they perceive to be the bedrock of a modernity that not only manifestly failed but also deserved to fail. This is especially true with reference to the triumphalist tonality associated with the chiliastic transcendence implied by the prefix 'post': postmodernity, post-coloniality, post-Enlightenment, even post-historicity, and their cognates, reminiscent all of them of finalist prophecies throughout the nineteenth and twentieth centuries, one of the most recently memorable of which is perhaps the eminently ideological notion of the 'end of ideology', propounded by Daniel Bell in the early 1960s to designate an ideological moment in the Cold War waged against the Communist bloc, which, in this perspective, was the only ideological formation.

The trouble with this fetishized prefix is that it indicates little beyond fixing a point in time. Postmodernism appears as a transcendence of modernism, but is in fact a cluster of rococo glosses on themes of a modernity accomplished with the exultant triumph of capital, just as this self-same capital in its countries of origin is, in large sectors, being dissociated from processes of production. In other words, postmodernism and associated notions appear to me to indicate not so much the transcendence of modernity in any serious or consequential sense, but rather a series of movements within the regime of modernity which abdicate the social, political and, very frequently, normative and aesthetic consequences and correlates of modernism. The mechanism whereby this abdication is actualized is by the censorship of history, the positing and organization of an amnesia, an insensibility to history – that is, to social and cultural reality – grounded in a sense of well-being which relegates history to those who might have need of it, and Heidegger's ideas to deconstructive *jouissance*. For historical reality and the position within modernity of postmodernism are substituted virtual realities of the present, the past and the Other, among which stands out the virtual reality of collective well-being in a West riven with structural crises, unemployment and social stresses sublimated in a triumphalism of the moment.

Ultimately, all these posterior conditions celebrated in postmodernism, post-Enlightenment, post-coloniality and so forth appear, in the perspective of history, to be no more than gullible, hasty and rather thoughtless redactions of post-communism, or rather the collapse of the Socialist bloc after the end of the Cold War. This made possible the economics of deregulation, and the acceptance of largescale unemployment and the economic values of the Victorian era, all premised on the collapse of the Keynesian consensus that regulated socio-economic life in the wake of the Second World War and in light of events that preceded it. It also resulted in misery and social involution in lands of the North (and of the South). Yet Western triumphalism marking the end of the Cold War was given the sense of conveying the end of an era. It is to mark a particular major conjunctural event that the thesis of the End of History is propounded, and herein are the variations spun on the theme of posterity. But the amplitude of the event is not such as to merit an epochal or even an eschatological regard, as is presumed for it by the End of History thesis and its progeny,[16] most particularly if we regard the end of the Cold War as a reconfirmation – not the dissolution – of the vigour of one side of this great conflict, and as the defeat of the main contestant. The war against Iraq does not mark a new era, but a continuation of one that has been with us for two centuries, one which, anthropologically speaking, could be regarded in its major forms of representation[17] as the performance of a ritual sacrifice marking the reconfirmation I have spoken of.

I need make no apologies for bringing facts of contemporary history into this discussion, as the terms of our theme – cross-cultural conversations and the conceptual and imaginary grounds on which they stand – are inseparable from conjunctural conditions. The presumption of posteriority, and the positing of this posteriority as a break, as the provision of a *tabula rasa* upon which the writ of transcendence is inscribed, has taken the form of an antithetical discourse: it is not only asserted that modernity has been transcended, but that it has been overcome, and it is not only claimed that the Enlightenment has been fortunately reduced to its true proportion as a historical episode in an absolute and irrevocable past, but that we are now living in conditions that render largely invalid the intellectual equipment ascribed to the Enlightenment. This is not least so because of the preposterous claim that the Enlightenment is the progenitor of all the acts of European barbarity in the twentieth century; it will emerge later that these acts, linked to Fascism (associated in the general mind with Germany; commentators normally forget the Balkans, Vietnam, Palestine and the thermonuclear attacks on Japan) were performed under the ideological signature of anti-Enlightenment doctrines. Finally, it is suggested that, instead of studying cultures – ours and those of others – in terms of universal ethnographic, sociological and historical concepts, we are to yield to a notion of individuality so irreducible that the multiplicity of historical masses is conceived in terms of 'incommensurability'. Thus post-objectivism, post-rationalism, post-historicism and post-metaphysical anti-foundationism are assumed far too readily to represent positions antithetical to objectivism, rationalism, historicism and foundationism; and all of them are postulated as antitheses of an entity known as modernism. In this respect, we are told of the need to decentre structural interpretations of cultures in favour of interpretations in phenomenological terms such as 'meaning'; we are urged to look at cultures as trans-historical masses in which change is inessential and continuity constitutive, and we are enjoined to look at these cultures not as structured historical units subject to the changes and mutations that occur in all histories, but as absolute subjects that found history and constitute its massive and glacial presence in an enormous movement of self-reference, irreducibility, of essential otherness to all that is not in essence its own.

I wish to claim a historical corrective to these stances and to speak against culturalism by contesting the strongly foundationalist premises on which it stands, just as the notion of an end of history is contested, among other things, by indicating its firm enracination in classical philosophies of history[18] – although one must bear in mind the cautionary note concerning the cultural analysis of new forms struck by Raymond

Williams in the statement that it is extremely difficult to determine 'whether these are new forms of the dominant or are genuinely emergent' in view of the relation between innovation and reproduction.[19] The notion of culture on which culturalist claims stand is, I submit, firmly grounded in an organismic metaphysics,[20] in which historical masses are regarded as entities defined by analogy to biological systems, and in which culture is conceived in terms of a bacteriological model. This vitalistic figure, whose metaphorical rhetoric founds the discourse of culturalism, is of course one which has always been associated with romantic notions of history, society and polity, and these in turn have always been associated with right-wing political movements in Europe and with retrograde anti-modernism subsisting within the interstices of subaltern nationalisms and within populism[21] (which, I should like to emphasize, given a common misconception, is distinct from being popular: populism is a mode of claiming full representativity of a people – which could correspond to a nation, but does not necessarily conceive the people as a nation – and of suturing what is claimed to be a disjunction between a people and a state, of bringing state and people into full correspondence on the assumption that the agency claiming this representative character does so by embodying the essence and inner being of this people: some Russian populists at the end of the nineteenth century decided the *Volksgeist* to be iconically realized in the *obshchina*, Hindu and Muslim fundamentalist populism regards this to reside in certain tokens of religious and social observance. In all cases, stress is laid on the exceptionalist nature of a given people, which is accounted for by a certain golden age which preceded the fetishization of modernity, capitalism and reason, and this primitivism is regarded as an atopia to be reappropriated within the social and political programme of populism).[22] The fact that these philosophies of history, society and politics do not figure prominently in standard textbooks of these subjects seems to stem from an organized collective amnesia, a rewriting of cultural history consequent upon the Second World War, which to some extent accounts for the prevalent ignorance about the intellectual roots of the present anti-Enlightenment positions.

Yet this ignorance is by no means absolute, most particularly in the field of literary theory, which, in some quarters, celebrates its irrationalist roots in Romanticism and in American Pragmatism.[23] The all-important nihilistic epistemology resulting from these positions is also informed by a profound seam of scepticism, most particularly cultivated in the Catholic anti-positivist polemic of the nineteenth century.[24] The

25

'persistence of certain rhetorics of disbelief',[25] including, as we shall presently see, the elision of subject-object boundaries and the ascendancy of language-game theories, is of course not a direct replication of Romantic discourses, but neither is it independent of them.

In social and political theory – our main concern here – these Romantic notions had been most fully developed in counter-position to the politics fostered by the Enlightenment. In Germany, France and England, these were associated with figures such as Herder, Bonald, Gobineau, Renan, Le Bon, Spengler, Burke, Coleridge and others, and formulated in terms both of culture-nation and of race. Thus Burke, for instance, spoke of the 'method of nature', of a historical mass as a 'permanent body composed of transitory parts',[26] in order to indicate an instinctivist tendency of the historical mass conceived as a nature. The far more systematic formulations of Herder fully deployed the organismic metaphor and conceived historical masses to be powered by *Kräfte*, vital genetic forces effected but not determined by ecological and other factors. Further, and within the same medieval conception, he conceived a historical mass – the nation – to consist of a permanent condition of perfection, an entelechy whose maintenance by internal vital powers is the condition for historical stability, indeed for abiding historicity.[27] Nations or cultures are therefore utterly and irreducibly individual, according to a naturalistic morphology of history described, with reference to the roughly congruent conception of Spengler, as 'a deliberate and painstaking attempt to extrude from history everything that makes it historical'.[28] History therefore becomes a vast space for the classification and tabulation of ethnological individualities in a manner that joined together Romantic philosophies of history with nineteenth-century anthropology.[29]

The same tropes and figures thus employed to theorize race are the ones that have, since the end of the Second World War, become employed in the theorization and celebration of cultural diversity, a development to which British cultural anthropology made a decisive contribution.[30] Such were and still are its high-cultural expressions. But it must also be said that these are closely tied to demotic and even primitive images of *Gemeinschaftlichkeit*, and the tribal idiom employed in demotic conversation, and in the demotic modes of the modern media, endows the luxuriance of high-cultural culturalism with immediate perceptive inflections which telescope the social perceptive field and produce immediate tokens of difference and of antipathy (blacks, Muslims, Algerians, Ausländers, and so forth) – even direct action against the objects of antipathy, as in organized social and political movements which mobilize on principles of culturalism conjugated with a variety of other matters: such as the new right in Europe and Serbian nationalism, Jewish fundamentalism (which construes culture in direct correlation with race and religion), Hindu communalism (which construes culture in direct relation with religion and its social, caste correlate) and cognate phenomena.

Be that as it may, the fact remains that the rhetoric culturalism, a rhetoric of identity which views difference as antithesis, can only subsist naturally in the context of a revivalism. So also postmodernism: I have tried to indicate that the profound ambiguity of postmodernism resides not only in the play of virtuality against reality in such a way that the posteriority of postmodernism inscribed in its name is postulated as absolutely novel, but it is in fact grounded in a particular, vitalist and irrationalist body of notions traditionally associated with right-wing politics, although not all strands of postmodernism politically partake of organismic nationalist mythologies.[31] Postmodernism resides also in a naïve body of references to pasts of which it partakes liberally, for it presents itself, in the field of social observation and commentary, as distinct from literature, as the repository of things *recovered*. There is at work a sort of conceptual irredentism, which claims to be recovering matters occluded by the falsity of actual history, the history of modernity, the Enlightenment and the world: matters such as identity, indeterminacy, subjectivity and authenticity, asserted in the spirit of *revanchisme*, often by former Marxists settling accounts with an erstwhile philosophical consciousness. It is, finally, this same revanchism that some Third-World intellectuals are reclaiming as a sort of saviour, a continuation of nationalism by other means; hence the positive assessment of exclusivist social retrogression, under the title of 'recovering inwardness', that is expressed in the propensity of subaltern nationalisms to defer questions of social progress, most particularly the emancipation of women, to the realm of inwardness, as a token negotiable in the process of resistance to colonialism, a sort of primal virtue preserved.[32] What is normally absent from this celebration of primal innocence is the fact that its mode of expression and articulation is so much part of modernity.

I shall now turn to what I claim to be an objective complicity between the three sides that sustain the culturalist rhetoric: Western xenophobia, postmodernist xenophilia and xenophobic, retrograde nationalisms and para-nationalisms in Eastern Europe and countries of the South, in which I include political Islamism and Hindu communalism. This is an objective complicity between exoticism and the rhetoric of identity and authenticity. By objective complicity I refer not only to their contemporaneity, their intersection at a given point in time, but also to a conceptual concordance, which I shall take up forthwith, and to a global political and structural complementarity, which will be taken up later.

There are a number of salient features that need to be brought up as essential, constitutive structural elements in this discourse of culturalism. It is certainly true that progressivist conceptions of history and of society were insensitive to the material force, indeed to the ontological weight, of matters cultural and national, in the broad sense, matters 'impervious to theoretical debunking'.[33] It is also the case that anthropological research, among other fields for the production of knowledge, is entangled in a web of textual, poetical and conceptual conventions that re-formulate 'others' in a manner which is 'inadequate' to their reality.[34] What anthropological self-reflection has not taken on board is the degree to which its objects of study, who may be savage but are certainly not stupid, play to the anthropological gallery. But all this is a far cry from deriving what is in effect a nihilistic epistemology from the impossibility of absolute knowledge, and from the assumption that knowledge of others is thus rendered radically questionable and confined to a self-expressive intuitionism, indeed, a solipsism, and the use of molluscar notions such as 'cultural ontologies'.[35]

We find in the assumptions of epistemological relativistic life-worlds of the spirit, first of all, an epistemological element deriving from the notion of *Verstehen*,[36] which initially founded certain elements of cultural and biblical criticism with Hender and Schleiermacher in the early part of the nineteenth century, then made its way through the sociologistic irrationalism of Dilthey to its diffusion, through various phenomenological and ethnographic procedures and pathways, into the mainstream of postmodernism, some of which was indicated in preceding paragraphs. This epistemological element propounds implicitly a social version of the innate-ideas concept, regards knowledge to be bounded absolutely by the immediate social and conjunctural conditions of its emergence, and postulates a certain correspondence, therefore, between thought and its social object, in such a way that being and knowing become, in principle, indistinct.[37] This implicit conception is constitutive of all rigorous privileging of the 'subject-position', of all ethnographies that pretend to allow natives to speak for themselves, of all fetishizations of 'incommensurability' and positive mystification of 'others'.

28

The indistinctness of knowledge here is such that Reason, in this *Lebensphilosophie*, becomes construed as life, which is at once subject and object of knowledge, such that 'history is life realized, and life is potential history'.[38] Reason thus becomes multiple, and knowledge of self, which constitutes self-expression – of the social self, the historical self or whatever other definition of subjective identity is preferred – is reduced to a solipsism. Trans-cultural communication becomes problematized as one requiring an act of *sympathy* which alone, according to this conception, allows access to a meaning that is, ultimately and in principle, inaccessible, it being the sense apprehended by an irreducible subject. And, of course, this is only to be expected when using the organismic, vitalist metaphor of organic self-possession and self-enclosure.

When highly theorized, this stance is expressed in terms of the notion of incommensurability, which I regard as a highly inappropriate surveyors' metaphor. I also consider the linguistic modelling of this question current in Anglo-Saxon philosophy (and its extension beyond Anglo-Saxon domains) inappropriate, for languages are untranslatable only if they are entirely private, in which case their description as languages will no longer be apposite. Communication, between individuals as between collectivities, takes place through the medium of vocabularies: regional vocabularies, social, historical, philosophical, erotic, ceremonial and so forth. Thus political Islamism is perfectly expressible in French and entirely accessible in the medium of Danish, and I believe we should be extremely wary of the relativistic temptation consequent upon the mystification of otherness: cross-cultural knowledge does not have conditions distinct from the conditions of knowledge in general and, further, a cross-cultural epistemology is not possible epistemologically, except in so far as it stands on the perception of othernesses both radical and virtual, and I will claim that this renders it undesirable. For the consequence and main instrument of cross-cultural epistemology is classificatory in quite a primitive sense, as it consists in the main of tabulating discrete differences and of classifying ethnographic detail into that emanating from the self-identical Ego and that arising out of an Other, into sheer alterity, in terms of a language of the self taken as the exclusive metalanguage of cultural typology,[39] whose elements are generically closed because they are constituted on the assumption of self-referential selves and self-referential others. The result of this is an antithetical discourse, whose elements in the description of others are constituted by inverting notions of the self: this is what constitutes the analytics of orientalist discourse, for instance.[40] Ultimately, this position arises from a moral relativism, and transcribes this into a cognitive relativism into which its holders argue themselves: an aesthetic problem which is not theoretical and can have no theoretical protocol, but one which is sustained by the will to an identitary rhetoric.[41] This position yields not only a relativism, but a correlative exceptionalism, which regards others as being beyond the remit of the normal procedures and constraints of human histories, societies, polities and cultures. In the final analysis, we have in the discourse of culturalist individuality a radical scepticism, as we have indicated above, affecting areas stretching from natural science (Feyerabend, for instance) to history, a scepticism unthinkable without the Romantic heritage, but equally disenchanted with objective knowledge because it is not absolute, as certain strands of scepticism are disenchanted with natural science because it is probabilistic, given to complexity and other forms of non-linearity, and does not have the occult determinism and certainty of magic. The question has been asked in ethnography, whether with the disappearance of the possibility of 'true' interpretations the possibility of misinterpretation has also vanished, and whether with the disappearance of notions of certitude the notion of error has also ceased to exist.[42] The same question is equally legitimately asked today in other fields of human and social sciences.

I turn from the epistemological constituent of identities and cultures to their ontological constituent, to the description of the substances and essences which constitute cultures, identities, selves, subjects. I have already discussed this matter in describing vitalism and organism, which form the grounds of this discourse on identity, subjectivity and culture. The constituent notion[43] of this substance, as was indicated briefly above, is that of a historical subject which is at once self-sufficient and self-evident, which is self-identical over time, whose rhythm and tempo are prescribed by internal organismic mechanisms of system maintenance and essential continuity. History is therefore the domain of the merely contingent, the inessential, and all change that is perceptible and which might appear consequential is not relegated to any proper notion of historicity, but is conjugated with the neo-Platonic metaphysical notion of materiality as privation. Time becomes the material element, whereas the essence – often confused with the textual or historico-mythological, as in the discourse of religious and national fundamentalism – becomes the spiritual, whose diminution can never result from the inside, but is ever caused by heteronomous interference. Thus – to think in organismic metaphors – we have historical masses construed as individual states or permanent conditions of phylogeny. They are conceived as supra-historical masses which speak in the tones of a chronophagous discourse. Thus societies and nations rise and fall, but do not change in any serious sense, and the wheel of fortune is animated, quite literally, by internal, intransitive, self-subsistent pneumatic impulses (Herder's *Kräfte*) and which together can be described by the term *Volksgeist*. The term is wonderfully apposite, certainly, but unconvincing, not only on account of a historical vitalism replete with associations with medieval notions of somatic composites sustained by the *anima*, which is said to make possible the realization of the very materiality of a historical mass, but also with regard to the psychologistic metaphor of the individual according to which the collective self is construed as an individual subject;[44] if I am allowed to think analogically, I might apply to this notion the recent considerations of a psychoanalyst regarding the notion of personal identity,[45] and I would maintain that the unconscious – the analogue for structured and mutable historicity – ruins the notion of a unified ego and consequently the very notion of an individual, for the ego is not a subject and can only be analytically defined in relation to its conditions. The same is true of collective identities: not only do they have no exclusive, absolutely and fully self-reflexive psyches, but such psyches, even if we admit them hypothetically, do not constitute subjects. This is not to exclude altogether, however, forms of behavioural coherence that might episodically display traditionalist regression and similar phenomena,[46] or that might have a wider anthropological salience.[47] What needs to be emphasized is that this social-psychological theme is often assumed to be self-evident, when in fact it requires clarification and proper elaboration.

As for the tongue in which the supra-historical subject of Romanticism speaks, it is none other than the rhetoric of authenticity: a rhetoric structured in antithesis, a classificatory *topos*, which is in reality not the unmediated voice of the nature of a particular history or culture, but rather the recherché self-presentation of this or that social force seeking hegemony; authenticity is highly inauthentic and presents, as described by Adorno in another context, a *für-andere* masquerading as an *an-sich*.[48] And we can clearly see how this works when we look at the representations of authenticity in countries of the south,[49] where we witness the wholesale invention of vestmentary, ethical and intellectual traditions amongst Islamist ideologues, or the deification of the Buddha in Sinhala nationalism, or again the invention of Hinduism and, subsequently, what has been termed the Semitization of Hinduism in the use of the God Ram by the Hindu right. In all cases, we witness an effervescent culture of classicization and of folklorization which, together, produce tangible tokens, or icons, of authenticity, read history through them and posit their realization as a political programme to establish a utopian order, a Shangri-La where everyone is authentic, where all is essence fulfilled, and where everyone smiles in contentment.

Fundamental to this conception of culture is an implicit assumption of homegeneity. The Other has a *Geist*, a soul, a genius, a totalizing notion whose appellation as 'culture' was inaugurated by Tyler, but which has also taken various other names, such as 'pattern', value, meaning,[50] the last-named one of the least meaningful notions in the cultural sciences. With the transitions from notions of society to those of representation, from evolutionism to incommensurability, a number of fundamental facts concerning social reality were obscured. Not least of which is that knowledge and representation, even in small-scale societies, are distributed and controlled, that cultures are webs of mystification no less than of signification, and that local diversity renders questionable notions of 'shared meaning', notions which are also compromised by the surface pragmatism of daily life. Facts such as these invite the inversion of the Geertzean thesis that ideology is a cultural system into the assertion that cultural systems are ideologies.[51] The notion of culture as an unmodifiable system to which novelties are impurities and in which all disturbances lead to crises – of 'identity' – has no justification in social reality.[52] Often construed partly as a result of linguistic and other technical forms of incompetence on the part of even some of the most authoritative social scientists,[53] this notion of culture makes certain unreflected assumptions about autochthonous utterances on tradition, including assumptions about a certain primacy given to discursivity. This is also grounded in an implicit causal hypothesis that utterances and actions arise from and are held together by some underlying intellectual project, so that the conservation of 'traditions' is regarded as an observed property of events rather than 'a hypothesis put forward [by the anthropologist – and by extension, the cultural scientist and historian – no less than by those who are taken for authentic speakers] in order to account for their actual repetition'.[54]

## II

I need not dwell very much on this authentic correlate of exoticism, and I need only make a few comments. The first is that the discourses of authenticity in the South are utterly heteronomous in origin, contrary to what is claimed, and equally autonomous. By this I mean that the tropes and notions of political and social thought available today form a universal repertoire that is inescapable, a repertoire which, though of Western origin, has in the last century and a half become a universal patrimony beyond which political and social thought is inconceivable, except very marginally. This was the result of a universal acculturation which has filtered through modern state structures, forms of discourse and communication, educational and legal systems, terms of political life and much more, which have become globalized, native not only to their points of origin, but worldwide. This repertoire has been described by another author in a slightly more restricted context as 'modular'.[55]

Against this, the discourse of authenticity reaches back into a reworked and re-elaborated past by means of a deliberate primitivism and nativism. This primitivism consists of two distinct elements: the one symbolic and specific to each group (like Sanskritism, the notion of the *sharī'a*, or the medieval insignia, coiffure and songs of Serbian nationalists); the other universal, being the form of social and political thought that is bounded by the universally and, for all practical purposes, uniquely available modules of social and political thought, of which organismic culturalism is one form, freely available and liberally used. No authentic social science or social philosophy is therefore possible, not only because its formal and institutional elements are no longer historically available, but also because what it implies is the collapse of knowledge into being in the monotony of solipsism and of sheer self-reference, the incommunicative perpetual nirvana of an Aristotelian god. All that actually exists of the latter is a clamorous celebration of some sentiment of transcendental narcissism, in a language, nevertheless, almost exclusively heteronomous.

It goes without saying that the language of primitivism subtends a project of cultural hegemony and of primitivist social engineering, and substantive examples of this can be multiplied virtually at will. Desirous of creating novel and anti-modernist (but only ambiguously so) conditions of social, cultural and intellectual life, fascistic political groups in the South propound a culturalism which is consonant with their political formation and renewed elite formation, and which is simultaneously consonant with the international information system as it has come to be in the last two decades: an information system characterized by elements of orality,[56] encouraged by visible bytes that classify, typify and daily reproduce tokens of exoticism which, as if by conveyance, are daily delivered to the countries of origin of this exoticism, cultivating a postmodernist taste for the pre-modern, buttressing the politico-culturalist advocacy of right-wing groups and their claims for authenticity, exceptionalism, self-enclosure. This is acted out not only on a global scale, but equally on a local scale, in which diversity of an ethnic and religious nature within Western countries is similarly construed.

The global political context of this is not a mystery. It is correlative with the redefinition of relations between what have come to be known as North and South, that is, between rich and poor, in terms of distanciation and the confirmation of the failure of textbook developmental projects, and with the collapse of the post-World War II Keynesian consensus. A local analogue within Western countries is an increasing tendency towards ghettoization, buttressed by policies of ethnic confinement and sustained by an ethnic stratification of labour, externally defined by the anti-immigration rhetoric of natural sympathies, a discourse with a recent past in the rhetoric of anti-terrorism which had pride of place during the Reagan years.

## III

I have throughout stressed the *objective* complicity between libertarian postmodernism and *tiers-mondisme* in the West, and the delivery, in the name of a culture become nature, of peoples of the South to regimes (such as those based upon Islamism) of social retrogression, and of Southern peoples in the North to archaic leaderships, not to mention the fatalistic naturalization of what we might call Balkanism, exemplified in the conflicts in Bosnia and Rwanda, previously experienced in the Lebanese civil war, all of which implicate international and local forces in the manufacture of minorities and ethnic groups. In certain political scenarios, this vision devolves to a bellicose search for enemies now that communism is no longer so regarded, and, not unnaturally, to nightmare visions, sedimented by the persistence of archaism, that conjure up renewed images of the Saracenic threat and Yellow Menace: hence the call to arms by a hitherto reputable US academic in the face of the 'Islamic–Confucian' threat, a threat to Western civilization by other civilizations defined entirely in culturalist terms.[57] I have proposed that the very notions of culturalism and the unreflected theme of cross-cultural conversations should be thoroughly questioned, and I have put forward the view that the politics of culturalist tolerance by necessity, given the contexts I have taken up, corresponds to a discourse on the congenital incapacities of Others – incapacities for modernism, democracy and so forth. If we are capable of understanding the discourses of madness, of the unconscious, of the ancient past, of ethnographic objects, and if we can interpret them consequentially, then surely we can understand 'other cultures' without needing to confine them to exoticism, and, thus constituted, we can take them for partners in 'conversation'. In order to do this, we need to look at them with the realities of history in view, if we are to go beyond politely listening and talking at cross-purposes, with due respect for the right of others to be impermeable to the understanding and adhorrent to the sensibility. Conversation should cease to be a form of cross-cultural etiquette if it is to preserve any liberating potential. Otherwise, by turning culturalist, it will leave the setting of terms to the most retrograde and violent forces of livid hatred both in Europe and beyond, and concede to them the claim that they represent all of us. Even authors of pulp fiction are aware that their writings are 'neologic spasms' preceding any concept whatever, slick and hollow 'awaiting received meaning'.[58] Intellectuals from the Third World in the West have a particular responsibility there, and they need to eschew the temptation of exoticist posturing, or of the postures of ambiguity, hybridity, and other ways of playing to the lofty circus. Hybridity, by pretending to be the mix of unmixables, merely confirms the presumption of the purity of its two termini, postmodernity and pre-modernity, exoticism and culturalism. Yet we have seen both to be radically impure, both complicit with each other inextricably; short of the purity of the angels, the only purity we can hope for in this situation of virtuality and of dissimulation resides in the quality of the critical gaze.

## Notes

1. This intervention was prepared for a conference convened under the title of 'Cross-Cultural Conversations', Århus, 1993.

2. For instance, Jürgen Habermas, 'Wahrheit und Wahrhaftigkeit', in *Die Zeit*, 8 December 1995, pp. 59–60, and particularly p. 60, col. 4.

3. Ernest Gellner, *Reason and Culture*, Oxford 1988, pp 14–15. It is noteworthy that Gellner abandons his cautionary attitude in his well-known claims concerning what he terms Muslim societies.

4. One could cite among the many illustrations of this the statement by the author of what purports to be a history of Muslim societies that in his book, he will emphasize culture and neglect the economy, as the former, he asserted, was the locus of historical individuation; yet it may be asked why, of all the possible loci, in terms of concept as of temporal and geographical scale, and for the circumscription of an historical individuality, culture is made to overdetermine all the other

markers of individuation, and result in a history that is radically defective when so detached from its structural bearings (I. M. Lapidus, *A History of Islamic Societies*, Cambridge 1988, p. xxiii).

5. On these matters, one could still most profitably consult Maurice Godelier, *Perspectives in Marxist Anthropology*, transl. Robert Brain, Cambridge 1977, parts 1, 2 and 4. One index of the sudden rise of culturalism is the fact that a fairly standard book on sociological theory published less than three decades ago has no entry for 'culture' in its index, and does not include culture as a major theme, which would be unthinkable today, not least because most publishers would not have it (Robert A. Nisbet, *The Sociological Tradition*, London 1967).

6. Pierre-André Taguieff, *La Force du préjugé. Essai sur le racisme et ses doubles*, Paris 1987, passim.

7. The working paper of the symposium for which this paper was prepared; see n.1, above.

8. Partha Chatterjee, *The Nation and its Fragments, Colonial and Postcolonial Histories*, Princeton, N. J. 1993, p. xi.

9. Umberto Eco, *Travels in Hyperreality*, transl. W. Weaver, London 1987, p. 129.

10. Marshall Sahlins, *How 'Natives' Think, about Captain Cook, For Example*, Chicago and London 1995, pp. 13–14, 180.

11. See especially Aijaz Ahmad, *In Theory*, London 1992, ch. 2 and pp. 204ff.

12. Colette Guillaumin, *L'Idéologie raciste. Genèse et langage actuelle*, Paris and the Hague 1972, pp. 2, 13; Taguieff, *La Force du préjugé*, pp. 19ff.

13. For the case of Britain, see Martin Barker, *The New Racism: Conservatives and the Ideology of the Tribe*, London 1984, pp. 14ff., 97, and chs. 3 and 4; Frank Reeves, *British Racial Discourse. A Study of British Political Discourse about Race and Race-Related Matters*, Cambridge 1983, passim.

14. See Erich Harth, *Dawn of a Millennium. Beyond Evolution and Culture*, London 1990, pp. 66ff.

15. See most pertinently, Pierre Bourdieu, *L'Ontologie politique de Martin Heidegger*, Paris 1988; and Richard Herzinger, 'Werden wir alle Jünger? Über die Renaissance konservativer Modernekritik und die post-postmoderne Sehnsucht nach der organischen Moderne', in *Kursbuch 122: Die Zukunft der Moderne*, December 1995, pp. 93–118.

16. For the vast complexity of the theme in the nineteenth and twentieth centuries the reader is referred to Lutz Niethammer, *Posthistoire. Has History Come to an End?*, transl. Patrick Camiller, London 1994, where the demotic notions of the end of history theme, exemplified by Francis Fukuyama's *The End of History and the Last Man* (1992), is aptly described as 'a kind of bandwagon operetta' (p. 91, n. 12).

17. On postmodernism and the Gulf War, see Christopher Norris, *Uncritical Theory. Postmodernism, Intellectuals, and the Gulf War*, London 1992.

18. Niethammer, *Posthistoire*, pp. 135ff.

19. Raymond Williams, *Culture*, London 1981, p. 205.

20. On the notions and metaphors of organism in European thought of the nineteenth and twentieth centuries, the reader is referred to the excellent discussion in Judith E. Schlanger, *Les Métaphores de l'organisme*, Paris 1971.

21. For the recent statements of these positions, see Albert Hirschman, *The Rhetoric of Reaction*, Cambridge, Mass. 1991.

22. See, among others, D. MacRae, 'Populism as an Ideology', in *Populism. Its Meaning and National Characteristics*, eds E. Gellner and G. Ionescu, London 1969, esp. pp. 155–8; A. Walicki, *The Controversy over Capitalism*, Oxford 1969, pp. 3, 35, 64, and ch. 1, passim.; V. I. Lenin, *Complete Works*, Moscow 1963, vol. 2, pp. 513–17. For the populist character of political Islamism, see other chapters in this volume, and Ervand Abrahamian, *Khomeinism*, London 1993.

23. See particularly Kathleen Wheeler, *Romanticism, Pragmatism, and Deconstruction*, Oxford 1993. For less enthusiastic accounts, see David Simpson, *Romanticism, Nationalism, and the Revolt against Theory*, Chicago and London 1993, and Terry Eagleton, *The Ideology of the Aesthetic*, Oxford 1990, chs 5 and 6.

24. For instance, Louis Foucher, *La Philosophie catholique en France au xixème siècle avant la renaissance thomiste et dans son rapport avec elle, 1800–1880*, Paris 1955, pp. 23–5, 36–8, 258; Robert L. Palmer *Catholics and Unbelievers in Eighteenth-Century France*, Princeton, N.J., 1939, pp. 106–112; D. G. Charlton, *Secular Religions in France 1815–1870*, London 1963, pp. 200–11. For a more restricted recognition, see Christopher Norris, 'Truth, Science, and the Growth of Knowledge', in *New Left Review*, 210, (1995), pp. 105–23. For the same origins for nineteenth and twentieth century Arab Muslim anti-scientism, see Aziz Al-Azmeh, *Al-'Ilmāniyya* [Secularism]. Beirut 1992, pp. 173–5.

25. Simpson, *Romanticism*, pp. 3–4.

26. Edmund Burke, *Reflections on the Revolution in France*, ed. Conor Cruise O'Brien, Harmondsworth 1969, p. 120; and cf. Simpson, *Romanticism*, pp. 57–8.

27. Johann Gottfried von Herder, *Reflections on the Philosophy of the History of Mankind*, abridged by F.E. Manuel, Chicago and London 1968, pp. 96–7, and *J. G. Herder on Social and Political Culture*, ed. and transl. F.M. Barnard, Cambridge 1969, pp. 272ff., 291ff. Cf. R.G. Collingwood, *The Idea of History*, Oxford 1946, p. 92.

28. Collingwood, *The Idea of History*, p. 182.

29. Johannes Fabian, *Time and the Other. How Anthropology Makes its Object*, New York 1983, particularly pp. 15–16, 19.

30. For the anatomy of these notions and the ease of transition between racism and culturalism, the reader is referred to Guillaumin, *L'Idéologie raciste*, ch. 1, Tzvetan Todorov, *On Human Diversity: Nationalism, Racism, and Exoticism in French Thought*, transl. C. Porter, Cambridge, MA, 1993, pp. 156–7, 219ff., and chs 2 and 3, passim, and Claude Lévi-Strauss. *A View from Afar*, trans. J. Neugroschel and P. Hoss, Harmondsworth, 1987, p. 26.

31. See Simpson, *Romanticism*, pp. 182–3.

32. On the anti-modernism of subaltern nationalisms, illustrated by a particular historical experience (Bengal), see Chatterjee, *The Nation and its Fragments*, p. 75 and chs 1 and 6, passim.

33. See the excellent discussion of the attitudes of Hegel and Marx to Romanticism by Gopal Balakrishnan, 'The National Imagination', in *New Left Review*, 211, 1995, pp. 59–61.

34. For some important instances of anthropological self-reflection, see James Clifford and George E. Marcus, eds, *Writing Culture. The Poetics and Politics of Ethnography*, Berkeley and Los Angeles 1986.

35. Witness for instance, the celebration of epistemological nihilism by Wheeler, *Romanticism*, pp. 244–5 and Conclusion, and Sahlins, *How 'Natives' Think*, pp. 157ff., 170 and passim.

36. The reader is referred, among others, to the account of Stepan Odouev, *Par les sentiers de Zarathoustra. Influence de la penseé de Nietzsche sur la philosophie bourgeoise allemande*, transl. Catherine Emery, Moscow 1980.

37. See my account of the epistemology of the 'Islamization of knowledge' theme, in 'Al-lā'aqlanīyya fi'l-fikr al-'Arabī al- adīth wa'l-mu'ā ir' [Irrationalism in Modern Arab Thought], in *Abwab*, 4, 1995, pp. 23–35.

38. Odouev, *Par les sentiers de Zarathoustra*, p. 142.

39. J. M. Lotman, 'On the Metalanguage of a Typological Description of Culture', in *Semiotica*, 14/2, 1975, pp. 97ff.

40. Abdallah Laroui, 'The Arabs and Social Anthropology', in *The Crisis of the Arab Intellectual*, Berkeley and Los Angeles 1976, pp. 44ff.; Aziz Al-Azmeh, 'Islamic Studies and the European Imagination', in this volume; Al-Azmeh, 'If āh al-istishrāq' [The Articulation of Orientalism] in *Al-Turāth bay n as-Sul ān wat-Tārīkh* [Heritage: Power and History], Beirut and Casablanca 1990, pp. 61ff. For consideration of similar attitudes and constructions in a reverse sense, see François Hartog, *Le Miroir d'Hérodote: essai sur la représentation de l'autre*, Paris 1980, and Aziz Al-Azmeh, 'Barbarians in Arab Eyes', in *Past and Present*, 134, February 1992, pp. 3–18.

41. The reader is referred to the robust account of I. C. Jarvie, *Rationality and Relativism. In Search of a Philosophy and History of Anthropology*, London 1984.

42. Roger Keesing, 'The Anthropologist as Orientalist: Exotic Readings of Cultural Texts', unpublished paper read at the 12th International Congress of Anthropological and Ethnological Sciences, Zagreb 1988, pp. 1, 5.

43. For what follows, see Aziz Al-Azmeh, 'The Discourse of Cultural Authenticity: Islamist Revivalism and Enlightenment Universalism', in this volume.

44. Marc Bloch long ago warned against this temptation in his review of Maurice Halbwach's *Les Cadres sociaux de la mémoire*, 'Mémoire collective, tradition, et coutume', in *Revue de Synthèse Historique*, XL (n. s., xiv), 1925, pp. 73–83.

45. André Green, 'Atome de parenté et relations oedipiennes', in *L'Identité. Séminaire interdisciplinaire dirigé par Claude Lévi-Strauss*, Paris 1977, p. 82.

46. For instance, Mario Erdheim, *Die Psychoanalyse und das Unbewusste in der Kultur*, Frankfurt 1988, pp. 237ff., 258ff.

47. For instance, René Girard, *Violence and the Sacred*, transl. P. Gregory, Baltimore and London 1979.

48. Theodor Adorno, *Prisms*, transl. S. and S. Weber, London 1967, pp. 152–5.

49. For Islamism in the Arab world, see Al-Azmeh, 'Islamism and the Arabs', in this volume; for India, Chatterjee, *Nationalism and its Fragments*, chs 4 and 5; for cognate themes, see Eric Hobsbawm and Terence Ranger, eds, *The Invention of Tradition*, Cambridge 1983.

50. See the sober reflections of Paul Mercier, 'Anthropologie sociale et culturelle', in *Ethnologie générale*, ed. Jean Poirier, Paris 1968 (*Encyclopédie de la Pléiade*, xxiv), pp. 907–9, 915, 918–20.

51. Roger Keesing, 'Anthropology as Interpretive Quest', in *Current Anthropology*, 28/2, 1987, pp. 161–3.

52. For instance, Ayse Caglar, 'The Prison House of Culture in Studies of Turks in Germany', Berlin 1990 (Freie Universität Berlin, *Sozial-anthropologische Arbeitspapiere*, no. 31), pp. 6–9.

53. For instance, the notion of *manna*, discussed by Keesing, 'The Anthropologist as Orientalist', pp. 3ff.

54. See most particularly the sinuous and rigorous considerations of Pascal Boyer, *Tradition as Truth and Communication: A Cognitive Description of Traditional Discourse*, Cambridge 1990, pp. 2–4, 10, 32–7, 79–86, 118; and cf. Marc Augé, *Le Sens des autres*, Paris 1994, pp. 28–9 and passim.

55. Benedict Anderson, *Imagined Communities. Reflections on the Origin and Spread of Nationalism*, London 1983.

56. I refer to the catalogue of characteristics treated by Walter Ong, *Orality and Literacy. The Technologizing of the Word*, London and New York 1982, pp. 37ff. and passim.

57. S.P. Huntington, 'A Clash of Civilizations?', in *Foreign Affairs*, 72, 1993, pp. 22ff.

58. William Gibson, self-declared author of cyberpunk novels, quoted in Julian Stallabrass, 'Empowering Technology. The Exploration of Cyberspace', in *New Left Review*, 211, 1995, p. 5.

# 2

# Civilization, Culture and the New Barbarians

The vast mood of disenchantment with civilization[1] is not merely one that seems to be activated at the end of millennia, even of centuries, with echoes of chiliasm even to the minds of those of us who are most resolutely convinced that the world might be disenchanted, that signs might be deciphered, that numbers could be made to stand before us demystified. I assert that the burden of the present moment consists in a state of liminality, not because of some reference to number mysticism at the beginning of a millennium and the end of another, but because, at a time when phantasmagoric scenarios like the end of history and the wars of civilizations are announced, deregulated Europe and the USA seem to be reverting to the mental world that predominated before the Second World War, and which, among other factors, precipitated that war. The postwar humanism that was made imperative by the evident calamities of war is everywhere on the wane. Some recent developments in empirical US social science research connect with much older lineages in studying educational underachievement, poverty and sexual preference, among other things, in terms of biological predisposition.

My subject concerns the primacy of reactionary rather than of liberal ideas in modern European history, and postmodernism which, for all its declared anti-foundationalism, is fundamentally a grand narrative of the irrational; I assert that the discourses on the barbarian within and the barbarian without are isomorphous, because both share a pessimistic anthropology beyond history, an anthropology which views human collectivities as governed by a natural history rather than one seriously involving human agency, by fatalism rather than historicity. I propose to bring to bear upon civilization and barbarity the ineradicable insistence of the present moment, and begin with the current mood of disenchantment with civilization.

Despairing of civilization, hankering after times past or utopias present among simpler peoples, the cult of nature, of the primitive and of the pre-colonial idyll, are not of course the preserve of western cultural studies academics or non-governmental organizations today. Nor is this primitivism of the civilized too often associated with reformist projects, which take the primitive as their model: this is so not only for the impossibility of repetition, but also because primitivism and the fascination with noble savages are more often the object of an air of ironic or melancholic despair of the present. Unlike the phantasy of Adamic and prophetic moments of foundation in monotheistic eschatologies and the fundamentalist transformation of these foundational moments into utopias and programmes for social, moral and political reform or revolution, some happy primitives are hardly examples to be emulated, fortunate in their primitive condition and with every right to remain in it as they may be judged to be. This discourse on the primitive is ubiquitous and quite timeless in its *topoi*. One might cite here the Scythians in the eyes of some Greeks, the Germans to all Romans, or indeed certain fundamentalist movements to the US State Department, as with the so-called Afghan 'resistance' before it spurned its original sponsors. Tacitus, for instance, a man not given to nostalgia or sentimentalism, thought the Germans loved indolence and hated peace, that they were not easily prevailed upon to plough yet were impatient for the harvest.[2] In the Arab Middle Ages, Ibn Khaldun, among many others but most famously, admired with melancholy resignation the unflinching virility and purity of heart of the very Bedouin who lays civilized cities to waste and terminates their hubristic effeminacy.[3] One and a half millennia after Tacitus, at a time when Celts in Britain were generally held to be barbarians and antitheses of what constituted civilized Britishness, Coleridge eulogized the primal innocence of Scotland's highlanders,[4] the 'Kilda's race', from a melancholy yet regretful distance:

On whose bleak rocks, which brave the wasting tides,
Fair nature's daughter, virtue, yet abides;

Suffic'd and happy with that frugal fare
Which tasteful toil and hourly danger give.

I have often heard members of the Berlin intelligentsia speak, in not dissimilar terms albeit far more prosaically and jokingly, of the '*echte Berliner*', with the sort of admiration that confirms aloof distinctiveness, just as Cockney speakers in the East End of London have often been regarded by less anonymous English as exotic, as civilization's Other. I have also often come across distantiating admiration of this sort for all manner of bizarre or dangerous political phenomena, such as political Islamism or Hinduism, deemed fitting and appropriate – indeed, natural, fated – for some other, more colourful, less civilized peoples.

The nineteenth and twentieth centuries have seen a firmer organization of discourses on the primitive – in some ways happy but more generally unhappy; praiseworthy but more often lamentable. That period also saw a consolidated and self-consistent anti-modernism, predominantly in a spirit of the Enlightenment and not often of the primitivist variety, although this varied regionally, with the German intelligentsia being more prone to historical nostalgia than others. The two past centuries constitute an epoch indelibly marked by scientism and its consequences, and the malaise of civilization as conceived in our epoch is hardly conceivable without reference to scientific attainment, as action upon or against nature as much as an aesthetic marker of social distinction. Scientism, of course, ought not to be altogether caricatured, despite its own efforts in this regard, and perhaps most zealously and piously among now forgotten nineteenth century German positivists like Maleschott and Buchner, in an attitude elsewhere delightfully captured in the character of Bazarov in Turgenev's *Fathers and Sons*, who regarded the dissection of frogs to be far more important than poetry, because it led to the truth.

Some form of scientism is without doubt a major premise of modernity. This applies as much to conceptions of nature as to bureaucratic and social-engineering notions of civility and social control. Anti-modernist trends have therefore often but not necessarily involved forms of anti-scientist scepticism; they took as the polemical model against which they measured the actuality and the relative uncertainty of scientific knowledge the very paradigm of extremist scientism; this paradigm regards science as a finalist and infallible form of magic. What I have just said applies just as much to the standard philosophical scepticism deployed by conservative Catholics and other anti-positivists in the nineteenth century such as Lamennais and Ravaisson;[5] it applies equally to philosophically trivializing Heisenberg's principle of uncertainty and its consequences in the course of this century, as much as to impressionistic invocations of chaos theory today – impressionistic and ignorant, as the highly deterministic chaos theory is read emblematically as a refutation of scientific determinism.

There is of course another cardinal principle for the mental culture of modernity, namely, historicism. This implied the valorization of history by associating substantive notions of progressive and elevating change to the passage of time. Historicism, calling up names like Hegel and Marx – as distinct from the historist doctrine, which was also perfected in Germany – is a notion of history and society as provinces of consequential change, not of substantive abidance or of naturalistic fatalism within the boundaries of self-subsistent and self-consistent cultures, or culture-nations, and historicism took on many forms, not least those of evolutionism, of progressivism, with or without teleological implication.[6]

Both cardinal principles of modernity, in tandem, had very strong, indeed and by way of antithetical inversion, constitutive implications for notions of the state of nature, the primitive and the barbarian. For these antitheses of civilization had, with modernity, come largely to be conceived as its antecedents, and were now regarded against a measure whose criterion is the accomplished work of time, a cumulative work which is in principle of benefit to all of humanity. Humanity was of course not an altogether new concept, and Dante, in *De Monarchia*, had already spoken of *humana civilitas* in a sense which remarkably anticipates modern usage. But the novelty resides in giving humanity a temporal dimension along a ladder which constitutes the civilizing process, a ladder which replaced the static hierarchies of medieval conceptions of Latin and Arabic, and which transformed the notion of civility and its various linguistic forms from the older, restrictive sense of defining a superior sociality and courtesy which predominated until well into the 18th century. Yet this notion of civility remained with a decisive presence, and constituted discourses on others insofar as these were discourses of social superiority where breeding was combined with science and reason.[7]

Under the regime of modernity, there were, *grosso modo*, two distinctive tempers that have dwelt upon the misfortunes of civilization in general. One was rationalist, despairing of the historical possibility of rationality and its generalization within society and among societies. The other was historist, anti-rationalist and indeed irrationalist; they decried reason and progress because they damaged the natural constitution of society, and were generally associated with conservatism. This second temper[8] has often been – and is still – associated with some form of anti-industrialism or romantic and pietistic anti-capitalism, and sometimes celebrates a prelapsarian past – of national vigour and simplicity, of order and hierarchy, of pure and primal religious life, or simply of the happy vegan life according to nature – as a time of plenitude and harmony. We can characterize the former as rationalist, the latter as romantic; the one associated with Jacobinism, the other with nationalism and Sturm und Drang. Whereas the latter can be very attractive in the arts and letters, it is manifestly dangerous and retrogressive in politics.

Now I do not wish to dwell long on these well-known matters, and I simply remind you of some features of particular salience to my description of the *fin-de-siècle* malaise with which we live today. Against the Enlightenment, accelerated by the French Revolution and by the internationalization of the republicanist model of social and political organization through Napoleonic action and example in Europe, Ottoman lands and Latin America – a profound seam of anti-Enlightenment speculation and action was in place. In Europe, most particularly in Germany and England – with Burke, Coleridge, Hamann and Herder among countless lesser others – it took the form of a diffuse but often virulent anti-Gallicism; in France itself the Enlightenment was vigorously combated after the Revolution by Royalists and Catholics like de Maistre and Bonald, in terms which became standard statements of hierarchical organism, and this was of course countered by very strong positivist and evolutionist tendencies.

Despite these tensions and antagonisms, the boundaries were not always fast and firm, and German organismic and vitalist theories of nations and cultures were nevertheless resonant and deeply influential. This is not least because historism, by substituting a particularistic anthropology of the *Volksgeist* for history, posits a natural history of society to which time is somehow incidental and insubstantive – a natural history which, in certain inflections, might also be regarded in the spirit of certain Enlightenment notions of deterministic naturalism: these were manifestly important to Gobineau and to all subsequent racialist theories. The consequence of this is of course a thesis which goes very much in the opposite sense to Popper's famous but ignorant critique of historicism, for it is historicism which makes it possible to think of human liberty concretely – not some ahistorical liberalism or English pragmatic beliefs in the crooked timber of humanity.[9] Another index of the complexity of this process is Michelet's appreciation of German thought, and his belief that he might interpret Germany's dangerously obscure and pantheistic wisdom to a rationalist civilization, taking Germany to be the India of the West, and believing himself to be a particularly apt interpreter of all that was good in German irrationalism on account of his being a Frenchman: France pronounced, according to him, the logos of Europe, just as Greece had previously articulated the logos of Asia to human posterity.[10] Let me note parenthetically that Romanticism was not always vitalist, revivalist or socially conservative: witness for instance the celebration of artifice by Huysmans and later quite differently by Proust, or of libertinism or the cult of decadence and decay, of the reveries of opium-eaters, or indeed a combination of many of these elements in modernist poetry, in Dadaism and in surrealism – all studied with remarkable prescience by Mario Praz.[11]

Having indicated certain elements pertaining to predominantly anti-Jacobin political Romanticism, let me turn to the theme of barbarism and of the precariousness of civilization, and work through it until properly woven together, in the manner of the present moment, with the disenchantment and re-enchantments of the Romantic. The salience of nineteenth century anthropology and philology for the discovery of the unromantic and disagreeable primitive within and without, and in a stratigraphic relation to civilization, cannot be overemphasized. The combination of an acute sense of social distinction and a strongly scientistic outlook towards civilized accomplishment, which made of reason an aesthetic marker of elevation, led people like Ernest Renan to speak of human advancement in terms of *echelons*, of layers in uneven social, historical and geographical distribution, according to criteria of race and national breeding. Jacob Burckhardt similarly spoke of reason in matters of religion for the few, but for the many allocated only magic.[12]

For his part, Sir James Frazer picked up on these fairly common ideas, and told a Glasgow audience that a nation was in reality two nations, with a small minority far ahead of the rest. The reason for this was that members of this minority have

> . . . thrown off the load of superstition which still burdens the backs and clogs the footsteps of the laggards. To drop metaphor, superstitions survive because, while they shock the views of enlightened members of the community, they are still in harmony with the thoughts and feelings of others who, though they are drilled by their betters into an appearance of civilization, remain barbarians or savages at heart.

All this had been confirmed to Frazer's mind as to the minds of others by the Romantic quest for knowledge: the folk-tales collected by the Grimm Brothers, for instance, indicated the

> ... astonishing, nay, alarming truth that a mass, if not the majority of people in every civilized country is still living in a state of intellectual savagery, that, in fact, the smooth surface of cultured society is sapped by superstition.[13]

Note that Frazer, like many others, did not flinch from calling a society 'civilized' when its vast majority was savage and barbarian, and that his yardstick was purely cognitive and exclusivist, disavowing any notions of human improvement or of the generalization of civility. This cognitive criterion was superimposed upon that other but correlative and indeed defining figure of nineteenth century barbarity: namely, poverty, whose existence, like that of cultural disadvantage, owes not a little to the kindness of the civilized minority. I will come back to this later with reference to today. With the exception of intellectual trends influenced by Marxism and positivism, cultural pessimism was all the rage at the *fin-de-siècle* that preceded ours: among very many others we could choose almost at random Frazer, Nietzsche and Dostoevsky: the one an anthropologist; the second a moralist and aesthetician; the last a Karamazovian narrator of the radical imperfection of humankind and of its entomological affinities. All three felt civilization to be something very precarious, resting uncertainly and improbably on a seething magma of barbarity, of primal humanity that, by virtue of the nature to which it is fated, eluded the Weberian dream of rational organization, or its amplification in Norbert Elias's civilizing process. It eluded the generalization of civility, the acquisition of a distinctive sense of time and temporality, the internalization of external coercion, and indeed involved the drawing up in the nineteenth century of rules for the regulation of hazardous, bloody games like football, and their transformation into sport. All of this, of course, falls within the terms of Weber's contention in *Politik als Beruf* – a celebrated but overrated text – concerning the monopolization by the modern state of the use of violence. None of these were generalized processes, as external observers witnessed as well, and I should like to refer here specifically to the savage satire of Shidyaq, a towering and wonderful Rabelaisian figure of Arabic letters in the nineteenth century, of the manners and customs of Parisians and Londoners, and his disquisitions on their common folk.[14]

Yet this restless human magma did not consist only of uncouth rustics, drunken tradespeople and domestic servants, but also crucially constituted crowds, imposed universal suffrage upon reluctant authorities, participated in revolutions, manned barricades, set up communes, executed priests, fulfilled the spectral promises made in the opening passage of *The Communist Manifesto* of Karl Marx and Friedrich Engels. It made a spectacle of historical change, and this was regarded by their betters as evidence of irrationality unrelated to social conditions of eruption. And it was indeed by means of irrationalist suggestions that this genie on the streets was wrapped up and domesticated, by means of jingoism, imperialism and war – the genie without, the colonial or the primitive, had not yet arrived as an active agency. But barbarians both inside and outside were alike, for Frazer as for many others: Adolphe Blanqui was only one of very many nineteenth century Frenchmen to compare Algeria and other colonies with various parts of metropolitan France as yet uncivilized.[15]

Over and above the fatalistic anthropology of Enlightenment's despair, of a Frazer for instance, were other, more finely targeted doctrines of pessimism, most systematically the social psychology of crowds sketched by Gustave Le Bon,[16] later taken up with different variations by various others, synthesized by Sigmund Freud,[17] and continued by Elias Canetti only 40 years ago.[18] The crowd became a metaphor for the exotic and barbarian commoner.

The first Freudian synthesis assimilated crowds to children, dreams, neurotics and primitives, in their propensity to accept suggestion, to sympathetic response and to the identification of the ego with the collectivity, all of which also calls to mind the contemporary theses of Levy-Bruhl concerning primitive mentalities, their dependence on suggestion, their mytho-poetic turn.[19] Freud later produced two grander syntheses.[20] Here, in a manner even less historical than hitherto, the task of civilization was construed not only against history but against nature herself. Civilization was defined ultimately as a defence against natural human proclivities to incest, cannibalism, lust and murder, very much in the manner of the pessimistic anthropology on which rested the deduction of the necessity of the state by medieval Arabic authors, and some centuries later by Thomas Hobbes. But Freud, unlike Weber, was not particularly interested in the state, and, not unlike theorists of ideology from Marx to Mannheim, or indeed Foucault two generations later, was in parallel concerned with the internalization of repression and its acceptance as natural. For this task, the delusionary character of religion comes to the aid of civilized order, fixing the mass of the people in a state of mental and emotional infantilism. Altogether, civilization, whose yardstick for Freud was a very conventional enumeration of mental and aesthetic indices of social distinctiveness, was only possible because of sublimation. He held in contempt the notion of distinction between culture and civilization.

Of course, this disquisition on the imperatives of instinctual repression, the internalization of inhibition and the development of the superego as prerequisite to order, is standard in modern western thought. It corresponds to the classical formulation by Kant, very much in the spirit of pietism, of the distinction between *Moralität* and *Sittlichkeit*, the latter arising from the hoped-for successful internalization of Elias's civilizing process. Hegel's formulation is of course equally classic, inspired by Enlightenment theories of despotism, particularly of oriental despotism, in which the despotic laws of orientals, most particularly of the Chinese and of Muslims, were enforced externally, materially and unspiritually, unlike those of the modern Prussian state.

It is interesting to note, parenthetically, that it is in these very terms of internalization that the religious legitimation of polity by refractory bedouins was conceived by Ibn Khaldun in the Fourteenth century[21] and that, at the end of the nineteenth century, the great Muslim reformer Muhammad Abduh restated the traditional Muslim thesis that Islam absorbed and transcended the two monotheisms prior to it, by setting them in an evolutionist and dialectical sequence. Within this order, Judaism rested on external, Levitical, coercion; Christianity was based in an enthusiastic sentimentalism; while Islam combined and transcended the two in the spirit of reason.[22]

Let us go back to the core line of the topic under discussion: the radical imperfection of culture; its precariousness and fragility in the face of a prior nature that is ever menacing; its need for constant maintenance in the face of the seething mass of barbarism just below the surface; and its inability, in Freud's view, to lead to happiness, not even through the security of religion. There is a certain amount of recent anthropological theorizing on similar topical material, some of which can be taken seriously. The anthropological work of Pierre Clastres on the origin of the state,[23] for instance, or more elaborately the theses, somewhat Freudian and Frazerian at once, of René Girard[24]: that religions, as quintessential guarantors of order, are based upon the performance of a primal sacrifice including ritual cannibalism; that the passage from non-humanity to humanity took and constantly takes the form of violent unanimity towards a surrogate victim; that modernity provides forms for the maintenance of this reality, including nationalism with its concept of hereditary enemies; and, finally, that Frazer's rationalism itself was a ritualistic expulsion and consumption of religion, his dismissal of religion as intellectual malfunction itself being fanatical and superstitious, and of a decidedly sacrificial character.

Of course, those who despaired of civilization, most particularly conservatives, took the short step from indicating the parlous fragility of civilized order to affirming inevitable, cyclical or linear decline, degeneration and atrophy. There was a large body of writing on degeneration in the early part of the last century – a fevered time by all accounts – and most particularly after the First World War and the revolutionary waves that followed it. For his part, the prominent Zionist Max Nordau, like many others, spoke at length in the 1880s and thereafter of decadence, of decadent art and poetry in a manner curiously anticipating the equally romantic Goebbels; he spoke even of biological degeneration. Degeneration of the lower orders of society came to stand metaphorically for their uncertain subordination in an age of revolution. John Maynard Keynes himself thought the lower orders to be given to primitive and irrational proclivities.[25] Alexis Carrell, celebrated eugenist and winner of the Nobel Prize for Medicine (who, after a career in New York laboratories, became the cultural and scientific oracle of the Marechal Petain at Vichy), deplored the proletarian degeneration of the energetic and intelligent northern stocks: emasculated by massification, and incapable of improvement or elevation. Carrell's once famous book, *Man: The Unknown*,[26] was highly influential for some prominent radical Muslim fundamentalist thinkers of the 1950s and 1960s, who appreciated both his ramblings about degeneration, and his staunch belief in a small guiding minority.

This environment of *Kulturkritik* in its various national and other forms, some of them melancholic, had as a counterpoint moods of affirmation: the affirmation of subliminal life in *Lebensphilosophie*, with the accent on the immediate, the protoplasmic, the primal, the irrational, the national, the abiding and that which is untouched by the wiles of civilization; this affirmation, as project or as statement of loss, was the *deus ex machina* of European irrationalism in this and other periods. Note for what follows, that the romantic evaluation of instinct whose repression by civilization is a mark of degeneration, from Nietzsche through Klages, Ernst Junger and other proto-fascist and fascist thinkers, not all of them German, was decisive for the postmodern critique of modernity inspired by Max Horkheimer and Theodor Adorno.[27]

Thus society or the nation as a physical organism – rather than as a mutable historical phenomenon involving human agency – could be substituted by the organismic metaphor of Romantic historism, whose substratum is spirit rather than race. Among others, Spengler's morphology of the historical organism[28] is conceived very much in line with a bacteriological notion of culture, which involves a deterministic natural history of the spirit, ending in what he called 'civilization', this being the atrophied, effete, degraded and degenerate form of a culture once great. The combination here of an icy deterministic Romanticism with a naturalistic irrationalism was particularly apt for the moment of its genesis. The Spenglerian heresy represented by Toynbee[29] was vastly more learned and plausible, and perhaps less amenable to direct political use. The predominance of such ideas, no less than the spread of this *volkisch Kitsch* to the Left by way of populism, was arrested by the Second World War, with the exception of the idyllic visions of some British historians.

Let us move more than half a century ahead, to the close of the millennium just past, to the present moment of deregulation and neo-globalization. The intervening period witnessed the rise of means other than authoritarianism and warmongering to deal with the barbaric magma below and to assimilate it. This was the Keynesian consensus that followed from the Second World War and from the vigour displayed by the Soviet Union – the necessity of employment for all, the welfare state, the New Deal, later in the United States, Johnson's Great Society and the idea of positive discrimination. These developments entailed not only the socialization and elevation of the commoner, but also his de-barbarization. In the Third World – and I am here starting my change of key – this was the great era of UNESCO, the UNDP, of national independence and non-alignment, of comprehensive development programmes – all of which led to the predominance of another discourse on outsiders, the debarbarizing discourse of universal development and of takeoff, except among circles in Europe which were then thought to be hopelessly anachronistic. The barbarian outsider, the colonial, was becoming an ex-colonial, and was no longer generally inert or only furtively active in his or her unreason. The barbarian outsider was being assimilated in turn.

The great swell of change in the 1980s, in which the Keynesian basis of the postwar order was jettisoned, became possible, with indecent haste, once the alternative historical, Jacobin project available since the Bolshevik Revolution was no longer available – capitalism had in previous decades taken over socialist ideas just as nineteenth century authoritarians like Gladstone and Bismarck took over ideas of universal suffrage. While Keynesian policies and ideas were triumphant, the more archaic fundamentalism of free market economics was confined to the margins: Friedrich von Hayek, most abidingly, no less than the younger Milton Friedman who spoke of a 'natural' rate of unemployment. Yet this turbulent magma is just now being reproduced in the name of the market, both within Europe and without, constituting what Toynbee called a new proletariat, internal and external, which owes nothing to civilization: with remarkable prescience, Toynbee used the term 'the postmodern age' as early as 1953, to designate the decline in the modernist European middle classes of the nineteenth century from about 1875, and the rise of these excluded and confined proletariats.[30] These were historical processes that precipitated the events of 1917–20, the rise of National Socialism and the Second World War. All of these events interrupted the post-1875 trend identified by the great British historian, and were compounded by the social prophylaxis of Keynesianism, leading to the century-long delay in the arrival of conditions of postmodernity as understood by Toynbee.

With the collapse of Communism – that ultimate form of irrationality during the Cold War, with its great fears and mass hysteria – and of the western Keynesianism to which it correlated, came the almost total disappearance of the notion of economic and social development for countries of the South. This was replaced by notions of structural adjustment in the economy and an emphasis on romantically anti-state, and therefore anti-national, locality in social development. All this was made in terms and in the name of a market considered to be the natural as well as the desirable state of humankind, and justified with a tawdry theology of the market as might be composed in a bazaar in a downmarket suburb of Sodom. Considered equally natural in this perspective are various areas of deregulation, which have come to comprise state, culture and society in deliberate involution: all of these are, of course, matters familiar from the cant of what we may call culturalist conservationism on a world scale. In the same breath, structural marginality and the existence of large permanent rates of unemployment, the segmentation of the labour market, geographical and other forms of segregation, became facts of life, facts of nature. Toynbee's proletariat becomes a vast metaphor for socio-cultural and, consequently, political marginality, both internal and external.

With this came the remarkable revival in the West of extremist nationalism, jingoism and militant racism, associated with a broad, effective, quite diffuse, revival *après la lettre*, as it were, of the classical repertoire of romantic, conservative, vitalist conceptions of society and of history. Notions of natural, almost biological boundaries of inter-group sympathy, of the impossibility of coexistence or integration, are all notions deriving from this repertoire, and are freely used by politicians in Europe as if they were matters of neutral self-evidence. What I am suggesting is that the present moment is marked by a culturalist turn, which totalizes the social inside, grounded in modes of thought about society and culture that describe themselves as postmodernist, and which sublimates the notion of race into the notion of culture and of specificity. Like the *Kulturkritik* I referred to and the *Lebensphilosophie* associated with it, this neo-Cartesianism of the irrational[31] claims the recovery of things hidden by civilization, the abiding premodernity of others palatable to postmodernist taste, backwardness restituted from the snares of the Enlightenment and the modernities it spawned, a prior order of nature, a vital force, rising up as a mystery of infra-historical organisms that dwell beyond time. Once deregulated in this fashion, culture follows the market in its awakening, in its irredentism, in its voracity. I am not making a rhetorical point here: the privatization of culture entails its simultaneous relegation, in practice and in principle, to foreign, global actors (in the name of multiculturalism) and to private backward political forces internally, in the name of authenticity and locality.

I know that the vitalist, organismic, romantic genealogy of seemingly liberal postmodernism is not immediately recognizable, and this is unsurprising. Collective amnesia and the organized public manufacture of memory made generalizable by formidable means of communication, and the devalorization of lived historical memory in favour of the virtual, are essential to postmodernist mystification, and this is not lost on one of its prophets, Lyotard – although I must say that this connection with romanticism and pragmatism is actually celebrated in post-modernist literary-critical histories of that particular calling. Standard textbooks of social or political theory give romanticism and vitalism decidedly minor positions in modern history, out of keeping with their historical weight.[32]

Western history in the last 200 years – political, social as well as intellectual – has only very partially been a history of liberalism and of reason; the terrible wars and atrocities of the twentieth century, from the slaughter of the two world wars, the war against Vietnam, on to ethnic cleansing and the murder of countless thousands of Palestinians and Lebanese by the Israeli Air Force, do not indicate an order of civilized sociality, no matter how many operas may be produced. Correlative with the social prophylaxis of Keynesianism, postwar democratic regimes successfully attempted to excise from public memory deliberate knowledge of ideological and conceptual tropes breathed by most Europeans for a century, and to displace an ample history and condense it into the shape of one particularly vicious monster, the Third Reich. This came to bear the entire burden of the banality of tribal evil; this and its consequences within West Germany would of course be greatly of interest in a Girardian perspective.[33] The ideological and conceptual tropes with great affinity to the tribal idiom of demotic conversation, now renascent under a variety of liberal multiculturalist and other labels, are closely related to those that predominated until the Second World War. It is thus that the internal proletariat again becomes naturally fascist or at least unashamedly xenophobic, and the external reverts to natural barbarity; for the construal of the barbarian within and without in terms of naturalistic determinism – the magma underneath, the outsider – amounts to an absolution from responsibility, which comes easily with the denial of human agency in matters cultural and civilizational.

That the barbarian within and without is the result of a certain atrophy of Enlightenment ideals, an index of their lack of accomplishment and generalization, that the civilizing process has not been thorough, is not something that I dispute with postmodernists. What I do dispute is the deduction of failure or even non-existence from imperfection, unevenness and incompleteness, and questions of causality: I do not subscribe to the preposterous connection made between the Enlightenment and Auschwitz now much in vogue. That the Enlightenment in some of its currents was idealistic is indisputable; that it was also elitist, authoritarian, often highly pessimistic and far removed from notions of human perfectibility, indeed very complex and often ambivalent – Voltairian, if you will – is also true. Like all major or otherwise consequential currents in history, it is diverse and almost any generalization about it might become partly false as soon as it is formulated. Condorcet and de Sade are equally figures of the Enlightenment, and one should therefore not regard the Enlightenment with the eyes of an antiquarian, but rather as a historical process which implicated institutions, states and entire cultural systems. Napoleon was perhaps its best representative: not only as a world-historical figure in the Hegelian sense, but as the first embodiment of the Enlightenment as a *longue durée* of international extent and depth, uneven in its articulations and undulations as this certainly was. Paraphrasing Braudel somewhat, its history is the sum of all its possible histories.

Moments of Enlightenment might have sought the elevation of the common run of humanity, but it is also indisputable that the increasing Tates of literacy in the nineteenth century were not merely acts of idealism of positivist programmes of social engineering, but at once more prosaically and profoundly, a mode of integrating Europeans into national states, of transforming Arabs and Turks into Ottoman citizens, of creating bureaucratic and other statist and cultural elites for the Napoleonic states I referred to through the educational system. But there is not much evidence that this process has had a necessarily civilizing effect, if measured against, for instance, actual mass reading tastes, or against the manifest recent atrophy of linguistic capacity which is manifest in Anglo-Saxon lands, but which is equally attested in Germany, France and elsewhere. With an apt hyperbole, H. M. Enzensberger spoke of High German gradually becoming a Germanic dialect poorly mastered as a foreign language in German schools and even in the universities.[34]

Enzensberger, quite legitimately in principle, related this linguistic atrophy to the decreasing need for what I should like to call deliberative and discursive literacy, and, crucially in the light of what has been said, to the relative disengagement of culture from social legitimation and distinction, with the result that secondary illiterates can reach leading positions in society and polity – he cited as examples the then–US-president and the federal German chancellor. I might add more: the atrophy of deliberative writing and the erosion of paradox, ambiguity and irony in the linguistically prefabricated, highly invasive formulaic modes of journalism, in which the cliché takes the place of the concept, and the kitsch becomes the representative. This is of course reinforced by the paradigmatic role of televisual communication sacrificing linear sequentiality and cumulativeness to lateral association. There is also of course a degradation in public esteem for education, especially of higher education whose institutions are being run down by governments around the world.

The decline of the book, and the stylistic and other constraints on books increasingly in evidence (in addition to what I have just said) point very much in my view to a revival of orality, in evidence among other things in the increasing stress on the demotic in public life and on a cultural production with a demotic turn. But of course this is no longer the naturally demotic, for the world has moved beyond this: Andy Warhol's cans of soup represent only virtually demotic culture, becoming culture only when circulated and marketed as such, just as the recent Vespa scooter's 1950s retro-features (made in 1996) are only recalled by today's buyers when marketed as memory. This same could be said equally about the fevered imagining of authentic cultural selves by Serbian nationalists, assorted fundamentalists of various hues, from the Hindu through the Muslim on to the Zionist Ayatollahs in the Occupied Territories, and of course the cultural studies establishment in universities in the United States and elsewhere. One might also mention the extraordinary revival of the motifemic fairy tale in fantasy novels, comics and films, and particularly in science fiction films replete with medieval and rustic stock images. This is indeed the world of the Grimm Brothers renascent, for literate adults no less than for children. Let me conclude this highly fragmentary catalogue by mentioning the atmosphere of infernal conspiracy pervading public life: phantasmagoric scenarios concerning the war of civilizations, the demonization with definite political purpose of, variously, the PLO until recent years, Saddam Hussein and of Muslims in general – as had been the case in the very proximate past, with the demonization of Communism, with prohibitionism and other public agendas in the political culture of the United States. These are all instances of mass-hysterical phenomena, like McCarthyism, various discourses on international conspiracies by Jesuits (in the eyes of the Left in Catholic countries), of Freemasons (by Jesuits). Another analogy presents itself even further back in history with the greatest of such phenomena: with the witch hunts in late medieval and early modern Europe, the continent was swept by vigorous campaigns to counter a conspiracy of lepers, assorted Saracens and Jews; it was thought, among other things, that the Saracens agreed to give Jerusalem to the Jews as a price for their participation in the undermining of order.[35]

From the barbarian within, I come again to the barbarian without. We have seen that the primitive, the barbarian, the outsider, the laggard and a host of other antitheses or failures of civilization are bound together, as a generic group of cultural categories, with similar conditions of emergence in the civilized imaginary. The tribally conceived northern inside, riven with contradictions and indelibly marked by savagery as I have indicated – as happily postmodern, as being beyond modernity in the sole sense (as I see it), of being based on a modernity accomplished and renewed, whose normative, epistemological and aesthetic equipment is no longer necessary for the maintenance and management of the public order (normative functions having been reallocated to very thoroughgoing forms of the manipulation of consent) – is, under conditions of acute post-Keynesian crisis, juxtaposed with a reconstitution and exists in conjunction with a culturalist construction of outsiders, as being themselves also in the mode of return to origins occluded. And just as notions of civic citizenship are being questioned, most saliently in the United States, on grounds of communitarianism, so also are people of the South regarded from this perspective, and within the categories of North American multiculturalist practices; in this way, members of various western intelligentsias present themselves as midwives of others' authenticity, construing what they term 'civil society' by dredging up pre-civil conceptions.

Altogether, this re-barbarization of the outsider takes the form of liberal sensibility.[36] In learned discourse it takes the form of appropriating the anti-orientalist theses of Edward Said: in this way orientals, especially those who describe themselves, quite implausibly, as postcolonial, in objective complicity with fundamentalist priests of authenticity, merge into the vicious cycle of this discourse of singularity; orientals are thus reorientalized in a traffic of mirror images between postmodernists and neo-orientalists speaking for difference, and native orientals ostentatiously displaying their badges of authenticity, in a play of exoticism from outside and self-parody from the inside. I have shown this in various writings to be a species of false memory, of invented memory marketed like the retro features of the 1996 Vespa. In this context, the discourse of culturalist specificity – instead of that of economic and social inequality and inequity – devolves into a post-1989 postulate concerning the congenital incapacity for modernity in a world of deregulation, hence for the inappropriateness of the economic, social and political treatment of economic, political and social problems arising from the recent forms of globalization and deregulation, and giving rise to the spectres of terrorism and immigration. The liberal-economic, free market proposals put forward as measures which will somehow, as if by the natural history of humanity so fated, cause this newer barbarism to disappear or at least render it invisible, seem in practice to be deepening the very socio-economic conditions that give rise to it.

The re-barbarization of the southerner transforms him or her, beyond history and the international inequity of resources, into tribal warrior, refugee, asylum seeker or illegal immigrant. The southerner thus rebarbarized turns into a terrorist and fundamentalist. Inept and incapable of development, the southerner becomes the pathetic victim of famine and anarchy, to which he or she is culturally predisposed. Uncivilized and only superficially touched by modernity, he or she becomes again prone to tribalism and to wars of ethnicity and religion, all construed as the results of a natural history beyond human agency. Once again, we encounter the banality of irresponsibility, and we encounter a barbarian construed as eternal when this construal itself is based on a system of relations which is mystified in the name of nature. Yet the 'midwives' of barbarian authenticity do not speak with the voice of nature, for nature has no voice, but of naturalism and of a deterministic natural history of the cultures of others; not of reality, but of virtual memory marketed. The aesthetic of exoticism and the distinctions based on wealth merge yet again.

I close by asserting that the conditions of the culturalist turn provide very hazardous conditions for the social sciences and humanities at the beginning of the millennium, twisting their gaze, providing ideological presumptions of inestimable force and consequence. Albert Einstein wrote to Sigmund Freud on 30 July 1932, in a sagely mode that I cannot begin to imitate, concerning war and mass suggestion, and we may take this in connection with crowds no less than in manufacturing postmodern communities of consent:

> Experience proves that it is rather the so-called 'Intelligentsia' that is most apt to yield to these disastrous collective suggestions, since the intellectual has no direct contact with life in the raw, but encounters it in its easiest synthetic form – upon the printed page.[37]

## Notes

1. There is a considerable literature on this notion, and I must rest content in referring the reader to P. Chaunu, *Histoire et Decadence*, Paris 1984. For broader perspectives, see E. Benveniste, 'Civilisation: Contribution à l'histoire du mot' in *Eventail de l'histoire vivante: Hommage à Lucien Febvre*, Paris 1953, pp.47–54; Febvre et al., *Civilisation, le mot et l'idee*, Paris 1930; and R. Kosellek, *Niedergang:. Studien zu einem geschichtlichen Thema*, Stuttgart 1980.

2. Cornelius Tacitus, *Germania*, transl. J. Rives, Oxford 1999.

3. Ibn Khaldun, *The Muqaddimah: An Introduction to History*, transl. Franz Rosenthal, Princeton 1969.

4. Samuel Taylor Coleridge, *The Collected Workds of Samuel Taylor Coleridge*, London 1969.

5. P. Spencer, *The Politics of Belief in Nineteenth-Century France*, London,1954; R. Popkin, *A History of Scepticism from Erasmus to Spinoza*, Berkeley and Los Angeles 1979; G.K. Malone, 'Apologetics', *New Catholic Encyclopedia*, Washington, D.C. 1967; L. Foucher, *La Philosophie catholique en France au XIXe siècle*, Paris 1955.

6. On this distinction, see, classically, R.G. Collingwood, *The Idea of History*, Oxford 1946.

7. The concepts 'civility' and 'civilization' are distinct notions. See A. Al-Az-meh, 'Civilization, Concept of', in *The International Encyclopedia of the Social and Behavioral Sciences*, Oxford, 2001, pp. 1903–1909

8. On the conceptual constitution and ramifications of this, see S. Odouev, *Par les sentiers de Zarathustra: influence de la pensee de Nietzsche sur la philosophie bourgeoise allemande*, transl. Catherine Emery, Moscow 1980.

9. The reference is of course to I. Berlin's *The Crooked Timber of Humanity*, but the expression itself comes from Kant.

10. Jules Michelet, *Oeuvres completes*, ed. Paul Viallaneix, Paris 1971.

11. Mario Praz, *The Romantic Agony*, transl. Angus Davidson, Oxford 1933.

12. Jacob Burckhardt, *Weltgeschichtliche Betrachtungen*, ed. J. Oeri, Stuttgart 1921. Quite apart from the original texts, the reader may be especially referred to M. Olender, *The Languages of Paradise: Race, Religion, and Philology in the Nineteenth Century*, transl. Arthur Goldhammer, Cambridge 1992.

13. The citation is from Robert Ackerman, *J.G. Frazer: His Life and Works*, Cambridge 1987.

14. A French translation of this author's work is *La Jambe sur la jambe*, translated by R. Khawwam, Paris 1990.

15. The citation is from Eugen Weber, *Peasants into Frenchmen: The Modernization of Rural France 1870–1914*, Stanford 1976.

16. Gustave Le Bon, *The Crowd: A Study of the Popular Mind*, New York 1960.

17. Sigmund Freud, *Group Psychology and the Analysis of the Ego*, transl. J. Strachey, New York 1959.

18. Elias Canetti, *Crowds and Power,* transl. C. Stewart, Cambridge 1962.

19. Lucien Levy-Bruhl, *Primitive Mentalities*, Boston 1966.

20. Sigmund Freud, *Civilization and its Discontents*, transl. J. Strachey, New York 1961a; *The Future of an Illusion*, transl. J. Strachey 1961b.

21. Aziz Al-Azmeh, *Ibn Khaldun: An Essay in Reinterpretation*, London 1982; G. Labica, *Politique et religion chez Ibn Khaldun*, Algiers 1968.

22. See Chapter 6, p.118ff.

23. Pierre Clastres, *Society Against the State*, New York 1977.

24. Rene Girard, *The Scapegoat*, Baltimore 1986

25. John Maynard Keynes, *The Collected Writings of John Maynard Keynes*, New York 1971.

26. Alexis Carrell, *Man: The Unknown*, Albuquerque 1991.

27. Max Horkheimer and Theodor Adorno, *Dialectic of Enlightenment*, transl. John Cummings, New York 1972.

28. Oswald Spengler, *The Decline of the West*, transl. C. Atkinson, New York 1928.

29. Arnold Toynbee, *A Study of History*, London 1948.

30. Arnold Toynbee, *The World and the West*, Lonon 1953.

31. Umberto Eco, *Travels in Hyperreality*, London 1987, p 129.

32. This was not the case in writings from the Soviet bloc, notably Georg Lukács, *The Destruction of Reason*, transl. P. Palmer, Atlantic Highlands 1981.

33. Girard, *The Scapegoat*.

34. H. M. Enzensberger '*Lob des Analphabeten*' in *Die Zeit*, 29 November 1985.

35. The matter is wonderfully traced by Carlo Ginzburg, *Ecstasies: Deciphering the Witches' Sabbath*, transl. R. Rosenthal, London 1990.

36. Among others, see the Prologue and Chapter 1; Aijaz Ahmad, *In Theory: Classes, Nations, Literatures*, London 1992, pp. 1–71; A. Callinicos, *Against Postmodernism*, Cambridge 1989; and P.A. Taguieff, *La Force Du prejudge: Essai sur le racisme et ses doubles*, Paris 1987.

37. 'Ich denke dabei keineswegs nur an die Ungebildeten. Nach meinen Lebenserfahrungen ist es vielmehr gerade die sogenannte 'Intelligenz', welche den verhangnisvollen Massensuggestionen am leichtesten unterliegt, wei! sie nicht unmittelbar aus dem Erleben zu schopfen pflegt, sondern auf dem Wege über das bedrtickte Papier am bequemsten und vollstangdisten zu erfassen ist.' The text is from a pamphlet containing correspondence between Freud and Einstein in the 1930s, Albert Einstein and Sigmund Freud, *Warum Krieg?*, Zurich 1996.

# 3

# The Religious and the
# Secular in Contemporary Arab Life

I see that, like myself, some of you are getting on a bit, and may therefore have retained, like many of our generation, some memory of what
things were like in the Arab countries fifteen or twenty years ago. And
since memories form, or fade away, in the context of the present and its
constraints, it would be a good idea to reconstitute some part of recent
historical experience so as to examine Arab societies, and their politics
and cultures, with some measure of objectivity; and give the benefit of
that experience to people who did not share it, those who might imagine
that nothing has changed and that the past, both recent and remote, is
identical to the present.

What I have to say is not very cheerful, but I would like to make a
contribution to a critique of Arab reality so that our countries can stop
being violated spaces, like Iraq during the tripartite aggression recently
or Palestine since 1948. Perhaps it may also help prevent any further
deportations of our Palestinian brothers, like the one that occurred at
Marj al-Zouhour in southern Lebanon.[1] I have to say, though, that I
have reservations about these Islamist patriots, and I do not believe that
national solidarity requires us to conceal our divergences or deny them.
Nothing much can be started without criticism.

Let us consider a series of illusions that are widespread these days:
the illusion of continuity and similarity between the present and
the recent past, or rather the idea that the present is being produced
by awakening identity – Arab for some, Islamic for others – as the
genie is produced by the lamp; the illusion that identity is permanent
and eternal (to use an expression which is not my own and which I
shall examine critically); the illusion that political and social activity, action to develop and liberate Arab countries, depends in the first
instance on the assertion of this identity; the illusion, finally, that the
real history of the Arabs in the modern era has been a mere illusory

moment, which has not had the slightest effect on the brilliance and purity of this identity.

Until very recently the question of religion had no great importance. The penchant for religion of some social categories, the Islamization of politics and the politicization of Islam, had little effect on public life. Religious culture, the religious referent in the public domain, Koranic or other religious quotations, religious sectarianism: all of these things generally existed on the fringes of daily life. It was thought that these phenomena were an expression of underdevelopment; they were considered reactionary, inimical to progress, civilization and freedom. And until the 1980s they remained restricted to a narrow range of adherents. They did not succeed in establishing themselves in private or public life: religious culture – and I insist on the word 'culture' to denominate something distinct from popular, everyday religious observance – remained the property of men of religion and frequenters of mosques. Its diffusion was the exclusive preserve of certain political groups, notably the Muslim Brothers, who during the 1950s had rallied around the pole constituted by Saudi Arabia with a view to fighting Arab nationalism, the Socialist project that had been grafted onto it and the resulting Soviet-Arab friendship. This friendship, incidentally, was far from artificial: it was a basic factor of our security. Contrary to what people would have us believe, the USSR and Arab socialism did not collapse because they were against nature, or against Arab values, but because they were subjected – for seventy years in the case of communism – to incessant and systematic attacks on the military, political, economic, ideological and cultural fronts, Islamist propaganda having spearheaded the ideological and cultural struggle against socialism in the Arab countries.

The political and social vocabulary of the peak period of nationalism and socialism was modernist and reformist, and did not include religious or pious terms. The fight against what is now called the West was then a struggle against capitalism and imperialism, not a fight against 'cultural imperialism' as it is understood now. The political and economic analyses then current dealt with the Arab nation as part of the Third World, and therefore subject to relations of exploitation with the West. Analysis did not depend, as it does today, on notions like the Islamic *umma*, or 'Satans' big or small, or on the idea of an opposition between the forces of faith and the infidels.

Domestic policy was centred on social development and broadening the range of non-political individual freedoms. Only marginal categories, opposed to modernity, called for application of the *sharī'a* and observance of obsolete precepts, or argued for a reduction of individual liberty (for women in particular). Only these groups saw the political field as a place for the application of primitive and barbaric penalties like amputating hands, stoning, flogging or crucifixion; only these groups gloried in archaic social customs like wearing the veil. Thus at the same time cultural policies were developing that preached – formally at least – an enlightenment, science and the universal values of civilization in the context of a global historical project. It was considered as a deliberately primitivist withdrawal to concentrate on the specific as opposed to the universal, or to cling to the idea that we might be a nation different from other nations, our essence defined wholly or partially by religion. The theory had not yet been invented that Islam was the solution to all ills because it lay at the origin of everything.

Do not deduce from these remarks that the nationalist period of Arab history was some sort of golden age whose disappearance ought to be lamented. To put it plainly, I am not one of those who believe in a golden age somehow impermeable to History and to society. I hold, on the contrary, that belief in an Arab or Muslim golden age which only needs to be restored and coaxed into a renaissance has been and still is a great weakness of Arab thought, Arab consciousness and Arab political discourse. I believe, furthermore, that the weight of this glorious past has resulted in an Arab politics based on passions, denial of reality and an erroneous way of thinking about public matters. This attempt to reconstitute the recent past, and to enlighten the younger generation on the reality of things during their childhood years, is undertaken to emphasize the point that evolution and change are the rule in all political and social processes and that these processes are never completed.

The nationalist period was marked by glaring flaws, of which political despotism was by no means the least (the freedoms referred to above are specifically individual, not political). It was characterized by the tendency of nationalist regimes, in Egypt notably, to ally themselves with social and religious reaction. No regime in modern Egyptian history has helped and supported al-Azhar, no regime has whetted its appetite for power, as much as the Abdel Nasser regime, for political reasons known to everyone. The nationalist regimes and their present-day surrogates lived simultaneously in several different worlds, extremely complex and strongly differentiated worlds; and there is no doubt at all that the worst fault of these regimes, from the viewpoint of Arab political and social thought, was their break with enlightened thought and the liberal heritage. This break, which has a whiff of vengefulness about it, was a consequence of the rejection of the liberal nationalist regimes which preceded the military nationalist regimes. Its effect was a caesura in the history of thought and sometimes in social development. And as a result the liberal heritage, along with its element of critical spirit and its openness to the history of other peoples and to democratic ideas, came to be regarded as 'reactionary'. Such, for example, was the epithet levelled by the influential Egyptian review *al-Talī'a* at Constantine Zureik, a genuinely liberal and supremely enlightened Arab nationalist thinker marginalized in his own country, Syria. The same process led to the eclipse – not just in the political domain but in the intellectual world too – of enlightened men like  āha  ussein and Alī 'Abd al-Rāziq, who resorted to rationalism in their examination of the Muslim Canon; an eclipse so complete that access to their work is currently restricted to its rubbishers at al-Azhar. We also witnessed the virtually total burial of the works of al-Sanhūrī, a man who had given the Arabs an accomplished, historically admissible body of juridical thought: he held the *sharī'a* to be a secular code of the same nature as other juridical systems in the world, and laid the foundations of the Egyptian civil code which inspired those of several other Arab states. Similarly, the nationalist tendency would only see the Bourguibist experiment from the perspective of its allegiance to the West and its relative indifference to the Palestinian cause; when in fact it was inconstestably the most serious attempt in modern Arab history to encourage social, intellectual and moral advance as part of the development

In trying to make a clean sweep of the past, the nationalist regimes thus contributed to the rejection of critical reformist thought. On the pretext that everything had to start from scratch, they denied intellectuals the ability to accumulate historical and social knowledge, without seeing that nothing useful can be achieved by denying the past and robbing the collective memory of its progressive capital. But it is true that the nationalist era coincided with a period of siege and encirclement; and that in the brief period before the Arab nationalist states turned in on themselves and changed into Mafias monopolizing power and wealth, it did not have enough time to complete its historical project, or enough perspective to retrace its steps. It thus accumulated errors. It did not stop at denying the recent past of the Arab countries (in the same way that, today, the whole of modern history is denied by the holders of Islamic authenticity) but, influenced by an ideology based on the concept of purity of the nation, denied that society had any historical characteristics at all, with the sole exceptions of decline and decadence. It saw the future solely as a continuation of its own essence. As a result, past and future were both diluted in such expressions as 'destiny', 'rebirth' and 'message' (these days this historical mystique is conveyed in expressions like 'total civilizational project'); and the political vocabulary became confused with a vocabulary of mystical character. People used oratorical forms in the belief that they were constructing our social and political future. In the name of Islam, it then became possible for marginal social and cultural forces opposed to the Arab states and the modernity of Arab societies to draw ideological nourishment from this political mystique; to absorb the nationalist discourse into their own Islamist political discourse, and forge the image of a totalitarian state based on an absolutist social vision that is just a mirror image of the nationalist absolutism they oppose. This development was the consequence of the end of the Cold War, during which the nationalist regimes were subjected to attacks by political and cultural Islam and, on the military level, successive defeats at the hands of the historic enemy Israel. This unleashed the forces of reaction which, earlier in the modern history of the Arabs, had occupied the position of victim. The progressive nationalist state thus undertook, in a hostile external context, equipped with very limited competence, to construct a history which it conceived as the restoration of a fantasized past.

Before pursuing this theme and showing how this imaginary construction is still being perpetuated today under a religious coloration of the past and of reality, let us pause for a moment to consider the nationalist state's construction of History. We have already remarked that the latest nationalist period of our contemporary history ended by glossing over the liberal recent past. In social, cultural, intellectual and educational policies and practices, however, it persisted in the direction indicated by the liberal phase (and before it the colonial and reformist phases of the Ottoman empire). The nature of these policies and practices can be summed up in a single word: *secularism*. The modernity which is a rampart of secularism had been a major dimension of the experience of Arab peoples before the appearance of the nationalist state; and this experience continued to feed on secularism.

No historical necessity has made secularism a central characteristic of Arab history since the second half of the nineteenth century; nor does the word secularism correspond to a concept drawn from a specific history, that of Europe, and applied to another history, that of the Arabs. But let us start by remembering that it is not possible to talk about a single European history, let alone a single Arab history. Nor is it realistic to talk about separate historical developments: European history is multiple, and its rhythms have been uneven, contradictory and complex. Secularism, in the area of thought, has only touched certain identifiable geographical and constitutional areas of this history. On the cultural level it became established, notably, in France and Mexico, where it was in competition with religious culture. On the legislative level it is overwhelmingly predominant in France and the United States, whose constitutions, although secular, coexist quite happily with very widespread religious practices. The fact is that secular thought has not been resolutely secular or squarely opposed to religion and religious institutions except in France, Mexico, the former Socialist countries and some strands of the European left. It was, however, non-religious in the sense that it was rooted in social, intellectual, juridical and cultural practices from which religious references were virtually absent. This was the case even in countries with an official church, like Britain where the monarchy still reigns by divine right, and in parties calling themselves Christian Democrat, like the ones in Germany and Italy.

Secularism is seldom presented as a political doctrine. But it is implicit in the social and cultural posture that does not recognize holders of religious office – and thus the religious referent – as a source of legislation, justice and teaching, and confines the clergy to exclusively cultural functions, however extensive the connections may remain between the secular and the religious.

The processes that took place in Europe also occurred in the Arab countries when the *fuqahā* were replaced by lawyers, the bearded and turbaned *shaykhs* by teachers (at first wearing tarbooshes, later bareheaded), the *qadīs* who ran the *sharī'a* by *efendis* (civil judges); and when the natural sciences, history and geography were adopted as the foundations of intellectual life in place of belief in *jinn* and devils, Gog and Magog, medical treatment by talismans and Divine Names.

This secularizing development took place in the form of a codification of the law and the redrafting of some precepts of the *fiqh* in the form of articles of law, all fused together into codes adapted to modern life and the standards of progress. Dropping some of the *sharī'as* worn-out notions, for example, the concept of testimony, especially in the case of women (based on attitudes from a bygone age which are, or ought to be, now regarded as meaningless), the *diyya* or blood price, and the interdict on bank interest or insurance operations, they placed legal capacities and sanctions – and responsibility – on a personal footing. Modified at the same time were notions of penalty, sexual offence and so forth, connected with archaic social situations. Apart from some progress in Tunisia and later in Syria, however, all the Arab countries have so far failed to transform issues related to personal status: inheritance and so on. But disputes on these matters have devolved, in varying proportions according to the country, onto the civil courts.

Arab countries started to become secularized when the *kuttāb*, the Koranic schools, were transformed into schools on the Western pattern, or when it was realized that this transformation was urgently needed, even if it was accomplished unevenly: fairly thoroughly in the Syrian provinces, less so in Egypt, where for various reasons – at first technical and later political – al-Azhar kept primary education under its thumb. In the Maghreb, French colonialism divided the education system into a modern sector closely modelled on the French system and another, archaic sector based on the *kuttāb*. The transformation was extended with the replacement of the *médersas*, which used to teach the *fiqh*, the Koran, the *hadīth* and elements of Arabic, by universities applying modern curricula. Such curricula were later, and rather reluctantly, introduced by institutions like al-Azhar and Zeitouna.

These changes laid the foundations for a development that might have been decisive if it had been allowed to occur: the passage from oral learning based on memorization and repetition – knowledge contained in handwritten texts and passed on during classes in the form of glosses and commentaries – to written scholarship contained in printed texts, and the methodical reasoning it made possible.

In the course of the upheavals that took place in the Arab societies over a century and a half, affecting their education system and juridical apparatus more or less profoundly, the body of *'ulamā* was evicted from the leading place it had occupied in public life producing, diffusing and exchanging the predominant mode of knowledge linked to the state. The holders of religious posts were not averse to considering themselves a quasi-clerical institution. Moreover they possessed all the characteristics of an institution: autonomous social networks and economic base (real estate, *waqfs* and salaries), and an internal hierarchy that linked the *qādīs* to the *nā'ibs*, to the institutional witnesses (*shuhūd*), to the administrators of the *waqfs*, to the preachers in the mosques and the other categories of staff in the religious and juridical institutions. The refusal to see the *'ulamā* as a true clergy is the heritage of Islamic reformist thought which, following the example of Mu ammad 'Abduh, held them to be a reactionary element. This school of thought did not recognize the *'ulamā* as having a clerical function, although historical analysis suggests the opposite.

Nevertheless Arab secularism, similar in this respect to other forms of secularism, was established by evicting the religious institution from its key positions in education, thought and justice, thus reducing its intellectual influence. In consequence, perception of the public, political and social domains through the prism of religion became marginal and was replaced by a new way of looking at the world, a perception that was modern, temporal, ideological, ethical, evolutionary, political; in a word, *nah a*. What this word really means is openness to the future and to modernity; it certainly does not define an introverted approach that preaches a return to the past, the sense in which the term *nah a* has tended to be understood for some years, since it was first incorporated into the Islamist discourse. These changes were accompanied by social upheavals on a very large scale, which affected the family structure and especially the position of women in that structure. Education spread, and with it a considerable decline in the number of women wearing the veil. Women – I refer here to town-dwellers, whose situation is different from that of rural women – started to perform manual and intellectual work and entered the system of production, as well as other sectors of activity such as the magistrature, government and so on. As a result public life developed along lines entirely different from those envisaged by the men of religion.

Modernity thus became a reality for the Arab institutions and Arab ways of thinking. It is perfectly reasonable to conclude that modern Arab history has seen a profound break with the past, mainly in the fields of thought and culture, whose sources shifted as the men of learning abandoned their turbans for tarbooshes, then mortarboards. But one first has to realize that Arab modernity and its side effects are not just superficial phenomena that only affect society in a marginal way. Arab societies have been dragged into world history by unbreakable bonds characterized by domination, dependency, political and cultural satellization, dislocation; but they have not been able to forge a new and durable articulation of their own internal economic, social and cultural bonds. The consequence is a sort of historical purgatory, belonging neither to their own past nor to anyone else's present. This helps explain the attraction of the backward and primitivist utopia preached by the Islamist political forces.

It is no less reasonable to perceive a historical break in a number of other fields: culture (new forms of writing like the novel, the play, the press article and modern poetry; painting; cinema and so on) and politics, which developed from a new perception of the public good, based on notions emerging from the ideologies that, in a modular fashion, have pervaded the whole world over the last two centuries. The most striking manifestation of this historic upheaval, and the resulting break with the past, is undoubtedly the fact that political Islam itself routinely resorts to notions borrowed from the modern (or even modernist) ideologies of European origin that pervade contemporary Arab culture and politics. The fact is that the references made by Islamist theoreticians to holy writ, and their use of the terms and narratives found there, are merely emblematic evocations. When we examine the Islamist picture of society, what we find is a concept in part closely modelled on a strain of Arab nationalist thought – that of *Misr al-Fatāt* (Young Egypt) or the Syrian Nationalist Party: a concept that holds society to be an organic bond without any internal differentiations capable of affecting its unity or direction. According to this outlook, the only differentiations affecting the nature and integrity of Muslim society are the ones caused by foreign influence. Thus they are not seen as the product of very complex social and historical processes, but solely as the result of attacks on the nature and integrity of the society the Islamists claim to be in harmony with their religious, political and social passions.

The historical vision of political Islam also recalls the theories of Herder and his disciples, and of Gustave Le Bon, authors critical of Enlightenment philosophy and particularly opposed to the idea that the labour of time is to be found in progress and evolution; and attached to the theory that civilizations, societies and cultures (Islam being, depending on one's point of view, any or all of these) follow a constant course, perhaps marked by periods of grandeur or decadence, but unchanging in nature and direction. It is as if the history of peoples were comparable to that of an animal species, each people remaining untamed and inward-looking, recalcitrant to evolution or progress, motivated by instinct and not by reason. It is not surprising that the concept of *a āla* (authenticity) has a central place in this theory that Muslims have predetermined characteristics, in the same way that doves do. They are supposed to be recalcitrant to qualitative evolution and to have experienced no concrete historical transformations; as if somehow outside History, once and for all time, they had been equipped with a collective spirit or *Volksgeist*, defined by piety and legalistic conduct, and fundamentally resistant to the social, political and cultural development implanted in their midst by modernity.

It goes without saying that this view contradicts historical reality. The *sharī' a* itself has evolved in parallel with the societies; and as far

as one can tell from an objective examination of History, it is not now
– nor has it ever been – a unanimously accepted code, but only a collection of principles and guidelines on what is legal, deriving what unity it
has from its relations with the governmental authorities in whose name
it is enforced. For the *sharī'a* is an emblem rather than a reality: just
a name, not an objective historical entity, and certainly not – whatever
the claims of people who don't really know anything about the history
of the Islamic *sharī'a* – a collection of articles of law which can reasonably be viewed as 'applicable'. As for the Islamist idea of political
action, what it boils down to is the Jacobin concept of the coup d'état,
favouring pure will over History and violence over conviction; History,
held to be constant, and society, held to be homogeneous, are seen as
the 'natural' foundations for an Islamic or Islam-based governmental
system that would emanate organically and in a natural way from an
ahistorical entity – the Muslim community. Such is the ideological scaf-
folding that determines the Islamist view of History, society and political action. It will not be at all difficult for specialists in politics or modern history to find parallels here with events and movements that have
arisen in other parts of the world during the modern era. Consequently,
if we strip the Islamist discourse of its symbolic trappings, its traditionalist and fundamentalist references, the utopian idea of a recoverable
past, we can immediately perceive the ideological similarity with other
populist movements, from Russian Narodniks to African populisms;
as well as the parallels with various right-wing nationalist movements,
especially the reactionary and extremist ones like the twentieth-century
German and Italian nationalisms, the Hindu nationalism that favours
the murder of Muslims in India, and some of the major branches of
Arab nationalism that are heavily tainted with fascism.

I am not trying to make out that the organizing principle of the Islamist ideologies has been imported from the West or inspired by it. I am
well aware of the multiplicity and variety of existing Islamist movements, and even of their mutual enmities and incompatibilities; but I
also observe a number of common points behind the different regional,
cultural and political positions, as in the case of an orchestra of many
instruments playing a complex piece with different melodies whose
musical phrases still harmonize. It is my view that the ideology of
Islamism has a history of its own, reflecting the political and social ideas and ideologies that are widespread in the Arab countries. It is these
ideas and ideologies that constitute Arab political culture and the related view of the world, defined by teaching methods and rules adapted to

political, intellectual and even literary discourse. Ideas of Western origin have implanted themselves in Arab countries and become our own; they are the foundations of modern political life, or rather they constitute the foundations of the current modern political discourse, something which is not simply symbolic or imaginary (as the contemporary fundamentalist discourse is). However, these implanted ideas and ideologies, which have a constitutive role in Arab political life, are produced and reproduced by us in extremely impoverished form.

This development took place in the Arab countries, as it did in the rest of the world – Asia, Africa, Latin America and Eastern Europe – under the impact of the Napoleonic model of the state and the 'French political ideas' exported throughout the world during the nineteenth century. Subsequently the long arm of European capitalism has subjected the entire world to a process of ideological and economic standardization. Without rejecting or denying this standardization of thought and ideology, which includes extremely beneficial vectors of development and progress, one should still bear in mind that Europe and America do not represent an unsurpassable apogee of progress. The globalization I am talking about should not be understood to mean an attitude of unchanging dependence in relation to the European historical experience, or an imitation of it, but rather as a starting point: the recognition of an undeniable historical fact whose extensive effects are not to be doubted. Europe gave the impetus for a global culture; but this does not mean that the European redaction of this culture, of Europe as of others, finds its apex in Europe, or its apogee. Indeed, with the rise of anti-Enlightenment trends, and their ubiquity, Europe is today a node of retrogression. Europe need not be taken for the limit of the universal culture that started in Europe.

So the entry of the Arabs to 'worldhood', their acquisition of a global outlook, has been implicit and natural. One indication of this is the secularity of the ideas lying at the centre of the Islamist conception of politics, society and History. We have already noted the direct Arab origins of this conception and the remote European influences on it; so we can reasonably assert that the alleged return to the roots of Islam is at best metaphorical, in any case symbolic, and involves a fair amount of falsification, the grafting onto the Islamic tradition of all sorts of modern historical, social and political concepts which the tradition is incapable of digesting. One can even go so far as to say that what have really been 'imported' are not modern political and social ideas, which are worldwide anyway, but certain aspects of the Islamic past which had already been discarded by contemporary Arab societies. Against this background, support for Islamist groups looks like a social and cultural movement aimed at founding a new society and subjecting Arab reality to the constraints of a worn-out collection of texts (whose connection with modern Arab reality is tenuous and symbolic at best), by methods that include terrorizing the citizens, especially women (as in Algeria, and Tunisia before 1989), assassinating intellectuals, planting bombs and so on (in Algeria again, and in Egypt and Lebanon).

The Islam of today's youth is not the Islam of their fathers and mothers; nor is it the Islam of historical tradition. It is the product of a highly specific reading of a small range of sources, interpreted politically to favour right-wing, fascist and hyper-nationalist ideology.

During the last phase of the nationalist period, the enterprise of institutional and cultural modernization which had begun in an earlier period was pursued in a somewhat uneven fashion. The idea, widespread in the Orient as well as in the West, that the Arab population is Muslim by essence and certain to return to a form of Islam embodied in the *sharī'a* (this alone being capable of solving all the problems facing the Arabs, their history, values and nature being foreign to secularism), is contradicted by the modern history of the Arabs. In fact these notions are mere fanciful assertions that lead some people to inject the imaginary into their perception of reality, to give credence to the rewriting of the recent past in terms of more ancient imaginings, to impose the remnants of a magical and religious outlook through the education system.

So why are the Arabs today living in an imaginary world that contradicts reality? What is it that drives some people so resolutely to ignore the temporality of the world and to deny the historicity of ideas wrongly perceived as religious? Why are more and more people embracing the idea that the only solution to the problems of Arab societies is to be found in a 'return' to the roots of Islam as conceived by Islamism? Why is refuting this assertion such uphill work? Why won't people admit that this assertion is an expedient for conquering political power in the name of a power supposed to be higher than the people, society and History: a divine power which, in practice, would mean iron control by political organizations claiming privileged access to the truth and to religious right? Why, lastly, do people try to make out that the constitution of an Islamic state or an Islamic society would be the political expression of Arab society's Muslim nature, a nature supposedly predating History and unaffected by the complex evolving reality that all societies are?

71

To give one example, the statement that Syria has a Muslim identity does not mean very much; not that the religious pluralism of geographic Syria, or the difficulty of defining identity, make it untrue. There is no doubt that Arab Christianity, especially in the Eastern churches, owes a lot to Islam. But conversely, traditional (and especially Ottoman) Islam borrowed from the surroundings in which it arose a number of traits that are undeniably Byzantine, including the religious organization and the relationship between religion and the state. So where do we look for a Christianity – or an Islam – that can be called pure and authentic? The social customs and religious folklore current in the Arab countries today are not derived exclusively from Islam, even though Islam in the course of its history has assimilated quite a lot of these practices and been influenced by them, while calling them Muslim. In reality they belong to the temporal domain and – in Syria's case for example – to a common history belonging to all the communities, and extending a long way back into the pre-Islamic era. If 'authenticity' had to be based on temporal primacy, then Syria would have to be deemed essentially Christian; for it was Christian before it was Muslim, and its ethnic origins are disparate (Arab, Turkish, Circassian, Kurdish and so on). Moreover if the nomadic Arabs (*a'rāb*), who have no connection with Arabism in the political or cultural sense, are excluded, it would appear that the most authentically Arab Syrians are Christians: the people of the Hauran and Mount Lebanon, including the Maronites who until very recently prided themselves on their Yemeni origins.

The question of identity is thus very complex. An individual – or a society – does not have a single, exclusive, permanent and unalterable identity that perpetuates itself without internal differentiations. The assertion that a society has an exclusive single identity is not a description of its nature; it is a political move aimed at taking control of the society and dominating it in crushing fashion in the name of this alleged identity, something that has already happened in Iran and Sudan and is threatening to happen in other Arab countries.

Let us now return to the decline of historical realism and critical spirit as the favoured tools for apprehending political and social facts. I do not intend to deal with the economic and social crises that have led to acute tensions, a broad social mobilization and the development of utopian movements that are called Islamist, but rather with the forms taken by these movements, which appear to support the idea of an Islamic nature exclusive to the Arabs, but ultimately serve to obscure secular reality.

I mentioned earlier that the nationalist period had coincided with a situation of siege. One of the main vectors of this encirclement, on the regional level, was the attempt to found an Islamic ideology opposed to nationalism, what might be called 'the Baghdad cultural pact'. Arab nationalism and socialism were judged impious, atheistic and inimical to tradition; they were accused of betraying the authentic values of society and introducing perversion and licence. The assault was led by people like Muḥammad Jalāl Kishk in Egypt, Ṣalah al-Dīn Munajjid in Syria and the Lebanese paper al-Ḥayāt (in its early period). Their scabrous discourse coincided with the appearance of Western (for the most part American) writings which, furthering the famous Truman doctrine, supported the idea that Islam would be a principal factor in the 'containment' of communism: specifically, the writings of Walter Laqueur; later American policy towards Afghanistan in recent years. The nationalist states, especially Egypt, responded by developing a discourse of their own that was liberally sprinkled with religious expressions and notions. In addition, the Egyptian government built al-Azhar up into an institution of world standing. So that especially in Egypt, but also for different reasons in Algeria, the nationalist state made abundant use of a sort of populist demagogy, even (especially during the Sadat period and immediately afterwards) allowing the media to be invaded by an obscurantist language hostile to progress, rationality and openmindedness: a culture that refers to *jinn* and demons, defines in religious terms what is permitted and what is forbidden, forces women to wear the veil and requires the men of today to model themselves on personages who have been dead for fifteen centuries. This tendency developed even faster during the late 1970s and 1980s as a result of the increased mediatic power of the Islamic oil states, the schooling of an extremely large number of Arab children in educational institutions belonging to these countries and the uncontrolled expansion of Arab universities which churn out extraordinary numbers of semi-literate alumni. Just in the last couple of years, whole chunks of Arab nationalist culture have been transformed for incorporation into the religious discourse; or rather, as happened in Iraq, the nationalist discourse has been reformulated in religious language, for the demagogic and illusory purpose of winning popular support and shoring up governmental legitimacy.

By these means, the nationalist state created the ideological and cultural conditions for the growth of movements that were opposed to it, and ran counter to its own historic point of departure. It thus allowed the religious discourse to occupy a central position. The whole apparatus of beards and turbans, and all that goes with them, became obtrusively apparent (albeit in a symbolic way, with broadcast prayer-calls but without abandoning the existing vigorous cultural and social policies), even in Tunis. But unlike other Arab states, Tunisia has not gone too far down this road; nor has the Syrian state, which is still hesitating to cross the threshold. The fact remains, though, that the demagogy of the turbaned state has played a major role in establishing an illusory view of reality, passed off as Islamic, which has effectively encumbered all thought concerning Arab or Islamic societies with primitive notions on their 'origin' and 'essence'. The types of political discourse emerging from the 'Baghdad cultural pact' have encouraged the theory that a society with a Muslim majority can only solve its problems by resorting to the so-called Islamic solution: a false syllogism that starts from a true premise – that the majority is Muslim – to conclude, quite unjustifiably, with the implicit assertion that Muslims are Islamists. The fact is that Islam is a dogma, a belief, a collection of rules of behaviour obeyed by the believer; while Islamism – political Islam – is a different matter altogether. The wide gap between the two practices can only be bridged by the ambition to take over the world by using religion and whipping up religious sentiment over worldly – which in the final analysis means secular – affairs.

The conjunction between the obscuring of modern Arab history and the campaign being waged against the secular core of that history has produced a tendency for the Islamic aspect of Arab society to be exaggerated in the popular imagination. A friend of mine has called this 'the over-Islamization of the Muslims'. I call it 'the over-Islamization of Islam': the view that Islam is a single, clearly established fact, unchanged and unchanging, with which the Muslims are totally impregnated. The truth of the matter is that the everyday Islam practised by ordinary people is very different from the maximalist, militant version; it is something lived in a way that doesn't need loud clamour, or pathological particularism, or excessive and exhibitionist differentiation through manner, behaviour, dress or level of hirsuteness. Nor can Islam, with its promises concerning the hereafter, do much to assuage hunger, create employment or resolve social crises. The ordinary Muslim asks for bread and is given only faith. That will not relieve his hunger for long, for it is opium rather than sustenance, administered, by the state or by sections of society, in a revival of the collapse of public and private values.

The nationalist state and the 'Baghdad cultural pact' cannot be held solely responsible for the eclipse of realism and the spread of illusion.

There is no doubt at all that television has played a leading role in the over-evaluation of the religious. Television programmes are followed with exaggerated attention, especially the daily world news programmes that swamp most of the Arab countries. These programmes feed the Arabs a deformed picture in which minor details, striking to the imagination, are routinely presented as essential features. For example, whenever a TV programme has a story about events in Beirut it shows pictures of frenzied demonstrations in the city's southern suburbs, whether they have anything to do with the story or not. Similarly, a documentary on Cairo will always represent that complex and seething town with a shot of an ox-cart, or rows of Muslims at prayer. Another shot of praying Muslims, this time in Marseilles, sets the tone for a piece on Arab immigrants in France. Perhaps this is the moment to note the apparently strange convergence between the fundamentalist discourse and the run-of-the-mill Western discourse (even sometimes that of Westerners who are well-informed, or think they are). Both are in agreement on giving prominence to exotic, eccentric or particularist features, an attitude which is not new and dates from the last century. The real novelty of the last fifteen years is that this Western discourse has appeared in connection with what (in the Reagan period) was called 'the struggle against terrorism', and has coincided, in Europe and the United States, with the rise of political irrationality on racial matters. It is quite clear that there is an objective correspondence, in thought as well as in politics, between Islamism in its relationship with identity and European racism in its relationship with the other: both are fundamentalist and isolationist, and both mythologize History. So there is nothing outlandish in the idea that Jean-Marie Le Pen is an ally of Islamic fundamentalism, the natural brother of the FIS.

The 'exoticist' discourse does not illuminate reality. On the contrary, for the last decade it has been a mechanism for widening the gulf between the rich, dominant North and a South defined by particularism, exoticism and barbarity. In an earlier period the expression 'developed societies' played the same role of buffer; today it is particularism, defined as 'cultural particularism', that constitutes a mechanism for erecting barriers around Europe, denying historical action to Arab societies and condemning them to remain submerged in their retrograde particularism, shut off from progressive movement, imagining themselves to be protected from all threats to their nature. In reality, their exaggerated attachment to what is past and what they fetishize as 'Heritage' means that they are effectively forbidden to perceive reality for what it is or acquire the means to evolve.

What is wanted, then, is to keep Arab societies buried in the illusion of their particularism and past glory, on the sidelines of progress, out of touch with reality, unable to remember their modern history and especially its positive aspects. What is wanted is that only the features of the 'timeless Arab' should be perceived, the alternative being prostration or dictatorship by the clergy, something a lot of Westerners would consider in keeping with Arab nature because it would correspond with an alleged authenticity. But what certainly affects me most strongly is the fact that former militants of the Arab left, nationalists who are disenchanted, sincere or naive, or who think they are being wily, have started giving credence to the Islamist discourse, implicitly accepting a correspondence between the Islamist conception of politics and so-called Islamic society.

It is worth pointing out, in conclusion, that the dangerous development now visible in outline is not inevitable. Arab societies are not by nature incapable of employing reason in the service of their national interests. It is not foreign to Arab identity to favour reason and national interests at the expense of passion and nostalgia. But unless we defend the central position of these views in our modern history, Arab countries will continue to be victims of a history that is slipping out of their grasp and being exploited by forces that want to keep the Arabs in a state of underdevelopment. There is only one name for this self-awareness emerging from a renaissance: secularism. The alternative choice would be a theocratic state, with the inevitable corollaries of confessionalism and irksome and damaging closure of the community: a marriage, a temporary marriage, of the pre-Galilean and the postmodern, fascinating to Westerners, but not good enough for us.

*Translated by John Howe*

## Note

1. This lecture was delivered in February 1993, soon after two events in the Arab world: an aerial attack against Iraq by Britain, the US and France (hence the allusion to Suez, called the 'Tripartite Attack' in Arab political vocabulary), and the expulsion by the Rabin government of a number of Islamist militants from the occupied West Bank, who set up camp at Marj al-Zouhour.

# 4

# Islamism and the Arabs

There is a growing tendency to reduce the politics of the Arab World to the play of infra-historical forces. A simple glance at recent writing and mediatic representations of Iraqi politics following the capitulation of the Baghdad regime would reveal that the complex processes unfolding are glossed quite simply, and with the supreme confidence of ignorance, as a contestation between various transcendental essences: Shi'ism, Sunnism, Kurdism, with epiphanies of merely peripheral consequence: the Kurdish Democratic party, the Baath party, the Takriti clan, the Da'wa party. Of even less consequence, and incomprehensible in terms of the above, are curious entities such as the Iraqi Communist Party (once the most powerful organized political force in the country). It is as if the social and political forces accountable in terms of history are elided to make way for *pneumata* simultaneously subjacent to history and super-ordinate to its flow.

## Islamism and Neo-Orientalism

The spirits that animate what in this image is the repetitive flow of Arab history and politics are, in the literate and semi-literate patois of today, firm *identities*, specificities which in their turn animate a discourse of radical irreducibility which constructs the theory that Arab society and politics constitute a mosaic: a metaphor for congenital antagonism between infra-historical entities, most particularly religious, sectarian and ethnic affiliations. These are presented as pure facticities, bereft of conditions, as identities intrinsically and definitively constituted prior to and beyond acts of constitution and without conditions of constitution, as social essences which, without mediation, become political forces: such are Shi'ite insurrections, Sunni regimes, Kurdish rebellions, without further qualification. These selfsame spirits are the transhistorical

77

essences to which all matters revert once history has, it is claimed, manifestly failed in subverting the continuity of these savage identities: history in its various ruses as nationalism, democracy and socialism. Thus it is claimed that universalist historical forces fail to make headway against the transhistorical *Volksgeist*, and are subject to almost immediate degeneration: nationalism to sheer religious xenophobia, democracy to corruption and manipulation, socialism to extortion and travesty. In other words, infra-historical forces, such as primary communal, religious or regional forms of social organization, are taken for the markers of suprahistorical continuity.

This metaphysical discourse on identity is not new. It was taken for granted in classical orientalist writing on the present condition of the Arab World, a discourse in which antiquarian erudition provided the material on which continuity and identity were established on bases which were ostensibly firm, and which proffered knowledge which enracinated the future, as well as the actually existing present – in contradistinction to the merely visible, in the Hegelian sense – in what it took to be its proper bearings, that is to say, in the past, in the vehicle of invariant *Geist*. What is new today, however, is three-fold: that this discourse of identity is taking place in the context of what is referred to as postmodernism and of the neo-orientalism associated with its movement, that it is buttressed with a pseudo-sociological explanation, and that it seems congruent with a political discourse of identity to the participants in this infrahistorical contestation. I will examine these in turn.

There are specific conjunctural conditions of possibility for the neo-orientalist discourse on the identity of the other – most notably, Islam, both within and outside Europe and North America. Not the least of these is the conjunction of the manifest failure of modernist notions of economic development in the major parts of the Third World (including the Arab World and other areas of Muslim majority). Nor is it possible to overemphasize the international reorganization of capitalist production under the regime of 'flexible accumulation', including the ethnic stratification of labour internationally and within advanced capitalist countries, and its attendant socio-ethnic stratification and ghettoization.[1] Along with these developments came changes in the character of the metropolitan state, from the 'national-social' one built on the Republican model to one which sustains a web of connections with society so diffuse as to become a 'state institution of the market'; this shift resulted in a redefinition of the notion of ethnic minority in Europe in far more accentuated form.[2] With these developments went the rise of the new libertarian right, most notably in the United States and in France with a 'new philosophy' in the mediatic and oracular mode, and the expansion of fundamentalism in the USA and of the racist right in Europe. The demise of communism dealt the *coup de grâce* to the nineteenth century with its modernist utopias of unilineal evolution and historical inevitability, but gave a new lease of life to its nationalist debris, particularly in Eastern Europe. It also exacted from certain intellectuals a ponderous and sometimes vengeful settlement of accounts with many an 'erstwhile philosophical consciousness'. The limitless *tiers-mondisme* of yesterday was sublimated and restricted not only to a consciousness of limits and differences, but to nihilistic assertions of closure officiated under the titles of relativism and liberalism. Such is the intellectual lassitude with regard to matters Islamic, that for the historical commonality provided by evolutionism in its various versions was substituted a notion of irreducible divergence. For historical rationality was substituted a banal historical relativism; for modernist developmentalism (or revolutionism) was counterposed a postmodernism of the pre-modern.

Ultimately, it is a finalist understanding of *difference* which underpins the above, a notion of difference that yields utterly to the wholly inappropriate surveyor's metaphor of incommensurability, to a notion of relativism which is open both to benign and to malign interpretations. In the former interpretation of relativism, an ethical assertion of mutual legitimacy masquerades as a form of the understanding, and constitutes an apology for otherness which cannot be cognitively maintained except after the most perfunctory fashion.[3] In the latter, we have an antagonism which by denial severely limits an identity[4] to an otherness/inferiority which is at once ineluctable and impermeable. In both, we have the language of the self – the self being an identity constituted by utterance on the Other in a particular conjuncture – taking itself for the 'metalanguage of a cultural typology'[5] whose terms are generically closed, thus yielding finalist notions of the West, Islam, and so on. The relations between these entities are relations of difference and intransitivity; their ensemble is sheer plurality, mere geographical contiguity and, ultimately, total war, the other face of the savage and chimerical notion of identity in the course of a history, our 'actually existing' history, which levels identities and devours them voraciously. For modernity – and, indeed, modernism in its various fields – is not confined to Europe, but is a universal civilization which from mercantile beginnings came utterly to transform the economies, societies, polities and cultures of the world, and to reconstitute the non-European world in terms of actually existing historical breaks.

Contemplating sheer difference in the manner described above transforms particularity into a metaphysic of particularism, anchored in a wonderfully archaic Romantic notion of history confined to the history of others. In the 1980s this relegation of the non-European world to irreducible and therefore irredeemable particularism was officiated, with increasing frequency and clearly as a mark of bewilderment, under the title of 'culture', which became little more than a token for incomprehension: each 'culture' is represented as a monadic universe of solipsism and impermeability, consisting in its manifold instances of expressions of an essential self, with each of these instances being a metaphor for the primary classifier – the West, Islam. Thus we have the invention of traditions, such as 'Islamic' dress, an 'Islamic' way of life, 'Islamic' positions on various political matters, simulacra all of them of the invariant essence of Islam, a name which is posited as the final explanatory principle.

The pseudo-sociology used to justify the above invention of particularity is no other than the theoretical elaboration of this mystification. One could refer here to works on Islamism which have won some acclaim[6] but which in my opinion are distinguished chiefly by banality. It transpires on scrutiny that this pseudo-sociology devolves to no more than the common epistemological correlate of all ideological formations, namely, to a protocol for reducing the *history* of the present to the *nature* of the invariant essence; indeed so unmediated is this movement, so scrupulous in its regard for invariant tropes, that one would be better guided by Vladimir Propp to the understanding of these works than take them in conjunction with Weber and others to illuminate Islamic and other manifestations of otherness. An ideology of particularist specificity guides the sociological imagination towards regarding quotidian banalities as epoch-making and marking the boundaries of a chimerical cultural ego to the inside of which there can be no entry.

The major fallacies on which this pseudo-sociology of the other is built are the notions of essential homogeneity, transhistorical continuity and closure. It takes place within the medium of variants of a discourse of 'authenticity', in which societies chosen as the field of application of the totalizing category 'Islam' – 'Islamic societies' – are thought to constitute a *Lebenswelt* with an essential and closed homogeneity. This leads to the confinement of political forms 'natural' to it to those in keeping with a putative Islamic essence. These forms are essentially, as mentioned at the beginning of this intervention, an expression of the Islamic – or Shi'ite, or Sunnite – nature of society, in which exclusivist notions of identity, rather than some ascriptive notion of citizenship, define political participation. These political forms also relate to society in a crude form of representation, premised on correspondence, and therefore on authenticity. In other words, and after the fashion of classical orientalism, society, polity and culture correspond immediately,[7] for it is only thus that they can together partake of an essence, and revert to nature.

Not surprisingly, particularly given a milieu of lapsed Marxism, the appeal to 'authenticity' commandeers Gramsci and presents itself as the reclamation of 'civil society' which Islamism is supposed to represent: a civil society, however, not as a 'Kingdom of Ends', nor as a moment of the superstructure (as in Gramsci) or of the structure (as in Marx), but as societal protoplasm teeming with ontological might. This is the precise genealogy – or, rather, aetiology – of the notion of a 'return' to Islam in the Arab world and elsewhere, a notion thoughtlessly used by almost all authors on Islamism and the Arab world.[8] The theme of 'return' has become a discursive *topos* which facilitates the elision of history, of society, and of polity, and is one which not only sustains this segregationist discourse in the West, but is also a prime instrument of the totalitarian Islamist political claim totally to represent society, as we shall see below.

There is one notion correlative to the trope of 'return' which is particularly pertinent here: the claim that non-Islamist political forces are not of autochthonous provenance, and not in correspondence with this protoplasmic identity. Thus socilism, liberalism and Marxism are not only extraneous, but *ipso facto* temporary, surface irruptions, the work of minorities out of keeping with the atemporal rhythm of the essence. This underlies the pseudo-sociological apology for Islamism popular in certain circles in France,[9] which defines 'civil society' as those sectors of the body social that have not benefited from the modern Arab state, and relegates to marginality other moments of the various Arab historical formations (highly transitional entities, all), including the state, the paramount agency of modern history in the Arab World as elsewhere. More empirically minded American studies adapt this rhetoric of authenticity. One author[10] maintains that, though internal differentiation indeed obtains in Arab societies and polities, the 'massive, glacial, and pitiable presence' of the religiously excitable plebs dictates an upper limit for any departure from fanatical frenzy: out of the bounds of 'civil society' are, therefore, Marxism, and liberalism. The future lies with 'Islamic liberalism' to which 'the Muslim bourgeoisie' is confined.

## Islam as a Political Category

It goes without saying that the position just outlined is part of what has been called 'cultural development aid', for under unpropitious conditions, such as the lingering social and economic crises besetting Arab lands – in keeping with their Southern identity – liberalism is seen as permitting a set of stable political arrangements which will 'either prevail worldwide, or . . . will have to be defended by nondiscursive action'.[11] The echoes of Fukuyama and his milieu are by no means fortuitous; both belong to the same moment – the present situation of monopolarity in international relations. The Islamist proclivity and apology of recent years in the West is a form of political intervention on the side of Petro-Islamic order yearning for realization in the wake of the cold war, which was played locally (in the Arab World) by the discourse of Islamist authenticity projecting an enemy in 'imported ideologies', initially socialism in all its varieties, and especially Nasserism, and today liberalism.

Islamist revanchism in the Arab World is not a 'return' to a primitivist utopia, although this is the manner in which it presents itself. Like its counterpart in Western writing, it subsists in a discourse of authenticity whose primary epistemological instrument is the recognition and registration of difference, and where the sacralization of politics is regarded not as a disguise, but as an unveiling. This is why Kepel,[12] for instance, rejects any consideration of the Islamist form of political expression in terms of ideology: he regards Islamism as neither mystification nor occlusion, but as revelation. It is in this same spirit that Islamist political organizations have throughout eschewed party politics, for they have always assumed, half in earnest and half with disingenuity, that they are above parties, being the authentic centre of whatever body politic they desire to dominate. Such domination is invariably interpreted as a return by that body politic to its Truth, the restoration of its nature and its spirit, the reassertion of its very Being.

Islam appears as an eminently protean category. It appears indifferently, among other things, to name a history, indicate a religion, ghettoize a community, describe a 'culture', explain a disagreeable exoticism and fully specify a political programme. I do not propose here to anatomize this category in the salient forms it acquires in the folds of the social imaginary in its various discursive loci, where it is constituted within a polarized system of binary classification in which 'the West' is taken as a normative metalanguage from which are generated, by negation, the tokens that together constitute the properties of 'Islam': fanaticism, irrationalist traditionism, atemporality, and their many metonyms, each betokened by common images, such as crowds, the veil, postures of prayer, and so forth.[13]

What I do propose to do in the following paragraphs is to bring back to history the category of Islam, and to unveil the universalist convergences yielded by the political discourse of Islamist exclusivism. The discourse of political Islamism shares many features with the category of Islam common in the social imaginary of 'the West' that I have referred to, and it will be seen that this is due to the fact that the two categorical formulations share common theoretical and historical conditions of emergence.

Political Islamism revolves around the advocacy of a political order which makes possible what is known as 'the application of the *sharī'a*'. An alternative formulation to this consists of inserting the advocacy of this political order – let us call it an Islamic state – in terms that lie at the interface between an eschatological solution in terms of a salvation history and the realization of a utopia. The *topos* where the order of perfection exists is one in frozen time, for it is none other than the order of rectitude that reigned at the time of the Prophet Mu ammad and of his immediate successors (the Medinan Caliphate), the order described in a voluminous corpus of quasi-sacred narrative scripture called the *adīth*. This utopian order is therefore a collection of paradigmatic single acts and pronouncements of impeccable rectitude and felicity, and it is the selfsame body of paradigmatic single acts that constitute and have constituted the mass of legal precedents upon which Islamic law is erected. Thus it must be clear that there can be no justification in speaking of the 'application' of the *shar'a*, as it is not a code, nor is it codifiable; rather it is a body of narratives relating to precedents to which is ascribed a paradigmatic status, acts most of which, although single, are by no means singular, as they have parallels elsewhere, in other traditions, or even, like various manifestations of sageliness, to be found universally.[14]

The first point established is therefore that the discourse of Islamist politics seeks the erection of a political order which makes possible the integralist implementation of a legalistic utopia whose elements are, for analytical purposes, both arbitrary and single, not being subsumable under any general category. From this, it would follow that there is no order of concatenation that binds these elements, but that the sole title by means of which they are joined together is their appurtenance to a name, Islam. In other words, Islam transpires to intend a repertoire of examples lent paradigmatic – indeed, sacred – status by subsumption under the normative cover of the name which sacralizes them and lends them a moral inevitability, and which alone carries the full amplitude of normativity within a set of elements, normative all of them, whose normative status is derived entirely form their association with the sacralizing name. Islam is therefore self-reference effected by transference; each element to which this sacral property is transferred – the veil, various regulations concerning dietary taboos and inheritance, elements of monotheistic dogma, certain types of commercial transaction, prohibition of usury, and so on – is in itself neutral had it not been for a value transferred to it. By this token, each of these elements is a metonym for Islam and stands for it fully. This is what makes it possible for 'Islamic' regimes to consider the establishment of an Islamic state definitive, when primitive punitive codes and the prohibition of usury, and a small number of other tokens of Islamicity are implemented. For it is this property of things Islamic – that they are only nominally so – that gives tokenism a very hard sense and, concomitantly, renders the indication of things as Islamic, an act which is only possible by the agency that effects the indication and the intention. The retrievable repertoire is immense; only a limited number of elements is reclaimed to betoken Islamicity, and this selection is a political act.[15]

The connection between populism and the Islamic repertoire is very close. Like populism, this repertoire can never in itself constitute 'the articulating principle of a political discourse'.[16] The signifiers of Islamism are not always 'floating', but for the most part they are exhumed by deliberate search among medieval works. Yet it is asserted by Islamists that these elements, *volens nolens*, form a continuous patrimony which belongs to all, like the elements interpellated in populism, and the node of interpellation, the nominative 'Islam', is made to indicate elements that are by no means 'popular', but are in fact arcane elements that are associated with the nominative and thus made to partake of the generality of intention attributed to it. Such are, for instance, certain manners of dress, like the 'Islamic' dress women are increasingly compelled to wear, the result of general textual indications and of pious Cairene dress designers in the 1960s. Elements from the past – manners of dress for instance – are made Islamic, and therefore 'popular', although they bear no relation to the manner in which people, Muslims included, dressed. This is underwritten by the primitivist trope that is a concomitant of populism,[17] and which is essential to Islamism, as it is this primitivism which provides it with its utopia.

Though neither 'popular' nor 'floating' except in part, the elements of this primitivist utopia are assimilated to the normative nominative 'Islam' and are thus represented as 'popular'. This is done on the assumption that that which is Islamic is perforce popular; that which is not in actuality popular is merely occluded, and its retrieval and reinsertion in the populist protocol is an act of rehabilitating nature which contingent history has left in abeyance.

This is the first point at which Islamist discourse in general is articulated with ideology and becomes fully political, going beyond its diffuse pietistic and ethical imperatives and nostalgias. For it is here that the elements in the Islamist repertoire are rendered elements in a specific notion of history, in a specific notion of society, and in a specific notion of political action.

History[18] takes place in two registers, one of which has a decided ontological distinction over the other: the authentic, and the inauthentic; that of the Islamic self, and that of its corruptions by otherness, such as non-Islamic people and religions, schisms, heresies and a manifold of enemies. The one is posited as original, hence necessary and in accord with nature, for Islam is a primeval relgion (*dīn al-fi ra*), and the other is posited as contingent, mere history, the passage of time as sheer succession and pure seriality, bereft of significance, and therefore of quality.

This ontologically differentiated history results in a discourse of absolute specificity and the rejection of any universalistic notions of history or of progress, much like Tolstoy and Mikhailovsky in Russia, and like certain forms for the expression of negritude or other forms of communalist and populist-nationalist expression. History for the highly influential Egyptian Sayyid Qu b (executed in 1966) is 'a memory determined by the authority' of the foundational age of Islam[19] – what we saw to be a utopia. All other history is contingent exoticism, for history that is ontologically weighty is limited to the history of the Islamic ego against which is set an absolute otherness. In principle impermeable, this ego is yet subject to degradation, which is of necessity contingent and solely attributable to exotic ruses and snares: of Manichaean and Muslim schismatics in the Middle Ages, of Jews/Marxists/Masons, allied to the evils of constitutionalism, Arab nationalism and other universal political principles in modernity.

Political Islamism seeks the retrieval of this essence superordinate over mere history; hence the names adopted by Islamist political groups, reminiscent of those adopted by ascendent and subaltern nationalisms: Renaissance (*Nah a, Risorgimento*), Salvation (*Khalā*), Awakening (*I yā', Yaqa a*), and their cognates. The present is a condition of radical degradation and deviance, and the task of the retrieval is the restoration of the pristine order, the primitivist utopia. The present is, at best, a Nicht-Ich, 'occidentosis'.[20] Absolute Unbelief makes it incumbent upon Islamist political *groupuscules* to shun their contemporaries and to reso-cialize their members according to the meta-social utopian model as an anti-society, and to condemn absolutely any attempt to 'ornament' this utopia or to render it acceptable to modern sensibilities or to formulate it in terms of modern political principles, such as nationalism, liberal-ism or socialism. Indeed, Islam 'regards the way of God and His Law as the fundamental principle to which people should conform, and to which reality must be adapted'.[21]

Thus we have a Romantic notion of history which is familiar in modern history – from Herder and his patrimony in Germany, to ide-as current in the Risorgimento, to the organicist conservatism of Gus-tave Le Bon. All these are widely attested to in the history of modern Arab thought, although irrationalism in modern Arab political and social thought has not yet been systematically examined. Indeed, we can also say that there are common conditions of emergence, and that there are convergences between modern Arab irrationalism and European irrationalisms. Islamist irrationalism is a new phenomenon – classical Islamic reformism was a curious mixture of organicist his-toricism and evolutionism, with a liberal-constitutionalist and utili-tarian interpretation of the scriptures.[22] Modern political Islamism, a product of the past two and a half decades, was born at a different conjuncture, which allowed it to articulate the elements of the Is-lamist repertoire with the concept of history available from Arab na-tionalist ideology, especially its expression in the 1930s and 1940s, associated with Baathism, and clearly formulated with reference to Nietzsche, Spengler, Bergson and others. With the Arab nationalist project defeated and in abeyance, especially after 1967, Islamist po-litical discourse tended in some instances to subsume a hypernation-alism in terms of the Islamist repertoire, or at least to bear it in its folds,[23] and indeed to fuse with the sort of nationalist advocacy put forward by a suddenly deeply pious Saddam Hussein in 1990–91. In all cases, the potency of the religious symbolic repertoire was primed

into the moulds of nationalist ideology that constitutes the actual political culture of the Arab World.

Islamist political discourse is loath to specify the political system that
the Islamic state would create and invigilate. It normally rests content
with emphasizing the uniqueness of this society, it being one where
God is the sole legislator.[24] Beyond the legal order which reenacts the
primitivist utopia, nothing remains but a savage vitalism: the social order will 'emerge vitally' from doctrine, and doctrine becomes 'the actual and active reality of the group'.[25]

This lack of specification appears odd in the light of the detailed regulation attributed to Islamic law. Yet this silence is not fortuitous, neither
is it without cover, and the cover is provided by the vitalist expression
often used. Vitalism yields two important consequences: a notion of
social homogeneity which implies a corporatist notion of society, and
a naturalistic concept of the socio-historical order and of the natural
inevitability of the utopian restoration.

Islamist political discourse always insists that the Islamic party is
not a political party on a par with other political parties, but that it is
distinguished by being consonant with the ontologically privileged
history outlined above. It represents the element of continuity, and is
therefore above and beyond political dissent, constituting instead the
very core of the Being-Social, the median point in an order which, if it
were to be in keeping with the ontological privilege of normalcy and in
conformity to the nature of things, must be homogeneous, undivided,
bereft of difference or of differentiation, an even surface from whence
authority and order spring vitally, a surface whose evenness renders
possible the direct and unmediated action of political authority. This is
amply shown in the attitudes towards democracy adopted by Islamist
groups that menace the fledgling democratic processes in, say, Algeria.
With a totalitarian valorization of the Rousseauian notion of the General Will, these groups postulate that the accomplishment of democracy
can only be signalled when an Islamic state is erected, thus making for
the full correspondence of state and society – some Islamists with curious minds or left-wing pasts state this in Gramscian terms, as do members of the growing group of Arab populist nationalists. The rejection
of party-political location thus acts as the grid through which the image
of the total state is made into a political programme and an agency
for totalitarian control, for the pronounced educational function of this
state is geared to the total homogenization of cultural and social space.
From this Islamist political parties derive their notion of democracy:

democracy becomes a totalitarian passion whereby the Islamist party substitutes itself for the body politic, conceived as a social protoplasm which remains formless until it is endowed with an Islamic order.

With the advent of this finalist Islamic polity, it is not only society to which the state is brought in correspondence. This correspondence is based on a sort of pre-established harmony, located in the proposition, mentioned above and universally stated by Islamist authors, that the Islamic order is primeval, in conformity with the predisposition of societies at all times and places, a sort of natural law, or even a cosmic order. For the rule of Islam is inevitable, as humanity must ultimately conform to the role allotted it by the Almighty, and deference to the Word of God in matters of social and political organization is simply a recognition of the sole order of society in conformity with the order of the cosmos.[26] The affinity between this pan-naturalism attributed to the restorative ideology, and the National Socialist cult of nature is manifest.[27] A common condition of emergence could be sought in a classical trope of all ideology, the naturalization of history. Another connection might be sought in Alexis Carrel (d.1944), the fascistoid Frenchman who has so entranced Islamist authors like Qu b and Shariati,[28] and who, like them, wrote at great length about the degeneracy of modern conditions, the solution to which he found with the neutralization of the proletarian multitude and the revivification of the germoplasm containing the 'ancestral potentialities' of the 'energetic strains' of North-Western Europe.[29]

Carrel also dwelt at length on the need for an elite – social and biological – for the salvation of civilization.[30] This elite, for Islamist political ideologies, is the group which sets itself apart from society and defends the rights of God as against the rights of mortals, and implements the eternal writ of God as against the unbelieving opinions of men, and which prepares itself for offensive politico-military action that aims at the correction of the world, and bringing it into harmony with the cosmos.[31]

The naturalistic argument for the inevitability of Islamic rule mentioned is not often manifestly deployed, although it is always implicit. Indeed, Sayyid Qu b, who propounded it, also propounded the position that no arguments from nature or from nationality can buttress the Islamist political position, which must rest on divine command, and this position is even more pronounced amongst Qu bist groups of the 1970s and 1980s.[32] In other words, the political imperatives do not relate to political conditions, according to this conception.

The most important consequence of this is that the realization of the category of political Islam is a very highly voluntaristic action. It is this voluntarist notion of political action which explains much of the apparent apolitical nihilism that marks the positions of Islamist groups. Direct, unmediated action aims to homogenize the surface of society, or assumes it to be homogeneous; it can be well described in terms of Hegel's analysis of the Absolute Freedom of the Jacobins in the *Phenomenology*. The world is the immediate substance of political action, and this political action is frozen in the moment of pure confrontation and contestation. Needless to say, there is no precedent for this conspiratorial notion of total political action in Muslim tradition. Instead, Islamist political activity stands in direct relation, because of common conditions of emergence in modernity as well as by direct example, to clandestine party organization and the tradition of the élitist *putsch* identified in the twentieth century with Bolshevism and its numerous progeny East and West, and this in turn goes back to the tradition in which gelled Babouvism and Freemasonry at the close of the eighteenth century, which gave rise to the Carbonari and the nineteenth-century revolutionary tradition.

Yet this degree zero of politics, this notion of contestation as total war, this immediate resort to terrorism, this practical end of the restorative concept of history, is the corollary of its beginning. The politicization of the sacred, the sacralization of politics, and the transformation of Islamic pseudo-legal institutes – the tokens of Islamicity – into 'social devotions',[33] are all means of realizing the politics of the authentic ego, a politics of identity, and are therefore the means for the very formation, indeed the invention, of this identity. The secret of Islam as a political category lies therein, that the image of the total state is reproduced under the guise of reaffirming a pre-existing identity endowed with an ontological privilege, an identity which is but the nominal node for the interpellation, by nominal association, of a host of tokens. It is this self-same node of interpellation that constitutes the hinge whereby are articulated the ideological notions of political Islamism – notions of history, the body politic, and of political action – and the tokens which fully stand for Islam. And what this Islam devolves to is the mirror image of the modernist state which originated with the Jacobins, was routinized and historicized in the Napoleonic state, and exported worldwide. The modernism of this proposed state is the fundamental feature of this supposedly pre-modern creature of postmodernism.

## Contestation and Democracy

Islamist discourse is therefore a celebrated witness to neo-orientalism, and the deliberate archaism of the former sustains the postmodernism of the latter. It transpired that Islamist political language is far from being *sui generis*; indeed, even if it were, it will still have been communicable, for communication is in fact premised on the non-equivalence of the interlocutors, and no degree of under-determination precludes successful communication, for indeed, it is indeterminacy which is 'the measure of information'.[34]

If we were to look with sober eyes at the history and politics of this discourse on history and politics, we would find ourselves amid a situation certain features of which have particular salience for our purpose, and I will outline these briefly before turning directly to the connection of all these matters with democracy.

The political origins of this Islamist discourse with its many varieties and inflections are easy to identify. It started in the 1950s and 1960s, as a local Arab purveyance of the Truman Doctrine, and was sustained initially by Egyptian and Syrian Islamists – both earnest ones, and socially conservative, pro-Saudi business and other elements opposed to Nasserism and Baathism. This was indeed the first great cultural and ideological enterprise of Petro-Islam, along with ideas of pan-Islamism as a force counterbalancing Arab nationalism, and Islamic authenticity combating 'alien' ideologies. The idea that religious affiliation is a potent weapon with which to wage war against state structures in the Middle East is not, of course, a new one, and has a history of trying to encourage the matching of religious and political affiliation – the first moment of this was Balkanization, the present one Lebanization.[35]

The Petro-Islamic enterprise has been hugely successful, especially with the substantial influx of the Arab intelligentsia to the relatively backward countries of the Arabian Peninsula, and the colossal ensemble of mediatic and other cultural organs that Petro-Islam has built up, and with which, most importantly, it has broken the secularist and nationalist cultural, mediatic and, to a lesser extent, the educational monopoly of the modern Arab state. It has resulted in the Islamic acculturation of certain social groups: not the recovery of an essence, but the manufacture of an identity. This is why Islamism is a force without resonance in places like the city of Sfax in Tunisia, whose internal economic and social structures seem to be in a good measure of continuity with the recent past, but with substantial influence in a city like Tunis, where sections of the population were traumatized by forces of social pulverization.[36]

On the basis of this hegemonic project, Islamism is now laying claims, like those countenanced for it by neo-orientalism, to the representation of the body politic – a surface construed to be as even as that of 'Islamic' society. It may be remembered that prior to the municipal elections in Algeria in June 1990, Abbasi Madani, the leader (now incarcerated) of the so-called National Salvation Front, said that he was confident of victory, and threatened untold violence and terror in case of disappointment. Apart from an attempt to terrorize state and electorate, the implicit assumption is that defeat of the Islamists would represent an act so unnatural that speech fails, and the only answer to which would have to be the 'non-discursive' assertion of nature, the self-realization of a transcendental narcissism. This pseudo-sociological notion of correspondence between Arab society and Islamist polity is now a central feature of the Islamist discourse on democracy and seems to sustain itself in an exclusively plebiscitary notion of democracy – democracy as a totalitarian passion for the identity of state and society, the liberal democratic form being the prelude to the abolition of liberal democracy.

This was not, of course, always so. The 'Islamic liberalism' which we saw advocated above, more than half a century out of phase, had a creative interpretation of Islam in terms of constitutionalism, rather than the other way round as is the case today. This consisted of a liberal exegetical effort, toward the Koran as well as early Islamic tradition, with a view to producing a concordance between the sense of this textual body and democratic ideas and institutions. This, in the work of Mu ammad 'Abduh (d. 1905) and others, was part of a modernist reinterpretation of Muslim texts of sacred or semi-sacred character, in which these texts were regarded as a code, open to the modernist interpreter, which yielded ideas in keeping with science, with evolutionism, and other ideas in currency including nineteenth-century European attitudes of sexual propriety. There were similar movements in the history of Catholicism, particularly in eighteenth-century France, and certainly before the influence of Bonald and Lamennais made itself felt. But this effort depends on an epistemological *legerdemain*, which operates by assuming the scriptures do not mean what they say. And this bluff was called by the ascendant fundamentalist Islam, in the past two decades, and the time for Muslim liberalism has certainly passed, although it still has many voices, some of them very creative and of considerable talent, but the most important of which is the Arab state, which has embraced Islamic modernism as its own.

So the question of democracy in the Arab World, as elsewhere, in countries with Muslim majorities and other parts of the South, is located elsewhere, beyond the bounds of mystification and within the boundaries of history and of politics: not as the realization of the Truth of society. Sectarianism is a sub-species of communalism, and communalism, a political phenomenon, is far more than the sheer register of the social and historical existence of communities. As in the liberal pluralism of Britain in the early part of this century, the liberal democratic position in the Arab World is formulated in opposition to the idealist theory of the state as coextensive with society and to the concomitant organicist paradigm of society I have outlined.

It is a fact that, despite claims of neo-orientalists and Islamists alike, Arab countries are subject to the social, cultural, political and ideological forms which, in the past two centuries, have become universal, albeit with varying rhythms, articulations and determinations. We have seen Islamism itself partaking of universality in its claims for specificity and irreducibility, with a pronounced sense of kinship to generic fascism and right-wing forms of subaltern nationalism; in Europe, it acts as a counter-fascism. This universalism is inescapable. Of European origin undoubtedly, expanding throughout the world by colonial and neo-colonial transformation of economies, societies, polities and cultures, this universalism leaves nothing intact, for the universal history of modernity is a voracious consumer of particularities. It brings together in this global concatenation even the most bizarre and archaic sectors of society and culture, whose abiding archaism – or, rather, I should say archaization, traditionalization – is their mode of contemporaneity in this global combined and uneven development, and provides a 'real time' ideological sustenance to political philo-Islamism in the West, a latter-day 'indirect rule' instrument. We cannot underestimate the role of Western mediatic representation in this archaization: exotic, marginal religious manifestations are presented as central, civil wars or insurrections which have political and other causes are presented persistently as sectarian – and these representations are transmitted back to their countries of origin, at once distorting realities, and actively inciting sectarian conflicts.

It goes without saying that unevenness is not confined to peripheries – European societies themselves form very uneven social, cultural and religious surfaces. There is no need to think of some particularly generic exotic quality in terms of which democracy in the Arab World should be understood or practised. This is so not because there is nothing specific there, for the banal truth is that everything is specific. Nor is it the case that there is a constant copying of matters European, although this copying indeed takes place. Universalism is quite simply the participation, *volens nolens*, in a historical movement which, though Western European in origin, is now a global patrimony. Its insertion in the peripheries is incomplete and uneven, because of the weak institution of social and cultural formation, a weakness which is the counterpart of 'authentic' assertiveness. There is no culturally specific theory of democracy, as there is no epistemology specific for studying others, except exoticism, whose epistemology I have outlined above; for the determinants of all knowledge are historical, not 'cultural'.

The conditions of democracy in Arab lands are therefore a matter to be seen in the light of social and political conditions generally, and in the light of the presence of blockages, not specific to the Arab World, which produce Islamist politics: in political, social, economic and normative conflicts, in the heterogeneity and weak institution of society and culture, in the constitution and reconstitution of variant identities, including secular nationalism, liberal and authoritarian, and of the various groups of the intelligentsia. The conditions of democracy should also be sought in the state: the state itself, in some instances such as Morocco, Jordan, Yemen, Algeria, Tunisia and Egypt, has been the agency which, with imperfections and varying trajectories, has lately promoted forms of democracy. In some cases (Jordan and Algeria) this was the sign of the state abdicating its political and educational functions and throwing a society, traumatized into the opium of Islamism, to an uncertain future. In other cases, a good measure of political rationality dictated political transformations towards democracy, however imperfect, provisional, or reticent – a rationality responding to growing public political awareness, to the capacity for political organization, to increasing concatenations of 'civil society', both by the *Bildungs-bürgertum* so important in modern Arab history, as by a talismanic aspect that democracy is acquiring in the eyes of Arabs, as an element guarding against future calamities.

Democracy in the Arab World therefore is not a mysterious matter to be unravelled by neo-orientalist expertise. It has nothing to do with 'identity', except in so far as it will add *citizenship* in the proper sense to the web of multiple identities that mark all individuals and collectivities everywhere and at all times, thereby completing the transition

from communal to civil society. This process, like all historical processes, is highly conflictual. Islamist politics is one party to this conflict,
a party which seeks to drain politics out of society and confine it to the
state. And we have seen that, this being the case, Islamist politics, with
its combination of 'pre-Galilean consciousness and post-Hegelian discourse',[37] is an eminently historical player subject to the ruse of history.

## Notes

1. David Harvey, *The Condition of Postmodernity. An Inquiry into the Origins
of Cultural Change*, Oxford 1989, chs 10, 11 and passim.

2. Etienne Balibar, '*Es gibt keinen Staat in Europa*: Racism and Politics in
Europe Today', *New Left Review*, 186, 1991, pp. 10ff.

3. I.C. Jarvie, *Rationality and Relativism. In Search of a Philosophy and History of Anthropology*, London 1984, passim.

4. Ernesto Laclau, *New Reflections on the Revolution of our Time*, London
1991, pp. 17–18.

5. J.M. Lotman, 'On the Metalanguage of a Typological Description of Culture', *Semiotica*, 14/2, 1975, pp. 97ff.

6. In France: G. Kepel, *Le Prophète et Pharaon*, Paris 1984 (transl. J. Rothschild, as *The Prophet and Pharaoh*, London 1985); in the Anglo-Saxon World
and Israel: E. Sivan, *Radical Islam: Medieval Theology and Modern Politics*, New
Haven and London 1985.

7. A. Al-Azmeh, 'Islamic Studies and the European Imagination', Exeter 1986;
this volume, ch. 8.

8. For a concrete corrective, see E. Davis, 'The Concept of Revival and
the Study of Islam and Politics', in Barbara Freyer Stowasser, ed., *The Islamic
Impulse*, London 1987, pp. 37–58.

9. Kepel, *Prophet and Pharaoh*; and O. Carré, *Les Frères Musulmans*, Paris
1983.

10. L. Binder, *Islamic Liberalism. A Critique of Development Ideologies*, Chicago and London 1988, pp. 358–9.

11. Ibid, p. 1.

12. Kepel, *Prophet and Pharaoh*, p. 225.

13. Al-Azmeh, 'Islamic Studies and the European Imagination', in this volume; and 'If a al-istishraq', in A. Al-Azmeh, *Al-Turāth bayn al-sul ān wa 'l-tārīkh*
[Heritage: Politics and History], Casablanca and Beirut 1987, pp. 61ff.

14. Al-Azmeh, 'Utopia and Islamic Political Thought', *History of Political
Thought*, XI/I, 1990, pp. 91ff and this volume, ch. 6; and *Al-Kitāba al-tārīkhiya
wa 'l-ma'rifa al-tarīkhiya* [Historical Writing and Historical Knowledge], Beirut
1983, pp. 93ff.

15. The above is based on Al-Azmeh, *Al-Turāth*, pp. 51ff. Cf. M. Arkoun,
*Ouvertures sur l'Islam*, Paris 1989, p. 46, who, following Lyotard, speaks of the
'degradation' of signs to symbols.

16. E. Laclau, *Politics and Ideology in Marxist theory*, London 1979, p. 194.

17. D. MacRae, 'Populism as an Ideology', in E. Gellner and G. Ionescu, eds, *Populism. Its Meaning and National Characteristics*, London 1969, pp. 155–6. The connection between Islamism and populism is also noted by E. Abrahamian, 'Khomeini: Fundamentalist or Populist', *New Left Review*, 186, 1991, pp. 102–19.

18. See Al-Azmeh, 'The Discourse of Cultural Authenticity', in E. Deutsch, ed., *Culture and Modernity*, Honolulu 1991, pp. 468ff; and this volume, ch. 4.

19. M.H. Diyāb, *Sayyid Qu b. Al-Khi āb wa'l-Idyūlujīyā* [Sayyid Qutb: Discourse and Ideology], Beirut 1988, p. 105.

20. The title of a book by the Iranian Islamist cultural critic, Jalal Al-i Ahmad, *Occidentosis. A Plaue from the West*, transl. R. Campbell, Berkeley 1984.

21. S. Qu b, *Ma'alim fi' - arīq* [Milestones], Cairo and Beirut 1981, pp. 41–2, 189, and passim; and the text of Islamist terrorist leaders in R. Sayyid Ahmad, *Al-Nabī al-musalla* [The Prophet Armed], London 1990, vol. 1, pp. 40–42, 53–103, 130, 148–9 and passim.

22. One can usefully consult A. Laroui, *Islam et modernité*, Paris 1987, pp. 127ff, and A. Al-Azmeh, 'Islamic Revivalism and Western Ideologies', *History Workshop Journal*, 32, 1991, pp. 44ff. On irrationalism in modern Arab thought generally, see Raif Khuri, *Modern Arab Thought*, transl. I. Abbas, Princeton 1983, and Aziz Al-Azmeh, *Al-'Ilmānīya* [Secularism], Beirut 1992, passim.

23. A. Al-Azmeh, 'Islamism and Arab Nationalism', *Review of Middle East Studies*, 4, 1988, pp. 33ff.

24. For example, Ayatollah Khomeini, *Al- ukūma al-islāmīyya* [Islamic Government], Beirut 1979, p. 41.

25. Qu b, *Ma'ālim*, pp. 43–5; and, *Al-Mustaqbal li-hādhā al-dīn* [The Future is for this Religion], Cairo n.d., p. 12.

26. Qu b, *Ma'ālim*, pp. 53, 110–11; and *Al-Islām wa mushkilāt al- a āra* [Islam and the Problem of Civilization], n.p. 1968, pp. 4–5.

27. See R. Pois, *National Socialism and the Religion of Nature*, London 1986, pp. 38–44 and passim.

28. Qu b, *Al-Islam*, pp. 7–30, 108 and passim; A. Shariati, *Marxism and Other Western Fallacies*, transl. R. Campbell, Berkeley 1986, pp. 15–16. See the detailed apologetic biography by R. Soupault, *Alexis Carrel*, Paris 1952. The connection between Qu b and Carrel has also been discussed by Y. Choueiri, *Islamic Fundamentalism*, London 1990, pp. 142–9.

29. A. Carrel, *Man the Unknown*, West Drayton, Middlesex 1948, pp. 252–4, 276 and passim.

30. Ibid., pp. 271–3, 277.

31. Qu b, *Ma'ālim*, pp. 11–12, 20, 72ff.

32. Qu b, *Na wa mujtama' islāmī* [Towards an Islamic Society], Beirut 1980, p. 11; Sayyid A mad, *Al-Nabī*, vol. 1, pp. 127–9.

33. The term comes from the Muslim Brother cleric M. Ghazālī, *Min hunā na' lam* [From This We Know], Cairo 1954, p. 44.

34. Y.M. Lotman, *Universe of the Mind. A Semiotic Theory of Culture*, London 1990, p. 227.

35. G. Corm, *L'Europe et l'Orient de la balcanisation à la libanisation. Histoire d'une modernité inaccomplie*, Paris 1989.

36. M.A. Hirmāsī, 'Al-Islām al-i tijājī fī Tūnis', in *Al- arakāt al-Islāmīyya al-mu'a ira* [Contemporary Islamic Movements], Beirut 1987, pp. 249ff.

37. D. Shayeghan, *Le Regard mutilé*, Paris 1989; Arabic translation as *Al-Nafs al-mabtūra*, London 1991, pp. 77, 89–90, 95–6.

# The Discourse of Cultural Authenticity: Islamist Revivalism and Enlightenment Universalism

I take it as an accomplished fact that modern history is characterized by the globalization of the Western order. Despite protests of a bewildering variety against this accomplished fact, it remains incontestable, especially as, with few exceptions of an isolated and purely local nature, these protests have taken place either in the name of ideologies of Western provenance – such as national independence and popular sovereignty – or substantially in terms of these ideologies, albeit symbolically beholden to a different local or specific repertory, such as the Iranian regime of the Ayatollahs. The validation of universalism does not arise from some transcendental or immanent criterion, but quite simply from affirming the rationality of the real.

The reasons for this are manifest: the conditions of Western economic and political conquest and hegemony in the modern age have engendered, for good or for ill, correlative conditions of equally real ideological and cultural hegemony. The East – and I only use this term for convenience – has been heavily impregnated with novel categories of thought, methods of education, contents of knowledge, forms of discourse and communication, aesthetic norms and ideological positions. It has become impossible to speak with sole reference to traditional texts and without reference to Western notions.

There is nothing particularly mysterious about this irreversible state of affairs, and the conditions for cross-cultural knowledge are not distinct from the conditions of knowledge in general. A cross-cultural epistemology is neither possible nor desirable. Knowledge is always of an object, and in this view the quiddity of other cultures is not substantially distinct from the objectness of any other object of knowledge – knowledge being empirical, aesthetic, historical, and its objects therefore being appropriate for these modes of apprehension and reason. Culture is a very coy object and is a term rather thoughtlessly applied to objects poorly apprehended or regarded as somewhat exotic and quaint.

One would therefore be better advised to speak of a universal civilization comprising a manifold of historical formations – the European, the Arab, the Indian. Each of these is highly differentiated, but these differences, or the cluster of such differences, are globally articulated and unified by the economic, political, cultural and ideological facts of dominance. Each historical unit is, moreover, multivocal, and Europe of course is no exception to this, despite the claims that are made on behalf of a triumphalist Hegelianism, somewhat impoverished by the elimination from it of history.

In this light, the notion of incommensurability and its cognates appears quite absurd, not only because historical units are not analogous to paradigms and apprehension is not analogous to translation. Neither are they homogeneous, self-enclosed and entirely self-referential entities, as would be required by the assumption of univocal irreducibility. The consequences of such assumptions exceed the simple elision of history and lead to a barren and naïve relativist temptation with at best a patronizing rhetoric of intercultural etiquette dressed up as a philosophical hermeneutic. More perniciously it leads to the absolute relativism that underlies apartheid and the culturalist pretensions of some political groups such as those that came to prominence with the conjuration of the Salman Rushdie affair.

This compulsory universalism can be illustrated with a particular case made all the more poignant because it is an advocacy of exclusivism and of incommensurable distinction. I have indicated that Europe has everywhere spawned ideological and cultural phenomena as diverse as her own. What appears in the East under the guise of traditionalism is normally an apologetic or a radically reformist discourse whose terms of articulation and criteria of validation are by no means traditional – traditions do not validate themselves, they are idioms. There are indeed deliberate archaisms and medievalisms that may appear in direct continuity with the past. Among these I would class the cultivation, for the purposes other than recondite anti-quarianism and historical research, of such matters as the magnificently ornate re-paganized Neoplatonism in vogue in Iran. This naturally evokes a chilling sense of the Gothic, but could with some effort be made comprehensible in historical conditions over-determined by European modernity. For it is a fact of the modern history of the Arab World, or of Iran and other countries with Muslim majorities – and it should be strongly emphasied that Islam is not a culture, but a religion living amidst very diverse cultures and thus a very multiform entity – that the predominant literate discourses in social and political life are local adaptations of Enlightenment and post-Enlightenment traditions, such as Marxism, naturalism, liberalism and nationalism.

In what follows, an attempt will be made to anatomize a notion of much potency in modern Arab social and political thought: it is hoped that a paradigm that will make comparable other exclusivist ideologies increasingly at work in the world, such as right-wing Hindu communalism, Zionist fundamentalism both secular and religious, and much else, will become explicit.

## I

In common with other subaltern nationalisms, as with defensive, retrenching nationalisms and with populist ideologies, the notion of authenticity is widely used both in formal discourse on matters political and social and in the interstices of casual comment. The notion of authenticity is not so much a determinate concept as it is a node of associations and interpellations, a trope by means of which the historical world is reduced to a particular order, and a token which marks off social and political groups and forges and reconstitutes historical identities. In these senses the notion of authenticity has analogues elsewhere, doubtless officiated under different names.

*A āla* is the Arabic term for authenticity. Lexically, it indicates salutary moral qualities like loyalty, nobility, and a sense of commitment to a specific social group or a set of values. It also indicates a sense of *sui generis* originality; and in association with the senses previously mentioned, *a āla* specifically refers to genealogical standing: noble or at least respectable descent for humans, and the status of equine aristocrats. Combined together and transferred to an attribute of historical collectivities, Arab, Muslim or other, *a āla* becomes a central notion in a Romantic conception of history which calls forth features commonly associated with such a conception. Of primary importance among these features is a vitalist concept of nationalism and of politics, replete with biological metaphor and, occasionally, a sentimentalist populism.

Ultimately, therefore, the notion of authenticity is predicated on the notion of a historical subject which is at once self-sufficient and self-evident. Its discourse is consequently an essentialist discourse, much like the reverse it finds in Orientalism, in discourses on the primitive, and in other discourses on cultural otherness.[1] In common with these discourses, the discourse on authenticity postulates a historic subject which is self-identical, essentially in continuity over time, and positing itself in essential distinction from other historical subjects. For the viability of a historical subject such as this, it is essential that its integrity must be maintained against a manifest backdrop of change of a very rapid and profound nature. It therefore follows that change should be conceived as contingent, impelled by inessential matters like external interference or internal subversion, the effects of which can only be faced with a reassertion of the essence of historical subjectivity. History therefore becomes an alternance in a continuity of decadence and health, and historiographical practice comes to consist in the writing of history as a form of classification of events under the two categories of intrinsic and extrinsic, the authentic and the imputed, the essential and the accidental.

It is therefore not fortuitous or haphazard that the title under whose name this discourse (and its political implications) is officiated should be revivalism, *nah a*, in line with similar historical and ideological experiences of which the *Risorgimento* readily comes to mind. For this entire ideological trope can be described as one of ontological irredentism, it being the attempt to retrieve an essence that the vicissitudes of time and the designs of enemies, rather than change of any intrinsic nature, had caused to atrophy. The counterpart of this was that the degraded conditions of today are mere corruptions of the original cultural essence, the retrieval of which is only possible by a return to the pristine beginnings which reside in the early years of Islam, the teachings of the book of God, the Koran, and the example of the Prophet Mu ammad. It must be added at the outset, however, that though revivalism was initially Islamist, and has tended to don the Islamist cloak in the very recent past, it received its most thorough grounding in the context of secular Arab nationalist ideology, which regarded Islam as but one moment of Arab glory, albeit an important one.

In historical terms, this constellation of notions came into currency in the second half of the nineteenth century, first with the Young Ottomans in Istanbul, and particularly Namik Kemal (1840–88), and shortly thereafter in the writings of the remarkable Jamal al-Dīn al-Afghānī (1839–97). Afghānī was not a profound thinker, but a very potent speaker and charismatic conspirator. His careers in Istanbul, Tehran, Kabul, Hyderabad, Calcutta, Cairo, London, Paris and St Petersburg have left an important imprint on pan-Islamism in the Arab World, which, in certain respects at his time, can be regarded as a form of protonationalism.[2] Afghānī left a body of miscellaneous writings, most notably his polemic against the pro-British Indian Muslim reformer Sir Syed Ahmad Khan (1817–98),[3] with whose ideas, it must be stressed, he was not really at variance. He inspired the journal *Al-'Urwa al-wuthqā*, a collaborative body of political, cultural and reformist writing published in Paris in 1882–83 with his then disciple, Mu ammad 'Abduh (1849–1905), who was later to become the Arab World's foremost and most subtle Muslim reformist.[4] A section of 'Abduh's writings are in tune with the general theses of Afghānī, but are far more finely tuned and retain none of Afghānī's occasional crudeness of conception, and 'Abduh's disciples numbered some of the Arab World's foremost Muslim reformist and nationalist leaders in the early part of this century. This same constellation of notions was channelled into the mainstream of Arab political and social thought through the nationalism which was later to become Turkish nationalism exemplified in Ziya Gökalp (1875–1924) and the Arab nationalism of his erstwhile associate, Sa i' al- u rī (1880–1968),[5] although rī was not a Romantic revivalist and populist like Gökalp, and Romantic revivalism was only to enter Arab nationalism between the wars, a process to which u rī, though at the peak of his career, was far too sober a positivist sociologist and educationist to contribute.

Before describing the anatomy of the notion of authenticity, it will be well to make a number of further historical specifications. It was rare after Afghānī for Islamist revivalism to take the Romantic form until very recently; its revivalism was concentrated on the revivification of a utopia which consisted of a clear set of precedents of a social, legal and moral order unconnected with an elaborate notion of history. It was only when Islamism associated itself with nationalism – the prevalent ideological impulse in the Arab World – and assimilated it in such a way that Islamism became a viable medium for the articulation of nationalism, that Islamism became Romantic and returned to the tropes of Jamāl al-Dīn al-Afghānī, who is idolized by today's Islamists. Finally, it must be stressed that it is extremely difficult to study precisely how Afghānī or his acolytes became Romantic. The notion of authenticity, which will be described presently, lies at the intersection of a number of concepts that are foreign to classical Islamic thought, which constituted the core of Afghānī's education. It is well known that the highlights of European thought were becoming quite familiar in Cairo, Istanbul and elsewhere from the early part of the nineteenth century and that they contributed to the formation of Young Ottoman thought.[6] But I believe it to be impossible philologically to trace European influence from such quarters of paramount importance for the notion of authenticity as Herder and the German historical school of law associated with Savigny and others at any time before about 1930, although some French thinkers in a roughly similar vein, such as Gustave Le Bon, were fairly well known.[7] If influence there was, it would most probably have come orally or implicitly in the body of occasional writing such as journalism; it is also very important to study the social and political conditions under which Romantic nationalism (or proto-nationalism) could grow spontaneously.

## II

The nation for Afghānī is akin to a body, and although he changed his mind over what constituted a nation, in the final analysis he devalued ties of ethnicity and, to a lesser extent, of language to the advantage of the bond of religion.[8] A nation consists of estates analogous to parts of a body, or of individuals whose organic unity is that of the parts of a vital organism. This organism is infused with a vital force like that which permeates its individual organs, and the power of this individual vitality is directly proportional to that in the whole organism.[9]

This organismic, vitalist paradigm has its major notions – if not its object, a socio-political order – in medieval Islamic natural philosophy. Equally important is that it naturally invites comparison with Herder's notion of *Kräfte* as inner sources of vitality and dynamic principles for the continued existence of nations; the question as to whether Herder's Romanticism is medieval in its conceptual inspiration is irrelevant to its modernity and to the vital part it played in nineteenth- and twentieth-century ideological tendencies. Though Afghānī's ideas initially were shaped in Iranian seminaries, they were received in Calcutta, Cairo, Istanbul and Paris, where they were filtered through contemporary social and political categories. Also like Herder's, Afghānī's paradigm concretizes this vital principle for the unity and cohesion of bodies national in culturalist terms and, like Herder's emphasis on *Bildung*, finds in civic and moral education the key to the maintenance and resuscitation of national glory. The vital spirit in empirical terms is a yearning in the hearts of men for glory and a leaning towards the consummate realization of values. And this vital spirit is operative only when it impels bodies national with a desire for excellence and distinction in wealth as well as glory and might (*'izz*).[10]

In situations of conflict brought about by pervasive Western interference in the Middle East, this perspective was not unnaturally invested with a social-Darwinist stance. It is well to bear in mind that the 'conflict theory' of political sociology was emerging in Germany at about the same time – proponents of this theory, as well as Afghānī, were keenly interested in Ibn Khaldūn's theory of the power of state, which they used in the construction of a nationalist Romanticism.[11] The struggle for existence, Afghānī tells us, pervades human history no less than in the animal kingdom and inanimate nature. The reason for this is that 'might is the visible aspect of life and of continued existence . . . and might is never triumphant and concrete except when it weakens and subjugates others.' As illustration, Afghānī cites the powers of nations, and specifically the subjugation of the Ottoman Empire by the European powers.[12]

What, in this perspective, is history? And what does the passage of time yield? It can be noted that the subject of history is the body national. Each body national, as in Herder, is a fixed nature which is, according to the characterization of Collingwood, less the product of history than its presupposition.[13] That unit which is historically significant is the national subject, and history is therefore one of alternance between true historicity manifested in might, and historical desuetude manifested in subjugation. Might results from cohesiveness and unity, and if this unity were to be lost the body national would lose its spirit or its general will, with the result that 'the thrones of its might will fall, and it [the nation] will take its leave of existence just as existence has abandoned it.'[14] It is indicative of Afghānī's style that he used the term *quwwa āfi a*, which I have rendered as 'spirit'. The expression, literally 'preservative power', is derived from medieval Arabic natural philosophy, in which Afghānī was deeply steeped and concepts from which he often used, where it designates the subliminal quality which keeps together a somatic composite.

The cohesiveness and unity of this body national infused with a vital impulse that yearns for glory is maintained so long as the factors which originally constituted this *Volksgeist* are operative. But once corruption sets in, once the essence is diluted, the auguries of national calamity become manifest. Thus the glorious classical civilization of the Muslim Arabs was corroded from the inside by the snares of esotericist sects, which paved the way for conquest by Crusaders and Mongols. Similarly, the fabric of the Ottoman Empire was weakened by Ottoman westernizing reformists in the middle of the nineteenth century. As for the

French, the glory of their royal past was corrupted by the seductions of Voltaire and Rousseau, which directly led to what Afghānī regarded as the calamities of the French Revolution, the Paris Commune and defeat in the Franco-Prussian War. In the same class of universally destructive, disintegrative impulses are socialism, communism and anarchism, which might cause the annihilation of humanity altogether, being the ultimate forces of corruption and radical antinomianism, the antithesis of order and civilization.[15]

There is no response to weakness and destruction save that of revivalism: the retrieval and restoration of the original qualities that made for strength and historical relevance. No progress without the retrieval of pristine beginnings and the cleansing of the essence from the adulteration of history:[16] such is the fundamental principle of revivalism; the example of Martin Luther was never far from the mind of Afghānī. The Islam that results from the elision of history and the deprivation of time of any significant ontological weight will shortly be taken up; but before this is done it is necessary to take a closer look at the categories that subsist in the trope of authenticity, of absolute individuality and irreducible historical subjectivity.

## III

The trope of authenticity described above as less a determinant concept than a node of associations is premised on a number of important notions and distinctions. Fundamental among these is a conception of history which posits a narcissistic continuing subject, mighty by virtue of its nature but enfeebled by subversion, inadvertence and what Hegel termed 'Oriental ease and repose'. This same subject will regain its vital energy and continue the maintenance of its nature – its entelechy – by a recommencement and by the revivification of its beginnings, which still subsist within it just as a nature, in the classical and medieval Arabic and European senses, inheres in a body.

But this subject is inconceivable in isolation from others, which exist alongside it, for the notion is essentially formed in the context of political contestation. These others are, to a very considerable degree, absolute in their otherness, in that they are antitheses of the subject, and, in order for them to be met, their subjectivity has constantly to be objectified, deprived of value except for that which, like forces of corruption, is inessential and contingent, hence transferable. Such was the attitude of Afghānī and all those who adopted the hopes associated with his name towards modern science and technology, of European provenance but not culture-specific and, moreover, necessary for the construction of national might. Throughout, the origin – the positive beginning – is adulterated, but still flows as a subliminal impulse amid degradation and corruption, for the fall from previous heights is inessential, and the essence of this historical subject is in fact suprahistorical and still subsists in the innermost core of the cultural self. The revivalist project is simply one in which this core is again brought to the surface and to the fore-front of historical existence, thereby restoring the historical subject to its true nature.

The truth of this nature is an ontological truth, one whose resistance to the vagaries of time is demonstrated by the revivalist belief in its capacity for resuscitation, and whose durability is the measure of its truth. Indeed, this nature, the vital impulse of the body national, is the very reality of the subject in history; corruption is conceivable only as privation. In the light of this, history consists of continuity over a time which knows no substantive causalities, for causality is only manifest in discontinuity.[17] This continuity is in a constantly antithetical relation to all otherness: to other nations, which by virtue of the very nature of bodies naturally seek to subjugate the nation-subject, and to corruptions within, for these are privations of the essence which seek to subvert, and thus to nullify, the vital energy which uplifts and allows for glory.

Time is therefore cleft between origins and corruptions, between authenticity and the snares of enemies. Forces of privation, of foreign – that is, inessential – provenance, have no intrinsic extensions: they do not extend to the core of the historical self, for they have no avenues that lead to the fund of subjectivity, either in the past or in the present. They have bearings neither in the past nor in the ontological reality of the present. In contrast, extraneous influences disturb the homogeneity of the subject and confound the bearings of its historical course by repudiating the original inner indistinctness and homogeneity which constitute the stuff of authenticity.

Authenticity, for a contemporary philosopher who has been attempting a left-wing reclamation of Afghānī along the lines of a Muslim liberation theology, designates the self in contradistinction to the other, the essential as against the accidental, the natural as opposed to the artificial. Only thus can individuality and specificity properly be said to designate any genuine distinctiveness in opposition to 'the loss of distinctiveness and dissolution in another specificity [of the West] which claims universality.' Authenticity and its associated notions are, further,

said to extend the cultural ego into history and endow it with 'historical continuity and temporal homogeneity and the unity of the national
personality.'[18]

Authenticity is therefore both past and future linked contingently by
the ontological void of today. The past is the accomplished future and
the future is the past reasserted; history is the past in the future anterior.
History is an even continuum, on the surface of which eddy tiny circuits
which counter the original energies of the continuum and work to suppress them, yet do not quite succeed in more than rippling the surface
and disturbing its evenness. Only thus can teleology be assured: for a
nature to consummate itself, for the future revival to close the circle of
historical appearance and coalesce with the original condition, the end
must be pre-given and inevitable in the sense that it is in accord with
nature.

The body national is thus neither describable nor recognizable if
measured against its contingent existence, or against the sheer temporality and lack of perfection which characterize it today. Time is devoid
of quality, corruption is purely vicarious, and the present is but a negative interregnum between a perfect origin and its recommencement,
which is also its consummation. History therefore takes place in 'two
modes of time, one of which has a decided ontological distinction,'[19]
the one relevant to the essence and a measure of its duration, and the
other which dissolves into transience and contingency. The former is
much like the time of myth as described by Schelling in his *Philosophie der Mythologie*, one which is 'indivisible by nature and absolutely
identical, which therefore, whatever duration may be imputed to it, can
only be regarded as a moment, i.e. as time in which the end is like the
beginning and the beginning like the end, a kind of eternity, because it
is in itself not a sequence of time.'[20]

The connection of these modes of time is the same as that of different
bodies national: a connection of otherness which, in a social-Darwinist
world, is one of subjugation and of antinomy, essentially of negation,
without the possibility of a mutual interiorization such as that inherent
in, for example, the Hegelian dialectic of master and slave. Indeed, the
polar structuration of the discourse on authenticity is what makes it possible not only to deny essential change in time, thus denying multiplicity over time, but also to deny what we might term spatial multiplicity of
any essential consequence, this being the social, political and ideological multiplicity at any one particular point in time, except in so far as
such multiplicity is perceived as subversive of a homogeneous essence

which requires evenness. Any unevenness, as has already been indicated, is perceived in terms of antithesis, privation, corruption, atrophy.

It goes without saying that, in the real world, this national subject, an essence which knows neither dysfunction nor transformation but only abeyance, must reassert itself against history. Hence it must bring in train an acute sense of voluntarism. If human history is not to be assimilated to that of brute nature, the only agency capable of restoring nature to its course and directing it to the consummation of its entelechy is the will of the reformer, who stands to his nation as does a physician to a body in distemper.[21] And since this body, the body national, is arbitrarily posited as *sui generis*, it follows that the liberty of the reformer can best be described by following the Hegelian analysis of Jacobinism: it is one possessed by a freedom based on pure self-identity, for which the world is its own will, and whose relation to the reality of the world is unmediated, and therefore one of pure negation.[22]

This will, in a pure, indeterminate element, is pure thought of its own self.[23] It is pure self-reference, a tautological circle, whose impenetrability to reason other than the reason of its own self-reference is very much in keeping with similar outlooks in the German *Lebensphilosophie* of the turn of the century, where life is at once the subject and the object of the mind.[24] The crazed waft of blood in the Rushdie affair is fully accounted for in this context. The authentic self is immediately apprehended,[25] and knowledge of it by its own is a sort of pure and perfect *Verstehen*, an almost innate endowment in the mind of the components that make up this body national, whose self-enclosure is epistemological and not only ontological. Indeed, the epistemological and the ontological correspond perfectly, for knowledge of authenticity is but a moment in the life of this authenticity. For what is such knowledge of a self-identical entity but a form of transcendental narcissism? Indeed, Afghānī specifically designates the *Bildung* of the renascent nation as one whose prime medium is an oratory which exhorts and reminds of the past.[26]

It should be clear from the foregoing that the subject being corrected by oratorical education, and which is Romantically conceived both beyond history and underlying it, is indeterminate if its conception is left as presented. There are no indications towards its determination except gestures towards historical particularities: events, names, dates. Beyond this there is reference to a name: Islam. There are analogues to this Romantic mode in virtually all cultures. In all these cases, in the absence of historical determination over and above the indication of a golden age wherein inhere exemplary glories and utopian exemplars, the discourse of authenticity is socially open, in the sense that its essential emptiness, what Hegel might have termed the boredom of its concepts, renders it very versatile and protean. As this ontological self-identity is epistemologically reflected in solipsism, the result is that the construction of identities here is fundamentally an act of naming.

Naming is not an innocent activity, but lies at the very heart of ideology, one of whose principal mechanisms is the operation of classificatory tokens that determine the memberships of socio-political groups. These operations also entail exclusions and inclusions by way of condensations, displacements and associative interpellation of some complexity.[27] The concrete images put forward as factually paradigmatic – the golden age, the glories of the Arabs, the Middle Ages in some European Romanticisms, the idyllic rusticity of Heidegger, of African nativist philosophers, or westernized Indian sages – serve as iconic controllers of identities and take on general values generated by a truncated and telescoped history; yet these are values which act as carriers of general attributes that no human collectivity can eternally possess and of paradigmatic value that is only imputed to them by the purveyors of the ideological messages.[28] The versatility of the general name – such as Islam – lies therein; the abstract act of naming engenders as many distinct identities as there are constituted social and political groups which might claim the name as their own. The reality of the historical subject lies not in the head but in historical reality, and the key to this reality is not the conformity to some self-subsistent essence or some invariant historical Islam which does not exist, but the group which adopts the name by adapting it to its particular form and understanding of the historical paradigm evoked by the name, a paradigm which is metonymically suggested and not specifically indicated by the name itself. The connection between name and historical reality derives its validation and credibility from extrinsic criteria, from the capacity that the group adopting the name has to enforce and consolidate its interpretation and to perpetuate it within institutions both epistemic and social.

## IV

This elaborate anti-Enlightenment philosophy of history and of politics which has been read from Afghānī's writings and which was constructed largely with the conceptual apparatus of pre-critical philosophy is not the only one which could legitimately be attributed to him. There are strands of other orientations as well. In his response to Renan's famous pronouncements of 1883 about the congenital incapacities of the Semitic mind and the inability of the Arabs to produce science and philosophy, Afghānī insisted instead that responsibility for the decline of the brilliant civilization of the Arabs was to be borne entirely by Islam. 'It is clear,' he wrote, 'that wherever it becomes established, this religion tried to stifle the sciences and it was marvelously served in its designs by despotism.' Islam, he added, is not unique in this respect; all religions are intolerant and inimical to reason, and the progress that the West had manifestly achieved was accomplished despite Christianity.[29]

Freethinking of this kind might be accounted for by many factors, not the least of which was that Afghānī led many lives. An Arabic translation of his reply to Renan was deliberately stalled by his then adept Muḥammad 'Abduh. But in order properly to appreciate the legacy of Afghānī's anti-Enlightenment polemic in its full extent, aspects of which will be taken up presently, it is important to draw attention to one other dimension of his position on Renan. For just as he said that Europe progressed despite Christianity, he also said that the Muslims cannot be denied a similar outcome in the achievement of excellence in science and philosophy despite the heavy burden of Islam.[30] The answer, which he never gave in the text of his reply to Renan, was reformism.

The Islam he attacked was the traditional Islam of the ecclesiastics. Like Luther, whom he greatly admired, Afghānī can be said to have 'overcome the bondage of piety by replacing it by the bondage of conviction . . . [and] shattered faith in authority because he restored the authority of faith'.[31] Afghānī, of course, provided some broad strokes, and actual reform – intellectual, social and legal – was to take place at the hands of Muḥammad 'Abduh, who can be said to have stood to Afghānī as St-Simon stood to Condorcet, giving primacy to 'social hygiene' over political power as the regulator of society.[32]

Such hygiene is to be had with the reform of religion, which, after all, Afghānī regarded as the backbone of social order.[33] And as Laroui has shown with customary perspicacity, this reformism – which he attributes entirely to Afghānī – is very much in the spirit of the Enlightenment. Of the fundamental motifs of classical Muslim reformism can be cited a utilitarianism in the conception of law, a naturalism in the conception of the world.[34] Indeed, the very core of the reformism is the repudiation of all authority that intervenes between the reformer and the origin to which reform is seen as a return: the Koran and the salutary example of early Islamic history. Islam, according to reformism, knows no authority save that of reason, and what passes for religious authority, such as the Caliphate and the various ecclesiastical offices, are nothing for 'Abduh but secular offices which carry no doctrinal authority.[35] Nothing is authoritative but the pristine condition of Islam.

With historical Islam thus marginalized, 'Abduh could embark on the reinterpretation of the Koran in the light of reason – the historical reason of the time: the fundamental criterion is contained in the notion that Islam is a religion of ease, tolerance and conformity with the conditions of human life, and is in this sense primeval, and thus the truest, historically the most versatile. Religions are subject to the laws of evolution, for the earliest of the true religions, with implicit reference to Judaism, is in conformity with the earlier stages of human history when right and wrong had to be arbitrarily dictated. A higher stage, implicitly with reference to Christianity, is clear when right and wrong are exhorted with reference to sentiment and to emotional arousal. Finally, with Islam, it is reason that is addressed.[36] Islam is thus transformed into a natural religion, and the reform of society is seen to reside in ridding it of the debris of history and revivifying the general sense of its original texts so they could have a contemporary relevance, in such a manner that Islamic law would become a particular variant of natural law. This reformed Islam is, incidentally, much in keeping with the laudatory ideas some Enlightenment thinkers held about Islam as a natural religion, superior to Christianity on this score, and in keeping with the natural course of social life.[37] After this naturalistic and utilitarian interpretation, little remains, in substantive terms, of Islam as it existed; what remains is a symbolic order.[38]

In the light of this legacy, it is hard to see what remained of Afghānī's irrationalist vitalism, which was the mainstay of his political theorizing and agitation, alongside his reformist notion of restoration. In historical terms, these two facets of his legacy have had separate careers, except to the mind of the Indian philosopher Sir Muhammad Iqbal (1876–1938). Iqbal combined German irrationalism and reformist naturalism and utilitarianism, after the fashion of Syed Ahmad Khan and the very similar efforts of Muḥammad 'Abduh, but he was of course working in a different tradition and circumstance to that experienced in modern Arab history.[39]

In fact, but for the possibilities inherent in the notion of reform as restoration, and therefore the implicit assumption of a subliminal historical continuity, which have been explored above, there is little in Islamic reformism of the Romantic politics of Afghānī. Reformist Islam has come to dominate official Islam, but until recently constituted only a subculture in the Arab World, where public life (with the exception of marginal and relatively backward areas like the Arabian Peninsula) has been dominated by nationalism, liberalism and various forms of socialism, and where the legal and educational systems, traditionally the mainstay of ecclesiastical authority, rapidly became secular.

What vitalist ideologies there were had an altogether different genealogy and had no reference to Afghānī. One would cite here some strands of Arab nationalism, such as the early doctrine of the Baath [Resurrection] Party now in power in Syria and Iraq. According to this doctrine, Arabism 'does not indicate spatial properties and betrays no passage of time'; it is 'the fount of theories, and is not born of thought but is wet-nurse of thought'. The national self, the historical subject, is itself a criticism of pure intellection and a reaffirmation of life.[40] Similar notions, buttressed with detailed historical researches, can be found in the writings of theorists of the Syrian Social Nationalist Party of the 1940s, 50s, and 60s, and the advocates of infra-historical micro-nationalisms, such as Maronitism in Lebanon.

Contemporary Islamism, a recent phenomenon which dates in earnest only from the 1970s, adapted the vitalist elements in nationalism, the prevalent political and ideological culture in the Arab World, and took advantage of its versatility, which has already been mentioned, to assimilate vitalism to its own purposes. It can be said that Islamism insinuated itself, with a good measure of success, via a process of renaming of the subject, whose identity is constituted by vitalist associations, into the nationalist ideological sphere and coloured itself accordingly. In so doing, it has resurrected the Romanticism of Afghānī and re-established him as the fount of authenticity and its main proponent and, indeed, its idol.

Islamist political and cultural movements have taken over Afghānī's Romanticism with different pitches and emphases. A few have made a thorough reclamation of its abstract Jacobinism, a tendency which we can see in the most acute manifestations in Khomeinist tendencies. Others have seen in it almost a fact of nature, seeing in the indication of raw identities a matter instinctively apprehended by any mind attuned to the workings of nature – in this case, the nature of Muslims; an otherwise excellent history of modern Arabic thought has been written from this perspective.[41] Yet others have adapted this Romanticism as a cultural form of an essentially nationalist impulse. To this latter trend belong the hybrid tendencies which seek to translate various aspects of a modern political programme into Islamic terminology in order to authenticate and thus authorize them[42] or to develop an authentic 'Islamic' method of social science whose metaphysical bearings are not Western, and which, not unnaturally, devolve to a restatement of some modern social science terms in a context where Islam acts as a myth of origin and charter of legislation, with an admixture of a vitalist epistemology.[43] In all these instances, Romantic Islamism is the name under which a hypernationalist cultural programme is officiated.

More directly relevant to the theme of this essay, however, is the reaction of universalist ideologies to the discourse on authenticity. The discourse of authenticity has rarely come into its own, outside Islamist circles, without being associated with some universalist discourse. Some illustrative examples drawn from the work of contemporary philosophers will suffice to show how this Romanticism was received and assimilated, although instances could be multiplied at will. Resistance to the notion of authenticity in the Arab World has been feeble in the recent past due to a number of manifest political circumstances, not the least of which being that the Arab World has not been immune from the worldwide resurgence of atavisim, ethnic and religious bigotry and fundamentalist religiosity.

One primary mechanism according to which linkages between universalism and particularist Romanticism are made is the simple act of naming that has already been encountered. The prominent philosopher, Professor Z.N. Mahmoud, a logical positivist by philosophical tendency and a liberal in politics, propounds a programme for the construction of an indigenous Arab philosophy starting from 'the self'. To this end, immediate apprehension is the epistemological key, for it is through introspection, he claims, that we can unveil the principles out of which arise 'our' judgements on all matters. Such is his manner of seizing the authentic, which he finds in instances from the Arab past, from which he then derives his liberal principles of liberty and rationality. The combination assures the Arabs not only of the capacity for science, but also human dignity.[44]

Not all attempts have been as crude and awkward as this self-authentication by a very skilled technical philosopher. What Professor Mahmoud did was to bring into prominence – he has a vast readership – a number of staple ideas in Islamist circles since the time of Mu ammad 'Abduh: that revivalism is the axial mode of cultural and political discourse and authenticity the sole means of actual success as of moral probity; that as a result, historical practice is an act of authenticating desires or programmes for the present and the future; and that this authentication involves reference to past events still somehow alive at the core of the invariant historical subject, events which are repeatable, in the act of healing the breach between past and future. Thus parliamentary democracy is presented as a simple revalorization of the *shūra*, a process of consulting clan chiefs in early Islamic times, and rationality becomes a reclamation of the work of Averroes and of Ibn Khaldūn, while freedom becomes a repetition of Mu'tazilite theological theses on free will, and socialism is made to stand in direct continuity with peasant rebellions of the tenth and eleventh centuries.

The past therefore becomes the paradigm of a present which must be authentic if it is to be in keeping with the *Volksgeist* and consequently merit serious cultural and political consideration. Past and future are unified by their substratum, the national essence, going beyond which is akin to breaking the laws of organic nature. It is this sense of historical continuity beyond history which has driven some Marxist philosophers to try to assimilate the discourse of authenticity. We can see this clearly in the monumental history of Arab-Islamic philosophy of Hussein Mroueh, assassinated not long ago. In it an attempt was made to separate two modalities of historical time, one of relevance today and the other redundant. The relevant one was, not unnaturally, 'materialist tendencies' which might afford a point of linkage between past and future.[45] The past is liberated of its historicity and posited as the fount of desired continuities with a desired future, and the past is again cast in the future anterior, as if the spell of teleology is cast.

The same is discernible in the apologetic tenor of some of the most sophisticated Marxist writings on Arab-Islamic thought. As against the charge by some writers that time in classical Arabic thought is atomized by occasionalism, one scholar cites the notion of analogy current in Islamic legal theory as well as in theology. Rather than seeing in analogy the primacy of the key term – the precedent – he slants his analysis in the other direction and finds in the practice of analogy a reaffirmation of historicity rather than the denial of history which it in fact is, for it is an affirmation of only one time, a time of superlative ontological weight, the time of the text and precedent.[46] The same author also follows a long tradition in finding in Ibn Khaldūn's metaphysical hierarchies a notion of class stratification, and discovers the Marxist theory of accumulation in the theological metaphors with which Ibn Khaldūn formulates his discourse on economic activity.[47]

Thus is the anti-Enlightenment polemic interiorized in the bodies of philosophies whose fundamental motifs had been derived from the Enlightenment, and thus is a heritage invented by the elimination of history as past and its retrieval as a form of the present. There is no great secret by which one can explain the invasion by the trope of authenticity and its setting of assumptions that others feel constrained to adopt. But for the understanding of this we must leave the terrain of philosophy for that of society and polity.

## Notes

1. See Abdallah Laroui, 'The Arabs and Social Anthropology', in *The Crisis of the Arab Intellectual*, transl. Diarmid Cammell, Berkeley and Los Angeles 1976, pp. 44–80; and Aziz Al-Azmeh, 'Islamic Studies and the European Imagination', Exeter 1986, this volume, ch. 8. For a close textual study of otherness in another historical context, see François Hartog, *Le Miroir d'Hérodote: Essai sur la représentation de l'autre*, Paris 1980.

2. The relation of Arabism and Islamism is exceedingly complex, and the reader is referred to the voluminous works of a conference on this matter: *Al Qawmīya al-'Arabīyya wal-Islām* [*Arab Nationalism and Islam*], Beirut 1981. See Aziz Al-Azmeh, 'Islamism and Arab Nationalism', *Review of Middle East Studies*, 4, 1988, pp. 33–51.

3. *An Islamic Response to Imperialism: Political and Religious Writings of Sayyid Jamal al-Din 'al-Afghānī'*, transl. Nikki Keddie, Berkeley and Los Angeles, 1968. See also Homa Pakdaman, *Djamal-Ed-Din Assad Abadi dit Afghānī*, Paris 1969. On Syed Ahmad Khan, see Christian W. Troll, *Sayyid Ahmad Khan: A Reinterpretation of Muslim Theology*, New Delhi 1978.

4. A. Hourani, *Arabic Thought in the Liberal Age*, London 1962, is a most serviceable introduction to its topic in English. For a rigorous technical study, see Malcolm H. Kerr, *Islamic Reform: The Political and Legal Theories of Muhammad 'Abduh and Rashid Rida*, Berkeley and Los Angeles 1966. It must be pointed out that studies on modern Arabic thought in English have achieved none of the seriousness of studies of comparable movements in India, of which one could mention V.C. Joshi, ed., *Rammohun Roy and the Process of Modernization in India*, New Delhi 1975; and Partha Chatterjee, *Nationalist Thought and the Colonial World*, London 1986. Fundamental for the study of modern Arab thought in a European language is Abdallah Laroui, *L'Idéologie arabe contemporaine*, Paris 1967.

5. See Taha Parla, *The Social and Political Thought of Ziya Gökalp*, Leiden 1985; and William Cleveland, *The Making of an Arab Nationalist: Ottomanism and Arabism in the Life and Thought of Sati al-Husri*, Princeton, N.J. 1971.

6. erif Mardin, *The Genesis of Young Ottoman Thought: A Study in the Modernization of Turkish Political Ideas*, Princeton, N.J. 1962.

7. Cf. the approximate sketch of Abdessalam Bin Abdelālī, 'Heidegger idd Hegel' [Heidegger contra Hegel], *Dirāsāt 'Arabīyya*, 19, no. 4, 1983, pp. 93, 96.

8. Jamāl al-Dīn al-Afghānī, *Al-A'māl al-Kāmila* [Complete works], ed. M. 'Umāra, Cairo n.d., pp. 130, 312–13; and *Al-'Urwa al-Wuthqā*, Cairo 1958, pp. 9–12 and passim.

9. Afghānī, *Al-A'māl al-Kāmila*, p. 147, and *Al-A'māl al-majhūla* [Unknown works], ed. Alī Shalash, London 1987, p. 78.

10. Afghānī, *Al-A'māl al-majhūla*, pp. 80–81.

11. For instance, L. Gumplowicz, 'Un sociologiste arabe du XIVe siècle', in *Aperçus sociologiques*, New York 1963, pp. 201–26 (originally published in 1898); *Geschichte der Staatstheorien*, Innsbruck 1905, par. 59; F. Oppenheimer, *System der Soziologie*, 2nd edn, Stuttgart 1964, vol. 2, pp. 173–4. See also Aziz Al-Azmeh, *Ibn Khaldūn in Modern Scholarship*, London 1981, pp. 157ff.

12. Afghānī, *Al-A'māl al-Kāmila*, pp. 443–4.

13. R.G. Collingwood, *The Idea of History*, Oxford 1946, p. 91.

14. Afghānī, *Al-A'māl al-Kāmila*, p. 153.

15. Ibid., pp. 157–64.

16. *Al-'Urwa al-Wuthqā*, p. 20.

17. Gaston Bachelard, *Dialectique de la durée*, Paris 1950, p. 52.

18. asan anafī, *Dirāsāt falsafiyya* [Philosophical Studies], Cairo 1988, pp. 52–7.

19. Wa a Sharāra, awla ba' mushkilāt ad-dawla fil-mujtama 'walthaqāfa al-Arabiyyayan [Some Problems Concerning the State in Arab Society and Culture], Beirut 1981, p. 71.

20. Quoted in Ernst Cassirer, *Philosophy of Symbolic Forms*, New Haven CT, 1955, vol. 2, p. 106.

21. *Al-'Urwa al-Wuthqā*, p. 20.

22. G.W.F. Hegel, *Phenomenology of the Spirit*, transl. A.V. Miller, Oxford 1977, pars 584, 590, 593.

23. G.W.F. Hegel, *Philosophy of Right*, transl. T.M. Knox, Oxford 1967, par. 4.

24. See the remarks on Dilthey in the excellent work of Stepan Odouev, *Par les sentiers de Zarathoustra: Influence de la pensée de Nietzsche sur la philosophie bourgeoise allemande*, transl. Catherine Emery, Moscow 1980, pp. 137–8.

25. Laroui, *L'Ideologie arabe contemporaire*, p. 66.

26. Afghānī, *Al-A'māl al-majhūla*, p. 81.

27. Aziz Al-Azmeh, *Al-Turāth bayn al-Sul ān wat-tārīkh* [Heritage: Power and History], Casablanca and Beirut 1987, pp. 91ff.

28. Cf. the analyses of Hedwig Konrad, *Étude sur la métaphore*, Paris 1939, p. 88; and Paul Ricoeur, *The Rule of Metaphor*, transl. R. Czerny et al., Toronto 1977, pp. 207–11.

29. Text in Keddie, transl., *An Islamic Response*, pp. 183, 187.

30. Ibid., p. 183.

31. Karl Marx, in Karl Marx and Friedrich Engels, *Collected Works*, London 1975, vol. 3, p. 182.

32. Cf. Robert Wokler, 'Saint-Simon and the Passage from Political to Social Science', in Anthony Pagden, ed., *The Languages of Political Theory in Early Modern Europe*, Cambridge 1987, pp. 335–6.

33. Afghānī, *Al-A'māl al-Kāmila*, p. 130 and passim.

34. Abdallah Laroui, *Islam et modernité*, Paris 1987, pp. 134–47.

35. Mu ammad 'Abduh, *Al-A'māl al-Kāmila* [Complete works], ed. M. Umāra, Beirut 1972, vol. 3, pp. 287, 289.

36. `Abduh, *Al-A'māl al-Kāmila*, pp. 448–56.

37. `Abduh, *Al-A'māl al-Kāmila*, pp. 282–311; and Mu ammad Rashīd Ri a, *Tārīkh al-ustādh al-Imām Mu ammad 'Abduh* [Biography of Mu ammad 'Abduh], Cairo 1931, vol. 1, p. 614. In general, see the excellent study of Kerr, *Islamic Reform*.

38. Laroui, *Islam et modernité*, pp. 127–30.

39. Mu ammad Iqbal, *The Reconstruction of Religious Thought in Islam*, London 1934, pp. 4–15, 42–55, 126–31, 148–54, 165–9.

40. Michel Aflaq, *Fī Sabīl al-Ba'th* [For the Baath], Beirut 1958, pp. 43, 44, 158.

41. Mu ammad Jābir al-An ārī, *Ta awwulāt al-fikr was-siyāsa fil-sharq al-'Arabī 1930–1970* [Transformations of Thought and Politics in the Arab East, 1930–1970], Kuwait 1980.

42. For instance, anafi, *Dirāsāt falsafiyya*; and *Al-Turāth wal-tajdīd* [Heritage and Renewal], Beirut 1981; and cf. Aziz Al-Azmeh, *Al-Turāth*, pp. 164–8.

43. For instance, 'Ādil usain, *Na wa fikr 'arabī jadīd: an-nā iriyya waltanmiya wal-dimuqrā iyya* [Towards a New Arab Thought: Nasserism, Development and Democracy], Cairo 1985.

44. Zakī Najīb Mahmūd, *Tajdīd al-fikr 'al-arabī* [The Renewal of Arabic Thought], Beirut 1980, pp. 274, 283.

45. usain Muruwwa, *Al-Naza'āt al-māddīyya fil-falsafa al-'arabiyya al-islāmīyya* [Materialist Trends in Arab-Islamic Philosophy], Beirut 1978, 3 volumes.

46. Mahmūd Amīn al-'Ālim, 'Mafhūm al-zamān fil-fikr al-'arabī al-islāmi' [The Conception of Time in Arab-Islamic Thought], in *Dirāsāt fil-Islām*, Beirut 1980, pp. 110–11. See Aziz Al-Azmeh, 'Islamic Legal Theory and the Appropriation of Reality', in Aziz Al-Azmeh, ed., *Islamic Law: Social and Historical Contexts*, London 1988, pp. 250–65.

47. Mahmūd Amīn al-'Ālim, 'Muqaddimat Ibn Khaldūn – Madkhal ibistimulūjī' [Ibn Khaldun's Muqaddima: An Epistemological Introduction], in *Al-Fikr al-'Arabī*, Beirut 1978, vol. 6, pp. 37, 41–2, 45–6.

# 6

# Muslim Modernism and the Canonical Text

The interpretation[1] of the Koran and of other foundational texts of Muslim religious and intellectual life was a crucial element in the development of Modernist Reformism associated with Mu ammad 'Abduh and his student Mu ammad Rashīd Ri ā, who remained faithful to the open-minded modernism of his teacher until a few years after the Imam's premature death in 1905.[2] As was the case with all religious thought confronting overwhelming and unfamiliar – or only recently familiar – ideas and modes of thought, Modernist Reformism in the lands of the Ottoman empire strove to reach an accommodation, and a double accommodation at that: salvaging the intellectual credibility of the Koran and other foundational texts on the one hand, and adopting the inevitable tropes and values of modernity on the other.

The interpretation of the Koran is but one strand in an intellectual enterprise of much wider bearing and profound consequence, and must therefore be placed within the wider context of this enterprise. One finds references to and uses of Koranic texts throughout the writings of 'Abduh, Ri ā and others who represent the same current. Recourse to books specifically composed as Koranic interpretations is inadequate. 'Abduh did, with reluctance and at his student's insistence, start a series of lectures on the subject, which Ri ā completed after 'Abduh's death and published as *Tafsīr al-Manār*; as its separate parts had been published in *al-Manār* over a period of many years,[3] this set the scene for a renewed exegetical literature in Arabic. But it is crucial to set these matters in the context of the wider implications of a discourse upon the meaning of the Koran. 'Abduh's reluctance can be interpreted as an implicit reservation against imputing to the Koran a systematic integrality which modernism might find indefensible.

# I

Undoubtedly the main feature that characterized reformist discourse at the end of the nineteenth century was its dependence on the optimistic evolutionism then current, associated with positivism and Darwinism. This serves to distinguish and to reclaim Reformism from the Revivalism that appeals to some at the close of the twentieth century. Evolutionist positivism was embraced because it helped to incorporate Reformism in an objective context by referring to some quality of natural determinism benefiting the advancement of nations. Darwinism in its turn was espoused because it was based on a simple concept of the struggle for survival, and also conveyed a 'scientific' naturalist image of nations preying upon each other, this being an apt metaphor for the imperialist onslaught on the Ottoman state and other Eastern countries.

Mu ammad 'Abduh, like his younger radical Arab secularist and atheist contemporary Shiblī al-Shumayyil,[4] adopted the Comtean model of the evolution of societies in three stages. In 1881 he came to the conclusion that human existence underwent three stages of development, the first characterized as natural existence, the second as social and the third as political:

> Man is seen to have been simple and instinctive, searching for sustenance, shelter and the other natural requirements which it was in his power to satisfy. Then concern for himself induced him to look to the preservation of his species, and his many needs compelled him to look for assistance from others. So he joined with others, united with them and became a town dweller. He progressed in this stage and began to consider his affairs and to attend to the concerns of his species. He thus became political. This is civil man with all his rights and duties.[5]

In this, 'Abduh reclaimed evolutionism as an objective context indicating a linear movement gradually progressing from the least to the most advanced within the context of social systems. He appropriated it in his own particular way to the field of the history of religions, in accordance with the concept of religion and education current in his age, and especially with thoughts inspired by Herbert Spencer, the evolutionist philosopher whom 'Abduh visited outside London and whose book on education he translated (from the French translation) but never published. Like Spencer, 'Abduh thought that the evolution of religion runs parallel to that of culture and society: total authority based on power is consonant with man's primitive stage, and the image of authority and the fear of death channel the imagination to the veneration and worship of idols founded on crude sense-perception. Man then evolved to the stage of prophethood, which ensues when mankind attains an intellectual maturity enabling him to distinguish the beneficial from the harmful. Finally, in the third stage, people regain the truth of prophethood, which they had in the meantime forfeited by following 'the steps of the devil of ambition and yielding to the seductions of politics'.[6] The context of the third evolutionary stage is not restricted to the general religious history of mankind, but also applies to the history of monotheistic religions, as was stated in the *Risālat al-Taw īd*. These religions develop from one that is founded on commands and prohibitions and the demand for absolute obedience, as 'Abduh pointed out that Judaism is, to a religion based on sentiment and emotion, as in Christianity, on to a religion which address the intellect – Islam – and combines both intellect and emotion in leading the way to happiness in both religion and worldly affairs.[7]

'Abduh was not the only one to follow the evolutionist concept of religion which placed religion, including Islam, in an objective, historical evolutionary context and in harmony with the progress of mankind. Indeed Jamāl al-Dīn al-Asad-Abādī (called al-Afghānī)[8] thought that man's imagination developed alongside his faculty for rational thought. Thus, primitive man worshipped the baser things of creation, such as stones, then progressed to the worship of fire, clouds and stars, finally coming to worship incorporeals. While the position adopted by Afghānī has certain peculiarities, it should nevertheless be seen in the context of an objective historical evolution afforded him by evolutionary theory, which was the prime conceptual equipment of the nineteenth century, and was consistent with the prevalent trends in contemporary Arab thought exemplified by 'Abduh, 'Alī Yūsuf and others.[9]

Thus, religions were thought to have developed and evolved in accordance with human evolution. In other words, the divine chronology of inspiration and prophethood followed the chronology of the secular and the mundane. Religion was an innate awareness of the existence of ultramundane invisible creatures. Man was 'by nature a rational and a religious animal'.[10] Indeed, one later Islamic Reformer proposed the idea that beasts are able instinctively to discern that which transcends the visible and the experiential, to the point where they can directly perceive the Creator, the Provider, as had, *mutatis mutandis*, Ibn Bāja nearly a millennium earlier.[11] And Francis Marrāsh (1836–73), in a text whose importance we shall refer to subsequently, stated that religiosity is an innate propensity which is as beneficial to the survival of the species as is reproduction.[12] Thus, the relation between religion and transcendental religious awareness was based in nature, without this religious appropriation of evolutionism pointing to the source of this innate necessity for religion or to its causes.

In accordance with the history of religions, current in the nineteenth century, Arab secularists of the same period pointed out that religion originated directly from fear: fear of death and fear of the over-whelming and unpredictable power of nature out of control, in response to which religion is created.[13] 'Abduh and others, however, did not take up a systematic anthropology of religion. Religion and the necessity for religion were matters only dealt with consistently in terms of theodicy, of a conception of divine benevolence, mercy and God's inevitable choice of that which is Best. As is well known, this is a medieval Muslim Mu'tazilite theological concept, appropriated due to its suitability for the evolutionism 'Abduh and his associates upheld, although it is not founded on a secularist theory of religious history, anchored instead in a properly religious view of prophecy and prophethood, used over and above historical discourse on religious history.

While the concept of the necessity of religion was appropriated in another form, it had more profound consequences for Arab political and social thought, for in this view religion became one of the prerequisites for defending a threatened body-social and a sign of a religious solidarity which, like racial solidarity, provides 'unanimity, unity of direction and demand for victory over those who contest it', as Afghānī put it.[14] The moral justification for religion, that it restrains the soul from carnal appetites and thus serves to impose order upon society,[15] was a necessary premise for the Romantic political revivalist discourse stamped with nationalism which emerged in Young Ottoman circles. It is found to have been particularly well developed by Namik Kemal[16] and given an internationalist perspective by Afghānī.[17] This moral justification then became one of the foundations of Turkish nationalist theory with Ziya Gökalp,[18] and was subsequently to return with renewed vigour in the neo-Afghanism of today.

This political discourse appropriated another principle from those associated with Darwinism, that is, the principle of the struggle for survival as applied to society and politics. In Europe, right-wing nationalist and racist thought (among whose authorities was Gustave Le Bon, of whom generations of educated Arabs were passionately fond) was based on the notion of the struggle for survival, due to the appearance of the notion of the survival of the fittest, and the identification of goodness and power. Afghānī proposed that man does not differ from the animals, plants or inanimate objects in the struggle for survival: 'for power is the manifestation of life and of survival, while weakness is the domain of extinction and death . . . Power is manifested and imposed only when it weakens and exploits something else.'[19] Mu ammad 'Abduh interpreted the text of *sūrat al-Baqara* 'If God had not checked one set of people by means of another, the earth would be full of mischief' by saying that this is

> one of the general principles [of natural history], and this is what in this age the learned refer to as the struggle for survival. They say that war is natural to man because it is one aspect of the struggle for survival . . . Some of those parasitic on the science of the principles of human society consider that the idea of the struggle for survival, which they say is a general principle, is due to the influence of the materialists of this age, that it bespeaks tyranny and oppression . . . and that it is opposed to the guidance of religion. If those who say this appreciated the concept of man or knew themselves, they would not say what they do.

As for natural selection and the survival of the fittest, this is

> one of the corollaries of what preceded. For God says that the nature of men is such as to prevent each other from achieving rectitude and human interest; this is the obstacle to the corruption of the world, that is, it is the reason for the survival of rectitude and the survival of goodness.[20]

In all cases, Islamic reformism's appropriation of what was known as social Darwinism was conditional upon the concepts of social Darwinism, even though the discourse assumed the form of argumentation based on interpreting verses of the Koran: yet these verses were, in this context, nevertheless nothing more than occasions for linking the imperative intellectual authority of the West with the symbolic authority of Islam as represented by the Koran. Thus, the discourse of reformism occurred in two worlds and issued from two worlds, and was incorporated in two worldly preconditions, one being the intellectual and the other the social and political.

Reformism became a programme for locating social Islam on the level of a normative Islam,[21] which was wide open in practice to the interpretations that considerations of general utility (from the reformist point of view) could convey. Thus, the issue of textual interpretation was made captive to the new circumstances, as every unrestricted utterance carries the meanings given to it by the person who appropriates it. Indeed, this unrestricted name, Islam, became an object in the struggle of interpretive space. Although the first Arab Muslim reformists wanted to liberate the meanings of Islam from the concepts that shackled it and prevented it from attaining currency, nevertheless in liberating it from its immediate and even ancient legacy (and this is the meaning of the call to *ijtihād*, a return to the first texts or the conduct of the original forefathers, with history defenestrated), they liberated it in principle from every context, and therefore made it amenable to every context. But in this manner they made of it a normative unity which could indicate histories, societies and ideals, that is, they made this indeterminate utterance a norm by which to measure all matters. It thus became a political sign able to achieve currency. At the same time they made Islam an occasion for the undisciplined ideological imagination. For when the normative was imagined as actual and positive, that is, when its actual existence was postulated, even though that existence had occurred in the bygone ages of the forefathers, it became possible to alternate between the normative and the pragmatic, to deny either the former or the latter, or to attempt to compel the one or the other to be interpreted according to principles which do not agree with it or with the possibilities of history and its point of view. This is the source of the utopia upon which Islamic politics today is based.

Islamic Reformism was founded on the postulation of a possible equivalence between the reality of a secular age and normative religion; theorizing that, given its innate nature, normative religion preceded the reality of today, and consequently should reclaim today as its very own. The title under which these equivalences are officiated is *fi ra*, human nature. Thus, Islamic Reformism had to subject both concepts to its reformist desire, by translating the one according to the other, a subjection which was undertaken on the basis of different norms, or a combination of norms in an 'objective Machiavellism' which characterized all areas of Reformist thought.[22]

The first Reformists did not deny their true sources, especially the liberal ones, and although the European ideas they possessed did not necessarily result from acculturation, there is nevertheless no doubt that circumstances were conducive for creating an environment for utilitarianism and its theoretical formulation.[23] Al- ah āwī was the first to read Rousseau, Voltaire, Montesquieu and Condillac,[24] and fully understood the European concepts concerning government restricted by law and absolute government.[25] *Talkhī al-Ibrīz fī Talkhī Bārīz* was a book widely read in Turkey after its translation in 1839,[26] and Namik Kemal had translated Rousseau, Montesquieu, Bacon, Volney and Condillac into Turkish.[27] As for 'Abduh, he was prompted to learn other languages so as to study the foreign works.[28] Before Rashīd Ri ā committed himself to restrictive salafism, he was strongly attracted to Western political thought, and emphasized that Muslims had adopted European political ideas and organizational procedures: 'This is concerned with the natural effect of their entering the country, whether this conforms with their intentions or otherwise.'[29] In 1906 he wrote:

> O Muslim, do not claim that this form of government [restricted constitutionalism] is one of the bases of our religion, having been derived from the Qur'an and the conduct of the Rightly Guided caliphs, rather than from association with the Europeans and knowledge of the affairs of the West. If it were not for considering the situation of these people, you and your like would not have thought that this was part of Islam, and the first people to call for the establishment of this basis would have been the *ulama* in Constantinople, Cairo and Marrakesh.[30]

He drew attention clearly to the simple mechanics on which the Reformist interpretation was based, mentioning the transmission of political culture, and then promplty went on to state that government restricted by law was 'clear and obvious in the Qur'an'.[31] He thus took the same course as European Protestantism, which produced a parallel interpretation to this; for this interpretation was not an attempt to make religion absorb the world, but rather to point out that the world was not free from divine intervention.[32]

In this way, the Koran functioned as a compendium whose verses rendered modern meanings. It thus became necessary to divest the Koranic text of the protection of its specific historical meanings, and to render it defenceless before the arbitrary ascription of interpretations, or to consign to it the flexibility of an unrestrained generality susceptible to a modernist interpretation, whose sense lies in characterizing modernity itself as fundamentally Islamic:

Persevere in reciting the Qur'an and understanding its commands, prohibitions, exhortations and so on, as it was recited before the believers and the unbelievers at the time of the Revelation. And be wary of interpretation, except in order to understand an expression whose original meaning you do not know, and if you want to understand an implied meaning.[33]

With the Koran thus made capable of rendering desired meanings, it becomes possible in turn to subvert reality, as Rashīd Ri ā described above, and to say with 'Abduh:

The longing of some people for consultative government and their dislike of despotism does not result from imitating the foreigners. It is because consultation is a duty of the *sharī'a* and despotism is prohibited by the *sharī'a*. For the law of Islam instructs that the rules of the Qur'an be followed and the *sunna* of the Prophet be adhered to. As for despotism, this contradicts the *sharī'a* as it is not restricted by law.[34]

Thus, official authority fluctuates according to context: it is secular and irreligious, a political constitutionality emerging from considerations of social utility, and also a religious legitimacy which considers constitutionalism and government to be restricted essentially by rulings and duties of the *sharī'a*. This resulted from an amalgamation of worldly rationality with Shar'ist rationality within the framework of a universality attributed to the latter, and absorbing the former in terms both of authority and theory; this is without regard for problems attendant upon translation from one domain of knowledge and politics to another completely different one;[35] the *sharī'a* thus became a metaphor for legality, abstracted from the people in authority and their desires. The Young Ottomans led by Namik Kemal participated actively in the discussions of the drafting of the constitution of 1876.[36]

In practice, the attitude of the Arab Reformists to constitutionalism differed according to their changing political circumstances. In all cases, however, the idea of government restricted by law was conceptualized by referring it to its imagined bases in the governments of Mu ammad and the Rightly Guided caliphs and in the Koran. Al-Kawākibī – quoting Alfieri, the Italian thinker at the time of the French Revolution, throughout his *Tabā'i' al-Istibdād* [The Nature of Despotism] – agreed with 'those who examined the natural history of religions' and considered that political despotism developed out of religius despotism, from which Islamic history was not excluded.[37] But he nevertheless excluded from historical inquiry that part of the history of Islam which he and his like considered to be an obligatory authoritative model. This part of history – the Koran and the early period of Islam, that is the golden age of impeccable conduct – achieved currency as though it were clearly defined. But this supposed distinctness was nothing other than a result of its protection from historical inquiry: the Rightly Guided caliphs ruled by the sword, by consultation of the aristocracy and by appointment to positions, and the Koran contains references to a theory of despotic government and a call for consultative government, without conveying precise meanings; it is impossible to derive a theory or even a prescription of the necessity of government, let alone institutions, from early Muslim history, as 'Abd al-Rāziq showed seventy years ago.[38] There is no guarantor for the validity of translation and interpretation – government restricted by law/consultative government or democratic/consultative government, as it is called today – except the desire of the person advocating the interpretation, who can guarantee his interpretation with a cultural and political authority which by its nature overwhelms observation, criticism and examination. There is therefore no justification in reason or in history for this translation, nor any credibility for it, except its being based on an exclusive normative status given to a name – Islam – which is represented by an absolutely normative source, that is, the Koran and the early period of Islam and on the desire to impose meanings on it that indicate modernism, such as participatory democracy or consultation of the aristocracy (learned and social) which Islamic.Reformism pursued in its first phase.

With this, history is ensnared: it is supposed to contain modernity. Modernity is also ensnared, by assuming its correspondence with that supposed past. Both are presumed equal under an ideological sign: Islam. Thus Reformism undertook the secularization of Islam, that is, applying its name to that which historically was neither part of it nor its intellectual and cultural authority, and implicating this name with a politically desired and intellectually pre-determined world. Islamic authority for this world thus remained purely nominal, yet it continued to be effective as an ideological and historical token pointing to the transitional character of Islamic Reformist thought, between the religious and secular cultures.

The Reformist discourse on the nature, remit and reform of the *sharī'a*, and on its relations with the new and changing circumstances, was most apposite to the endeavours by Islamic Reformism to derive discussion about the affairs of the world and its concerns from religious discourse, and, in the same sleight of hand, to incorporate this discussion into a discourse secular in its actual bearings, although with religious justifications for the priority of secular authority superimposed.

But Mu ammad 'Abduh did not consider these matters in detail, for his contribution was largely in practical legislation and general statements, such as his saying that the *sharī'a* was, 'when Islam was real Islam, flexible enough for the whole world. But today, it is too narrow even for its followers, so they are forced to look elsewhere and seek to protect their rights with something which is beneath it.'[39]

There can be no doubt, however, that Mu ammad 'Abduh was the inspiration behind the contributions of his pupil Rashīd Ri ā before Ri ā's transition to the Wahhabi allegiance. It did not occur to Mu ammad 'Abduh to link his ideas, which we referred to, with a view of the presumed pure Islam as a description of a prelapsarian society that was prior to modernism, including legalist modernism. Rather, he desired to link preservation of some Islamic character to life alongside the changes which have overtaken the *sharī'a*. Thus, the restoration of the *sharī'a* by reclaiming internal possibilities attributed to it as sources of legal contemporaneity became a most important matter, by which *sharī'a* was protected from ruin in principle after its ruin in practice had become an imminent threat underwritten by secular legal reform. It was for this reason that Rashīd Ri ā wrote:

> God instituted the laws of nature in spite of us, and He entrusted us to institute the laws of the *sharī'a* and gave us freedom of choice concerning it. So if we with our freedom of choice do not reconcile the two sets of laws, then that which has now become obligatory will remain fixed, and that which is now optional [the *sharī'a*] will become obsolete.[40]

In this discussion the concept of the laws of nature was decisive, for the independence of the world, with its particular norms and precepts (even though they might occasionally be associated with proximate or remote divine providence), was the most important intellectual acquisition of modern man, beginning with nature and ending with history and society. From them al- ah āwī tried to obtain an interpretation of the Mu'tazilite notion of rational approbation and disapprobation (*ta sīn, taqbī* ). He applied this notion to the enactment of laws in Europe on the basis of the concept of the modern notion of natural rights or the 'universal rules of nature', although he felt compelled, however inconsistently, to associate this with the Ash'arite proposition that the real mover is God. Although these rules, he said, preceded the norms of the *sharī'a*, nevertheless most of these norms are not at variance with them.[41] Namik Kemal proposed a similar theory, just as throughout the history of Islamic Reformism until Ibn Bādīs this imputed equivalence between the universality of the *sharī'a* and natural law based on change became a standard position and an invariable thesis.[42]

This necessitated two closely interrelated procedures: the first was to sacrifice in principle the *sharī'a* based on the legacy of Islamic *fiqh*; the second was the statement that this sacrifice is in keeping with the basis of the *sharī'a*. In this way, detailed jurisprudential rules would be removed, while the general principles would take their place. These general principles would then be referred to the principles of jurisprudence (*uṣūl al-fiqh*).

The first part of this procedure was to limit severely the obligatory elements of this religio-jurisprudential legacy. These were limited to devotions and fundamental articles of faith, 'without worldly rulings, which the *sharī'a* entrusted to those in authority in order for them to relate to the general principles which it has laid down for these rules. For particulars are not delimited and the *sharī'a* does not determine them. On the contrary, they differ according to the differences in custom, time and place.'[43]

According to this interpretation, the detailed rulings of the *sharī'a* are limited to certain fixed punishments for particular crimes (ḥudūd). As for the rest, these consist of general considerations for the protection of life, property and virtue, such as the necessity of justice, decency, moral refinement and the illegality of fraud.[44] The Reformists do not tell us in what respect these general matters constitute Islamic law as such or what distinguishes them from the general rules of the majority of societies in the world and their moral and legal bases. But it is evident that there was an attempt to link these general rules of rectitude with some of the principles of *fiqh*, which are taken here to be general tokens rather than, as they truly are, parts of an integrated system existing in an Islamic judicial system and Islamic jurisprudential institutions. The most important of these principles is a general rule which is incompatible with the principle of change, and which states that the Islamic *sharī'a* will remain until the end of time and that its survival is dependent upon the Five Generalities (*Kullīyyāt*) adumbrated by Shaṭibī after Ibn Rushd and al-Ghazālī. Rashīd Ri ā adds other procedural rules, which he ascribes to his teacher: attention to meaning rather than to words; the necessary justifies the forbidden; need takes precedence over prohibitions; rules change with time; specifying laws according to custom is akin to specifying them according to the text.[45]

It will have been noted that the unequivocal judgements of the text were not connected in a methodical or detailed way to this recourse to the Five Generalities, which seem to form a general basis for virtually every legislative system in the world. Rather, they are incorporated within the framework of a vague general concept of natural rights. Al-Shā ibī's appropriation by Rashīd Ri ā, was something of this sort. But the appropriation of Najm al-Dīn al- ufī (d.1276), from whom Rashīd Ri ā published an important text in *al-Manār* in 1906, was more significant. For the Hanbalite al- ufī established the obligation to give priority to public interest (*ma la a*) over the Text and the concensus of opinion (*ijmā'*), when these conflicted. With this he more explicitly supported the position of al-Shā ibi, which was based on the need for every legislation to conform with 'what is customary in such matters' and to suspend legal obligation if this involved difficulty beyond what is customary, that every principle of the *sharī'a* (the Koran, the *Sunna, ijmā'* and *qiyās*) which 'is not in conformity with custom is not a reliable [legal] principle'. On the contrary, practice and custom form the basis of the doctrine of unrestrained public interest.[46]

This abrogation of the text, and in practice of the *sharī'a*, in the interests of the secular view of the world, not only gained the praise of Rashīd Ri ā but also secured the approbation of other Reformists, such as Jamal al-Dīn al-Qāsimī in Damascus and 'Abd al-'Azīz Jāwīsh in Egypt.[47] The broadening of the domain of the world and narrowing of the domain of religion was the substance of the *ijtihād* which the Islamic Reformists advocated.

The call for *ijtihād* was combined with the rejection of *taqlīd*, that is, the rejection of historical Islamic traditions in favour of the basic texts understood as the repository of natural right, and the rejection of imitating the schools of law. It was also combined with a call for syncretism (*talfīq*): to take from the various schools, even those which were moribund such as the āhiriyya, such rulings as suited the present age. Supporters of his included al- ah āwī, Khayr al-Dīn al-Tūnisi (without success), Afghānī, Mu ammad 'Abduh, Ibn Bādīs and Rashīd Ri ā, who in Turkey was considered to be the leader of those who remained neutral and catholic (*lā-madhhabiyya*) in matters of jurisprudence.[48]

It is difficult to establish the relative importance of the general doctrines concerned with public interest (and their legal justification: legal purpose or the Five Generalities). Despite constant confirmation of the priority of public interest, that is, of the secular consideration of legal transactions, Rashīd Riḍā nevertheless completely refrains from bracketing the Text and the *Sunna*. Rather, he continuously stresses the importance of applying the *ḥudūd*, and in none of his writings does he deal with the respective jurisdictions of the *sharī'a* and secular law, always emphasizing that the former is based on one of the four sources of jurisprudence, while the latter is based on individual reasoning (*ra'y*). Indeed, he considers that secular law has limits of applicability, the most important of which is 'non-violation of the *ḥudūd* of God, for the ruler may not make legal what is prohibited nor prohibit what is legal'. One must rather act according to those precepts of the *sharī'a*, unless resisted by an obstacle from public interest; but this does not entail rejection or replacement of the *sharī'a* by discretionary judgement (*istiḥsān*). Thus it is impermissible, for example, to increase the share of inheritors, for instance those of women, to serve a particular interest or for a certain reason.[49]

In this way, Rashīd Riḍā confirmed the modernity of the *sharī'a* in the possibility of its being bracketed in principle, but he rejected this in practice. He was prevaricating: he only saw in the principles of the *sharī'a* confirmations of natural right, the norms of society and change, for he emphasized the role of necessity in the formulation of the public interest, and the incorporation of such necessities within the framework of the aims of the *sharī'a*.[50] At the same time Rashid Rida stated that within the *sharī'a* and its particular laws there was something public interest could not transcend. He therefore secularized the *sharī'a*, and refused to see in this secularization anything but a validation of the *sharī'a*, understood in terms of its consisting of general aims. We have seen that these are not particular to the Islamic *sharī'a*, but rather contain the laws of all nations, or almost all. Thus, the world was made to contain religion on the basis of worldly norms, and religion was made to contain the world due to the necessity of the world's proceeding according to religious law.

In this way, the Reformist compromise, based on nominal translation, was undertaken: religion is the world. There is therefore no secularism, as it complicates the connection between these two and indicates their differentiation in reality. Thus, the circle was squared and the square was circled, and the Reformist translation was based on the evasion of contradiction, the suppression of difference, the eradication of differentiation.

The prevarication of history necessary for the Reformist interpretation applies equally to what was transmitted from the past. For precisely as the present is naturalized into religion on arbitrary bases, so is arbitrariness exercised in the application of historical judgements in accordance with the requirements of the present, in exercising a pragmatic historical criticism. The relentless criticism of adīth by Rashīd Ri ā was most particularly of this sort. Rashīd Ri ā's call for legal judgement on the basis of 'true' adīth was only regarded by him as obligatory as long as it was not inconsistent with public interest. When a adīth was inconsistent with public interest, it was considered to be in contradiction with the general foundations supported by the Koran and the Sunna, in which case it would, in this view, necessarily be an isolated adīth, which only expresses an individual opinion without conveying certainty.[51] Thus, judgements on historicity and veracity were based on considerations of current utility, and adīths were rejected for considerations of utility with no allusion to their historical deficiencies or strengths. This was exactly what 'Abd al-'Azīz Jāwīsh did famously; Rashīd Ri ā criticised him for his rejection of 'true, universally acknowledged' adīths when their meaning did not please him,[52] even if Ri ā had declared that not all of al-Bukhārī's 'true' adīths were true and that their questioning by some was a well-founded challenge on the whole.[53]

Among the adīths Ri ā challenged on legal grounds – elsewhere stating that others were invalid on rational grounds – was the adīth of the gharānīq,[54] which today is known as the Satanic Verses and which Mu ammad 'Abduh had previously challenged because, in his view, it violated Muslim principles in its implied denial of the impeccability of the prophet and his communications from God, but without saying that it was incompatible with reason. Critical scholars (mu aqqiqūn) such as al- abarī and Ibn ajar had accepted this adīth, the latter thinking it probable because it was transmitted via three chains of transmission, which fulfilled the conditions of authenticity, despite the fact that the chain of relators did not go back to the prophet.[55] In the same sense of social utility, Rashīd Ri ā corroborated Ibn Khaldūn's declaration that the body of adīth regarding the awaited Mahdī (Messiah) was 'weak' (da 'īf) because, in his view, it belonged to the 'Babi innovation', and averted the attention of Muslims from political and military preparation.[56]

Comment on some of the verses of the Koran by Protestant propaganda[57] came in the same vein. Mu ammad 'Abduh made strenuous efforts to counter the discrediting of the Prophet: some of the salient theses of this propaganda were that the Koran was 'full of the affairs of Mu ammad himself . . . had it been the word of God as they [Muslims] claim, it would not be fitting for the Creator of the Worlds and the Maker of Creation to demean Himself by revealing that which concerned none of His creation except Mu ammad and his wives'; that the Koran went into exhaustive detail concerning 'Ā'isha's supposed deception, the Copt Mariya, and Mu ammad's marriage to Zaynab bint Ja sh after her divorce from Zayd b.  aritha.[58] Indeed, 'Abduh did his utmost to take on some aspects of the new criticism of the Old Testament in order to raise doubts concerning that book.[59] He was followed in this by his student, who pointed out that the 'history' of the Torah was acquired from Assyrian and Chaldean mythology, but he did not indicate that in this he was in agreement with one of the Protestant books which challenged Islam and which remarked that the Chaldean or Egyptian legends are the source of the Jewish information on Ishmael, by means of whom the Jews ingratiated themselves with the Arabs, 'using them as a means to drive the Byzantines from Jerusalem or to establish a new kingdom for themselves in Arab lands in which they could take refuge'.[60]

A mad Fāris al-Shidyāq had preceded both 'Abduh and Ri ā in this critical effort by almost half a century, when he wrote *Mumā akāt al-Ta'wīl fi Munaqa āt al-Injīl* (which is still in manuscript form and unpublished), which was based on the legacy of nineteenth-century European criticism of holy texts.[61]

Concerning these matters, the Reformists continued in their selective zeal, and in this way imitated their Protestant critics, for while the latter employed strict historical and rational criticism of the text of the Koran,[62] they exempted the Bible from it in exactly the same manner as our Reformists had exempted the Koran and the conduct of the Prophet from the strict historical criticism they considered permissible to apply to the Bible and the Torah. Muslims and Christians still affirmed clearly the historicity of narratives about the past contained in the holy books, and this included free-thinkers like Salīm 'An ūrī, who based his assertion on the Torah when affirming the plausibility of Solomon's construction of Palmyra.[63]

But not all the dealings of Islamic Reformism with the basic texts involved this kind of protective prevarication. Indeed, there were signs of a serious view of historical criticisms of selected historical texts, such as al-Wāqidī's *Kitāb al-Maghāzi*.[64] This was a view whose methodological premises were only properly applied in the works of the Indian Reformist Sayyid Ahmad Khan (1817–98).[65] But the Reformists had to confront the new scientific, natural and historical knowledge, which was based completely on secular authority and which was unequivocally incompatible with the text of the Koran. They therefore relied on the same strategy that was employed in the interpretation of the *sharī'a*, that is, to begin by restricting the domain of binding certainty and narrowing the sphere of religion vis-à-vis an expanding world endowed with an independent secular authority completely dissociated from Islam or any other religion. Thus, at the hands of Rashīd Ri ā, some of the prophet's utterances became matters of guidance and not of command, expressing an opinion and not issuing from God. Examples of such utterances were those concerning agriculture, medicine and the other mundane affairs.[66] The second step concerned matters which could not be so easily disregarded, such as the statements of the Koran, and used scepticism as a method to establish soundness. For when reason and transmission are in contradiction, transmission must either be relegated to fideism (*tafwī* ), that is, to say that only God has knowledge of this, or be subjected to interpretation. As for interpretation, it must comply with the rules of the Arabic language, according to Mu ammad 'Abduh, who based his statement on a long legacy in which the soundness of his position on interpretation was confirmed. At the same time he also emphasized that the results of this disciplined interpretation would conform with those established by reason.[67] Thus, with interpretation restricted to philological exegesis and discounting allegory in the name of fideism, a literalism is affirmed which goes against the very grain of this reformist effort.

In other words, it was necessary to rely on the Reformist interpretation which established a priori the correspondence of scientific truth and the text, and to affirm the veracity of each separately and on independent bases, then to put the two together in complete congruence and in this way to square the circles. One example of *tafwī* concerns the *jinn*, for the Koran affirms a world of *jinn* parallel to our own but does not provide any evidence for the reality of these invisible beings, although the text does mention that they were created 'from fire with no smoke'. But this reference to fire does not demonstrate a truth, according to Rashīd Ri ā, who does not tell us the reason for his statement, apart from remarking that the creation of man from dust and foetid mud does not, for its part also, demonstrate the truth. He thought that one should not conjecture about divine mysteries but believe in Koranic verses without interpretation[68] by consigning them, according to the venerable Hanbali position, to the knowledge of God alone.[68]

The reader will note that the introduction of this principle to the rest of the Koran must inevitably have momentous consequences which make the text tantamount to inarticulate speech with no discernible meaning, and that the application of this principle to the method of Islamic Reformism depends totally on the ability to exercise dominion over this process of *tafwī*. This power to control and to differentiate verses subject to *tafwī* can only be achieved by an authority over the text, an authority of exegesis and interpretation which might be based on *ijmā'* and possibly on independent opinion. In both cases, the precondition for the exercise of this dominion is its political basis in the name of an authority which renders final judgement in matters of religion, that is, the religious institution.

What is true of those verses that point to the existence of transcendental and invisible things is similarly true of matters about which certainty can be achieved, such as knowledge of history and nature. These are matters in which a contradiction appeared between the Koran and what the educated people of that age had learnt in the new and modern educational system.

A case in point is the story of Noah and the Flood. The examination of this story represented a transitional stage between *tafwī* and interpretation, it being open to the possibility of doubt and contestation and therefore to *tafwī*. Muḥammad 'Abduh considered that the tale of the flooding of the world is a narrative with no Koranic authority, being based, rather, on an isolated *ḥadīth* which does not afford certainty. He then cited the argument of some theologians and philosophers that the existence of shells and fossils of fish on the tops of mountains proved that water rose up there 'and this would never have happened unless it had covered the world'. He went on to cite the opinion of the majority of contemporary authorities, saying 'the flood was not universal, for reasons which would take too long to explain'. 'Abduh then concluded as follows:

> No Muslim may deny that the flood was universal merely because of the likelihood of such an interpretation of the verses of the Qur'ān. On the contrary, no one who firmly believes in religion should reject something demonstrated by the literal meaning of the verses, and

*ha īth* whose *isnāds* are trustworthy in favour of this interpretation, except by rational evidence which positively shows that the literal meaning is not the one intended by the text. Arriving at this conclusion is a matter that requires deep study, great application, and extensive knowledge of stratigraphy and geology. And this depends on various rational and traditional sciences. Whoever speculates irrationally without sure knowledge is reckless, should not be heard, and should not be permitted to propagate his ignorance.[69]

The fundamental point which this position affirms is the possibility of resorting to interpretation, indeed its necessity, when it is asserted that the literal meaning is 'not the one intended'. In this way the spirit of modernity is correlated with that of the text, and the definitive authority of the text entails endowing that authority with a meaning derived from modernity, which is incompatible with it on grounds of anachronism. Certainty and the text thus become counterparts. When interpretation is not undertaken, and when the content of the text does not concur with the actual history of nature or mankind, it is said that the meaning of the text is merely general or that it does not aim to inform but rather to guide:

Human history contained in the Qur'ān is like the natural history of animals, plants, and inanimate objects in it, and like its statements concerning the stars. What is intended by all this is to demonstrate by example the omnipotence of the Creator and His Wisdom, and not to set forth in detail the natural sciences or astronomy which God has enabled man to understand through study, contemplation and experiment to which He has directed him by both instinct and revelation. For this reason we assert that if we presume that the affairs of history and nature mentioned in the Qur'ān only conform with what all or some of the people discerned or believed at the time of Revelation. then this is not to discredit it. This is because these matters are not of themselves significant. What is intended by them is rather to guide and benefit people with what we have indicated.[70]

Religious reason therefore resorted to interpretation, that is, imposing upon the text meanings which it could not sustain, being derived from the knowledge and circumstances of an age vastly different to that in which it emerged. The Koranic text, and especially the verses alluding to astronomy, came to be understood as if some of its statements were based on a code, whose key was modern scientific knowledge, which in turn is connected to the encoded words by the bond of iconic allusion. Thus, modern means of communication, such as the radio and the telegraph, become keys for understanding the communications between Solomon and the Queen of Sheba which the Koran mentions.[71] Similarly, the statements dealing with heaven and its splitting point to the possibility of a change in the structure of the universe and an imbalance in its order when God wills, by means of cosmic events such as the collision of planets.[72] The division of the Red Sea and the drowning of Pharoah's army are explained as Moses's crossing the sea at a shallow point and the incoming tide inundating Pharoah and his army.[73] As for the defeat of Abraha before Mecca by the Abābīl birds, Mu ammad 'Abduh viewed it in the following terms:

> It is possible to conceive that this bird was a species of mosquito or fly which carries the germs of some diseases, and that these stones were of dried poisonous mud which the wind had blown and which had stuck to the legs of these insects. If these came into contact with a body they would enter its pores and cause sores that eventually lead to the decay and decomposition of that body. A multitude of these weak birds might be considered as the mightiest soldiers of God in His destroying whatever people He wills. And this small life-form, nowadays called the microbe, is the same thing. The groups and communities of these [microbes] are so numerous that only their Creator can count them. But God's ability to defeat tyrants does not depend on birds being on vast mountain tops, nor on their being a kind of griffin, nor to their being a unique species, nor to knowing the number of stones and why they have such an effect, for God has armies of everything.[74]

Indeed,  usayn al-Jisr adopted a scientific interpretation of miracles, interpreting the splitting of the moon in terms of earthquakes, and relying on the chemical transformation of air into water to explain the prophet's miracle of giving some of his followers water to drink from his fingers while travelling.[75]

Rashīd Ri ā used the same method to explain the evil eye, likening it to 'magnetic hypnotism [Mesmerism]', which acts on people from a distance.[76] He had a strong belief in spiritual influences, including the summoning of spirits, black magic and his own personal power to perform marvels.[77] Perhaps the most instructive illustration of the mecha-

nism of Reformist interpretation is the position of Rashīd Ri ā regarding the nymphs (al- ūr al-'i ) of Paradise. For he renounced the entire
Islamic legacy and, with a Christian puritanism, he emphasized, in con-
sonance with the concepts of sexual morality prevalent in nineteenth-
century Europe, that the nymphs were not women specially created for
the pleasure of men in Paradise, but rather earthly wives accompanying
their husbands.[78]

Thus, writing about the scientific interpretation of the Koran, on the
assumption that religion cannot produce what can be refuted rationally,[79]
became a widespread genre, beginning with usayn al-Jisr. Relying on
him were Mu ammad Shukrī al-Alūsī in Iraq – despite his opposition
to interpretation generally – Jamāl al-Dīn al-Qāsimī in Syria and the
students of Mu ammad 'Abduh in Egypt, especially al-Shaykh an āwī
Jawharī (1870–1940), who followed usayn al-Jisr in his philosophical naivety and who produced an exegesis of the Koran in twenty-six
volumes based on the discoveries of modern science. Many others before them had written about the subject, such as Mu ammad b. A mad
al-Iskandarānī al- abīb, who published a book in Damascus in 1300
AH entitled *Tibyān al-Asrār al-Rabbāniyya fi l-Nabāt wa'l-Ma'ādin wa
l-Mawāshī al- ayawānīyya* [Revealing the Divine Secrets of Plants,
Metals, and Animals] and another entitled *Kashf al-Asrār al-Nūrāniyya
bi l-Qur'ān* [Revealing the Koran's Secrets].[80] And the so-called scientific interpretation of the Koran was to have a long and profuse history,
starting with the massive scientific interpretation of an āwī Jawharī,
'Abduh's former pupil, moving on to Mu ammad Farīd Wajdī's integration of this type of exegesis within general exegesis, and on to later
developments.

But there can be no doubt that precedence in the field of scientific
interpretation belongs to Francis Marrāsh. usayn al-Jisr's book *al-
Risāla al- amīdiyya*, which was the source of much that followed,[81]
was dependent on Marrāsh's *Kitāb Dalīl al- abī'a*, which was serial-
ized in one of the Ottoman official journals and which preceded al-Jisr's
work by approximately two decades. Al-Jisr's book shows the influence
of Marrāsh in its arrangement of chapters, manner of argumentation and
reasoning, and its view of science and religion. Painstaking research is
required to determine the exact nature of this relationship. This cannot
be done here, but we hope that such a study will be undertaken.

The Marrāsh/al-Jisr line appropriated an extensive body of arguments which European apologetic religious thought had produced to
defend religion in the face of positive science. The universality and

use of these arguments in religion had arisen in clear defence of religion and the incompatibilities with reason it contained. Modern Muslim thinkers followed the practice of their predecessors in viewing nature as a sign of perfection and of the existence of divine being, and as a field for the manifestation of God. From this the systematic arrangement of nature and the interdependence of its parts can be concluded. With the Reformists, the recollection of Islamic philosophy was closely connected with the legacy of modern European Christianity in demonstrating the existence and intervention of God in nature, something the Catholics studied particularly when countering the criticism of religion in the eighteenth century[82] and which was found to a lesser degree in the natural theology of Protestantism.[83]

But it was the Catholics, especially in France, who produced the most extensive apologetic legacy, for the works of such as Lamennais and Bonald in the nineteenth century were adopted as part of the modern intellectual religious legacy, the legacy of philosophical scepticism.[84] From this arose the doctrine that the principles and laws of natural science rested on mere assumption, that knowledge acquired via the senses was unsound, and that beyond human knowledge were affairs which rationality could not comprehend.

Francis Marrāsh was the connecting link between Catholic apologetics and modern Islamic thought in his opposition to the finality of science, of which the above-mentioned book by    usayn al-Jisr was the basic text. Marrāsh had acquired these concepts while studying medicine in Paris at the beginning of the 1860s. At that time a Catholic philosophical movement, under the leadership of Dr Tessier and Dr Fredault,[85] was active in the medical school in Paris. It inherited the legacy of Lamennais and others, and defended religion by stressing its conformity with science, coupled with a sceptical position about the certainty of science: a sceptical position, we should say, towards scientism, for the scepticism posits a fully accomplished and perfect science that is counterposed to the radical incompleteness of actual scientific practice, which suggests this attitude laments science because it falls short of magic. This philosophical doubt, alongside a natural theology which infers the existence of God by means of nature, characterized the whole legacy of Arab Islamic and Christian thought opposing science[86] in a form which has continued until today under the celebrated title 'Science and Faith'.[87]

The two strands – scepticism towards science, and the scientific validation of the Koranic text in the name of *i'jāz* – are continuing today, having taken divers courses. Ultimately, they led to the formulation of the notion of the 'Islamization of Knowledge': not only of natural sciences, but equally of social and human sciences.[88] Correlatively, this trend has been inimical to the development of the more historically apposite tendencies in the exegesis of Modernist Reformism, namely, those calling for turning to the Koranic text with the equipment of modern historical, philological and analytical scholarship. In this vein, some of the best and most innovative attempts to study the Koran scientifically have been marginalized during this century.[89] Most particularly galling is the hysterical and inquisitorial manner in which the work of Mu ammad A mad Khalaf Allāh[90] and, forty years later, that of Na r āmid Abu Zaid[91] was received.

## Notes

1. This article is based largely on arguments and materials presented in the third chapter of my *Al-'Ilmāniyya* [Secularism], Beirut 1992. I am grateful to Dr Ronald Buckley for preparing a draft translation from the Arabic.

2. For accounts of this exegetical enterprise in general, see Jean Jomier, *Le Commentaire coranique du Manâr*, Paris 1954; and the relevant chapters of J.M.S. Baljon, *Modern Muslim Koran Interpretation, 1880–1960*, Leiden 1961 and of J.J.G. Jansen, *The Interpretation of the Koran in Modern Egypt*, Leiden 1974. For a systematic critical consideration, see 'Abd al-Majīd al-Sharfī, *Al-Islām wa'l- adātha* [Islam and Modernism], Tunis 1990, pp. 63ff., 183ff.

3. *Tafsīr al-Qur'ān al- akīm* [Exegesis of the Koran], 12 vols; in what follows, I have quoted from the 4th edn of vol. 1 (1373) and the 3rd edn of vol. 2 (1367), which contain the text of 'Abduh.

4. Shiblī al-Shumayyil, *Ta'rīb li Shar Büchner 'alā Madhhab Darwin fī Intiqāl al-Anwā' wa uhur al-'Ālam al-'U wī wa I lāq dhālika 'alā al-Insān* [Arabic Translation of Büchner's Commentary on Darwin's Doctrine], Alexandria, pp. ha' – a'; *Majmū'at al-Duktūr Shiblī al-Shumayyil* [Dr Shumayyil's Collection], 2 vols, 2nd edn, Cairo 1910, pp. 85–8.

5. Mu ammad 'Abduh, *Al-A'māl al-Kāmila* [Complete Works], ed. Mu ammad 'Amāra, Beirut 1972–3, vol. 1, p. 337

6. Ibid., vol. 4, pp. 558–61, cf. vol. 1, pp. 281–7.

7. Ibid., vol. 3, pp. 448–50. Mu ammad Rashīd Ri ā adopted this notion in his *Mu āwarat al-Mu li wa'l-Muqallid* [Dialogue between a Reformer and a Traditionalist], Cairo AH 1234, pp. 2–3.

8. Salīm 'Anhūrī, *Si r Hārūt* [The Magic of Hārūt], Damascus 1885, p. 117.

9. Fahmī Jid'ān, *Usus al-Taqaddum 'ind Mufakkirī al-Islām fi l-'Ālam al-'Arabī al- adith* [The Conception of Progress according to Muslim Thinkers in the Modern Arab World], Beirut 1979, pp. 167–73 and passim.

10. `Abduh, *Al-A'māl al-Kāmila*, vol. 3, p. 487.

11. 'Abd al- amīd b. Bādīs, *Kitāb Āthār Ibn Bādīs* [The Works of Ibn Bādīs], compiled by 'Ammār al- alibī, Algiers, vol. 2, p. 22.

12. Francis Marrāsh, *Shahādat al- abī'a fī Wujūd Allāh wa'l-Sharī'a* [Nature as Witness to God and Order], Beirut 1892, pp. 43–4.

13. Al-Shumayyil, *Ta'rīb li Shar Büchner*, p. ha'; *Majmū'at al-Duktūr Shiblī al-Shumayyal*, p. 14.

14. Jamāl al-Dīn al-Afghānī, *Al-A'māl al-Kāmila li Jamāl al-Dīn al-Afghānī* [Complete Works], ed. Mu ammad 'Amāra, Cairo, p. 312.

15. Ibid., pp. 141–8, 171–3; Marrāsh, *Shahādat al- abī'a*, p. 3.

16. Concerning the thought and activities of Namik Kemal, see Niyazi Berkes, *The Development of Secularism in Turkey*, Montreal 1964, pp. 209–22; and erif Mardin, *The Genesis of Young Ottoman Thought: A Study in the Modernization of Turkish Political Ideas*, Princeton 1962, ch. 10.

17. Berkes, *Secularism*, p. 222.

18. Taha Parla, *The Social and Political Thought of Ziya Gökalp, 1876–1924*, Leiden 1985, pp. 29, 42, 46.

19. Afghānī, *Al-A'māl al-Kāmila*, p. 443.

20. *Al-Manār*, vol. 8, no. 24, February 1906, pp. 929–30. This text is also in *Tafsīr al-Manār*, vol. 2, p. 497, but it is not found in 'Abduh, *Al-A'māl al-Kāmila*, vol. 4, p. 720, where it should occur.

21. 'Alī Umlīl, *Al-I lāhīyya al-'Arabiyya wa'l-Dawla al-Waṭanīyya* [Arab Reformism and the National State], Beirut 1985, pp. 13–15, 58–61. See also 'Abduh, *Al-A'māl al-Kāmila*, vol. 2, p. 459 and passim; Ri ā, *Mu awarāt al-Mu li wa'l-Muqallid*, p. 64 and passim; Ibn Bādīs, *Kitāb Āthār Ibn Bādīs*, vol. 2, p. 79.

22. The expression is that of Abd Allāh al-'Arwī, *Al-Idiyulujiyya al-'Arabiyya al-Mu'āsira* [Modern Arab Ideology], transl. Muhammad 'Ītāni, Beirut 1970, p. 73. It is restricted to one particular context and in it is seen a reflection of the attempted connection between two different temporalities and the occurrence of two societies in two distinctive historical moments.

23. Cf. Laroui, *Islam et modernité*, Paris 1988, pp. 134–47.

24. Rifā'a Rāfi' al- ah āwī, *Al-A'māl al-Kāmila li Rifā'a Rāfi' al- ah āwī* [Complete Works], ed. Mu ammad 'Amāra, Beirut 1973, vol. 2, pp. 190–92.

25. Ibid., pp. 94–5, 102, 201–3.

26. Berkes, *Secularism*, p. 121, n. 46.

27. Jurjī Zaydān, *Tarājim Mashāhīr al-Sharq fi l-Qarn al-Tāsi' 'Ashar* [Biographies of Illustrious Easterners in the Nineteenth Century], Beirut 1970, vol. 2 pp. 120–21.

28. 'Abduh, *Al-A'māl al-Kāmila*, vol. 3, p. 174.

29. Mu ammad Rashīd Ri ā, 'Manāfi' al-Urubiyyīn wa Ma arruhum fi'l-Sharq' [The Benefits and Evils of Westerners in the East], *al-Manār*, vol. 10, no. 3, 12 May 1907, p. 193.

30. Muhammad Rashīd Ri ā, *Mukhtārāt Siyasiyya min Majallat al-Manār* [Selected Political Writings], ed. W. Kawtharānī, Beirut 1984, p. 97.

31. Ibid., p. 99.

32. Simon Schama, *Embarrassment of Riches*, London 1987, p. 97.

33. 'Abduh, *Al-A'māl al-Kāmila*, vol. 1, p. 589.

34. Ibid., vol. 1, pp. 351, 355; Ri ā, *Fātawā*, no. 295.

35. Ibid.

36. Afghānī and 'Abduh, *Al-'Urwa al-Wuthqā wa l-Thawra al-Ta rīriyya al-Kubrā* [The Sure Bond], Cairo 1967, p. 117; 'Abd al-Rahmān al-Kawākibī, *al-A'māl al-Kāmila li 'Abd al-Ra mān al-Kawākibī* [Complete Works] edited by Mu ammad 'Amāra, Beirut 1975, p. 147; Ri a, *Mukhtārāt Siyāsiyya min Majallat al-Manār*, p. 134.

37. Berkes, *Secularism*, p. 223; Mardin, *The Genesis of Young Ottoman Thought*, pp. 105, 202.

38. `Alī 'Abd al-Rāziq, *Al-Islām wa u ūl al- ukm. Bahth fi'l-khilāfa wa'l-ukūma fi'l-Islām* [Islam and the Principles of Government], 2nd edn, Cairo 1925.

39. Al- ah awi, *Al-A'māl al-Kāmila*, vol. 2, pp. 473–4; cf. the observations of Umlīl, *Al-I lāhiyya al-'Arabiyya wa'l-Dawla al-Wa aniyya*, p. 116; 'Abd al-Latīf, *Al-Ta'wīl wa'l-Mufāraqa* [Interpretation and Difference], Casablanca 1987, p. 37; Louis Awa , *Al-Mu'aththirāt al-Ajnabiyya fi'l-Adab al-'Arabī al-adith* [Foreign Influences on Modern Arabic Literature], Cairo 1962, pt. 2, pp. 133, 134, 125–126.

40. `Abduh, *Al-A'māl al-Kāmila*, vol. 3, p. 323.

41. Ri ā, *Mu āwarat al-Mu li wa'l-Muqallid*, p. 55.

42. Al- ah āwī, *Al-A'māl al-Kāmila*, vol. 2, pp. 191, 479–81.

43. Ibn Badis, *Kitāb Athar Ibn Bādīs*, vol. 4, p. 20.

44. Ri ā, *Fātawā*, no. 36.

45. Ri ā, *Mu āwarat al-Mu li wa'l-Muqallid*, pp. 53, 58–9.

46. Mu ammad Rashīd Ri ā, *Tārīkh al-Ustādh al-Imām al-Shaykh Mu ammad 'Abduh* [The Biography of Muhammad Abduh], vol. 1, p. 614.

47. Abū Is āq Ibrāhīm b. Mūsā al-Shā ibī, *Al-Muwāfaqāt fi U ūl al-A kam* [Concordances and the Principles of Jurisprudence], ed. Mu ammad Munīr, Cairo 1341, vol. 1, pp. 63–4.

48. āfir al-Qāsimi, *Jamāl al-Dīn al-Qasimī wa 'A ruhu*, [Al-Qāsimī and his Age], Damascus 1965, p. 233; Mu ammad Mu ammad usayn, *Al-Ittijāhāt al-Wa aniyya fi'l Adab al-Mu'āsir* [Nationalist Trends in Contemporary Arabic Literature], Beirut 1965, vol. 1, p. 361.

49. Al- ah āwī, *Al-A'māl al-Kāmila*, vol. 1, pp. 544–55; al-Afghānī, *Al-A'māl al- Kāmila*, pp. 329–30; Ri ā, *Mu āwarat al-Mu li wa'l-Muqallid*, pp. 135–6; Ali Merad, *Le Reformisme musulman en Algerie de 1925 a 1940: Essai d'histoire religieuse et sociale*, Paris 1967, pp. 222–8 and passim; Berkes, *Secularism*, p. 381; Arnold Harrison Green, *The Tunisian Ulama, 1873–1915: Social Structure and Response to Ideological Currents*, Leiden 1978, pp. 116–7.

50. Ri ā, *Mu āwarat al-Mu li wa'l-Muqallid*, pp. 136–7.

51. Ibid., p. 126.

52. Ri ā, *Fātawā*, no. 506.

53. Ibid., no. 737.

54. Mu ammad Rashīd Ri ā, 'Bāb al-Intiqād 'alā al-Manār' [On Criticism of al-Manār], *al-Manār*, vol. 28, no. 6, 28 August 1927, p. 474.

55. Abduh, *Al-A'māl al-Kāmila*, vol. 5, pp. 283–9.

56. Ri ā, *Fātawā*, no. 44.

57. Mu ammad 'Abduh and Mu ammad Rashīd Ri ā, *Tafsīr al-Fāti a* [Exegesis of the Fāti a], Cairo 1319, pp. 100–23.

58. The appendix in Jirjis Sale, *Maqāla fi'l-Islām*, [A Discourse on Islam], transl. Hashim al-'Arabī, Cairo 1909, pp. 364–375.

59. `Abduh, *Al-A'māl al-Kāmila*, vol. 5, pp. 22–3 and passim.

60. Mu ammad Rashīd Ri ā, *Shubuhāt al-Na ārā wa Hujaj al-Islām* [Christian Sophistics and Muslim Proofs], Cairo 1904, pp. 2–15, 33–6; and the appendix in Sale, *Maqāla fi'l-Islām*, pp. 323–5.]

61. `Imād al- ul , *A mad Fāris al-Shidyāq, Āthāruhu wa 'A ruhu* [Shidyāq: His Works and His Age], Beirut 1980, pp. 76–8, 246, n. 87.

62. See the appendix in Sale, *Maqāla fi'l-Islām*.

63. An ūrī, *Si r Hārūt*, p. 71.

64. `Abduh, *Al-A'māl al-Kāmila*, vol. 2, pp. 424–5.

65. See especially Christian Troll, *Syed Ahmad Khan, A Reinterpretation of Muslim Theology*, Delhi 1978, ch. 4.

66. Ri ā, *Fatāwā*, no. 209, pp. 731–3.

67. `Abduh, *Al-A'māl al-Kāmila*, vol. 3, p. 282.

68. Ri ā, *Fatāwā*, no. 111.

69. `Abduh, *Al-A'māl al-Kāmila*, vol. 2, pp. 512–13.

70. Ri ā, *Fatāwā*, no. 45.

71. Al-Afghānī, *Al-A'māl al-Kāmila*, pp. 268–9.

72. `Abduh, *Al-A'māl al-Kämila*, vol. 5, pp. 365–6.

73. Ri ā, *Shubuhat al-Na ārā*, p. 5.

74. `Abduh, *Al-A'māl al Kāmila*, vol. 5, p. 529.

75. usayn al-Jisr, *Risāla al- amīdiyya fi Haqīqat al-Diyāna al-Islāmiyya wa Haqqiyyat al-Sharī'a al-Mu ammadiyya* [The Hamidian Discourse], ed. Khālid Ziyāda, Tripoli, n.d., pp. 64–5.

76. Ri ā, *Fatāwa*, no. 209.

77. A text of Rashīd Ri ā in Shakīb Arslān, *al-Sayyid Rashīd Ri ā aw Ikhā' Arba'in Sana* [Ri ā: Forty Years of Fraternity], Damascus and Cairo 1937, pp. 85–6.

78. Ri ā, *Fatāwa*, nos 193, 196.

79. `Abduh, *Al-A'māl al-Kāmila*, vol. 3, p. 357.

80. Yūsuf Ilyān Sarkīs, *Mu'jam al-Matbū'āt al-'Arabiyya wa'l-Mu'arraba* [Index of Arabic Books], 2 vols, Cairo 1928–31, p. 438.

81. Al-Jisr, *Risāla al- amīdiyya*, pp. 180–206.

82. Robert L. Palmer, *Catholics and Unbelievers in Eighteenth-Century France*, Princeton 1939, pp. 106–7, 108–12.

83. John Hermann Randal, *Takwin al-'Aql al- adīth*, transl. George Tu'ma, Beirut 1965–6, vol. 2, p. 222.

84. Louis Foucher, *La Philosophie catholique en France au xixème siècle avant la renaissance thomiste et dans son rapport avec elle, 1800–1880*, Paris 1955, pp. 23–5, 36–8, 258.

85. Ibid., pp. 257–261.

86. Marrāsh, *Shahādat al- abī'a*; al-Jisr, *Risāla al- amīdiyya*; Louis Shaykhu, 'Tanāqud al-Dīn wa l-'Ilm' [On the Contradiction of Science and Religion], *al-Mashriq*, 3, 1990, pp. 304–5, 308–9.

87. The fullest and most systematic statement of the sceptical position in modern Islamic thought known to me is by the last Shaikh al-Islam of the Ottoman state

who fled to Egypt in 1924; it is virtually never quoted: Mu tafā abrī, *Al-Qawl al-Fa l bayn alladhīna yu'minūn bil-ghaib wa'l-ladhīna lā yu'minūm* [On the Decisive Distinction between Belief in the Beyond and its Denial], Cairo [1361] 1942, esp. pp. 30ff. For criticism of 'Abduh and other modernist interpreters, see ibid., pp. 44–90.

88. For comprehensive comment, see Azīz Al-'A meh, 'Al-lā'aqlanīyya fi'l-fikr al-'Arabī al-hadīth' [Irrationalism in Modern Arab Thought], in *Abwāb*, 4, 1995, pp. 22ff.

89. Al-'Azmeh, 'Al-Us ūra, al- ass, wa't-Tārīkh' [Myth, Text, and History], in *Al-Islām wa'l- adātha*, London 1990, pp. 259–84.

90. *Al-Fann al-qa a ī fi'l-Qur'ān al-karīm* [Narrative Art in the Koran], 2nd edn, Cairo 1975.

91. Most particularly, *Mafhūm an-na ; Dirāsa fī'ulūm al-Qur'ān* [The Concept of Text; A Study in Koranic Sciences], Cairo 1993.

# 7

# Utopia and Islamic Political Thought

It is easy to underestimate the complexity of utopia in Islamic political thought, the diversity and variety of elements it calls forth to the mind with and without justification. It is easy not fully to appreciate the problems attendant upon ascribing to Islamic political thought a utopian element, not least because the notion of utopia is itself problematic and easy to banalize, and because in Islam utopian elements are elusive and difficult to disentangle from mythological, eschatological, legal and didactic contexts. More important, in addressing the question of utopia and the state in Islamic political thought, one has to confront the problematic status of political thought in Islam, and one must try to approach it in a way other than by analogy with modern political thought. Islamic political thought is a topic much addressed, but very little understood, and the general impression one gains from modern studies is one of essentialism, recursivity and repetitiveness[1] – there are exceptions of course. So one must reflect, in however preliminary a form, upon the notion of Islamic political thought, which is really not so much a coherent, deliberate and disciplined body of investigation and inquiry concerning a well-defined and delimited topic, but is rather an assembly of statements on topics political, statements dispersed in various discursive locations; there is no 'political theory' as such in Islamic political thought.

This contribution will therefore scan a period of over a thousand years and probe the edges and boundaries of its subject matter; it hopes to offer a number of specifications, distinctions and notions which are essential if one were to be able to begin thinking about utopia in Islamic political thought. Impressing upon the reader the importance and necessity of these preliminary distinctions and specifications will, in itself, be a worthwhile task. Of these specifications I will start with one which I have already elaborated elsewhere.[2] This concerns the state – *dawla* in

143

Arabic. Both lexically and in terms of actual usage until modern times, the term denoted a particular kind of patrimony, the proprietorship of command and authority within a specific line. Very rarely is the state, *dawla*, actually discussed – as distinct from being mentioned – in works that concern politics, be they works of public law, of ethics, or *Fürstenspiegel*. The precise field of use and elaboration of the term and the notion *dawla* is historical literature.[3] In historical writing, *dawla* refers to the continuity over time of power exercised by a string of successive sovereigns, and to the facility by which single sovereigns exercise exclusive power: thus we have the *dawla* of the Abbasids, and the *dawla* of Hārūn al-Rashīd. This abstract *dawla* is constituted of a body politic, in the original sense: a sovereign, his troops, his bureaucrats. What must be stressed is that this concrete body is distinct from a body social and from what later came to be known as civil society. This is absent from Islamic political thought except as an abstract locus of order and disorder which receives the action of *dawla*, and is only implicitly conceived in Islamic law. *Dawla* only relates to that which stands apart from it in a very abstract fashion; in this connection the sovereign, *sultān*, is the sole political subject, whose action upon society is univocal.[4] The exclusivity and totality of sovereign power is habitually compared to that of God, not unlike the practice in pre-modern European traditions. In Mamluk times, for instance, the jurist Ibn Jamā'a (d. 1333) carried through an interesting transposition which elevated the force of this analogy: whereas dogmatic theologians had previously demonstrated the unicity and omnipotence of God by, among other things, analogy with the unicity and omnipotence of royal power, he demonstrated these same characteristics of royal power by analogy with the divinity.[5]

The state in this context is therefore little more than the everyday incarnation of power, the monopoly of abstract power to command and coerce. We must, incidentally, view the notions of the celebrated Ibn Khaldūn (d. 1406) in this context: whereas it is still the common wisdom on this matter that Ibn Khaldūn was in essence a sociologist who derived state from society, close textual scrutiny and attention to that which is thinkable and unthinkable in his historical world would reveal that it is abstract power, not society, which is the primary substance of his discourse.[6]

One derivative of power is the field of its use: politics, *siyāsa* in Arabic. *Siyāsa* denotes absolutist management, the direction by reason of unreason. It is used in relation to animal husbandry. It is the management of natural disorder by the order of culture, and regal power is the ultimate state of culture in a natural world of men marked by a *bellum omnium contra omnes* which necessitates the establishment of power – this power is variously termed *wāzi'* (Ibn Khaldūn), *waz'a* (Jā i – d. 869), *shawka* (Ghazālī – d. 1111, Juwainī – d. 1085), *qahr* (Ibn Jamā'a) and *ghalaba* and *taghallub* (Ibn Taimiyya – d. 1327), or generally *mulk* and *sultān*. *Siyāsa* is therefore not the field where power is contested and arrived at: *siyāsa* presupposes the power of which it is a *modus operandi*. It is true that Muslim writers on politics from the earliest times like Ibn al-Muqaffa' in the eighth century, to Ibn Khaldūn more than six hundred years later, adopted some Persian notions and distinguished between three types of kingship and of *siyāsa*: that based on religion, that based on reason, and that based on caprice.[7] This is not a typology of state forms as is sometimes maintained, but is an operationalist classification of *siyāsa*. *Siyāsa*, politics, does not establish power and authority, but presupposes it and is premised on its absolutist exercise. The relation of all these notions to political and historical reality is an interesting matter, but I must resist the temptation to discuss it now.

Be that as it may, in Arab-Islamic writings pertaining to politics, *siyāsa* is of course encountered in two types of discourse. The first is the flourishing *Fürstenspiegel* genre, the tradition of which persisted from Sassanian times well into the Ottoman Empire. The principles of *siyāsa* in this body of writing consisted of sententious statements and of *exempla* which could best be reclaimed from the past for advertence, exhortation and emulation. The repetition of these *exempla* amounts to the repetition of movements by which skills are acquired, and these books are in effect technical manuals, not theoretical treatises on the science of politics.[8] This was indeed appropriate to the circumstances, for these texts were normally delivered at court orally, and oral education proceeds by means of narratives and proverbs rather than by more general statements – this is as true of the Abbasid court as of Cathar education studied by Le Roy Ladurie or education based upon the Homeric epic studied by Havelock.[9] Central among the topics addressed in these *Fürstenspiegel* is '*adāla*, justice – this was not here a legal category of course, but a descriptive notion denoting a harmonious arrangement of things in such a way that everything would remain in its place. Their result would thus be optimally beneficial to the king. At the centre of this just and harmonious order is hierarchy: a just manner of management is just when it guides the affairs of men in a way commensurate with how things turn out to be in terms of their relations of hierarchy – the argument is circular, but it is not mine, and circularity is here concomitant with the attitude of hyperrealism such as that professed by *Fürstenspiegel*.

The other type of discourse on *siyāsa* is the one where we will have our first encounter with the notion of utopia: this is *siyāsa shar'iyya*, that based on *Shar'*, the Islamic *nomos*, the *dharma* of the Muslims. This, like that of the *Fürstenspiegel*, is anchored in the prior assumption of absolute power, and is another *modus operandi* of power. The discourse is primarily legal discourse. It is perhaps necessary at the outset to correct an assumption often made in modern scholarship, which supposes that *siyāsa shar'iyya* is a late development, consequent on the atrophy of the caliphate and to be set in Saljuq and Mamluk times.[10] Henri Laoust has quite correctly taken it further into the past than is normally thought, and described the *Ahkam sultaniyya* of the eleventh century Māwardī (d. 1058) as a work of *siyāsa shar'iyya*.[11] I would take it three centuries further back to the time when the *sharī'a* was still in genesis as a distinct body of ideological and legal motifs, and specifically to the suggestion by Ibn al-Muqaffa' (d. 759) that the Abbasid Caliphate should suppress legal differences and institute a body of statutes by which they would regulate the affairs of the world. In other words, there is not a phase of unadulterated religious polity in Islamic history, nor was there ever this presumption by Muslim politicians or jurists.

Moreover, the *shar'ī* character of *siyāsa* is not altogether formally distinct from the notion of justice just discussed, though it is distinct in provenance and in its substantive details. Formally, like the *exempla* of the *Fürstenspiegel*, these details are premised as pregiven power and authority, and are so constituted as a particular means of administration and the husbandry of human beings in their private and collective lives. They are, as the titles of countless treatises tell us, *a kām*: statutes, ordinances, judgements, rulings.

In provenance, they emanate in part from divine and otherwise revered commands and interdictions as manifested in the Koran and in narratives about sayings and actions of Mu ammad, and in part from the varied and sometimes discordant rulings of jurists and early Muslims. These, together with the small amount of explicit legislation attributed to divine and prophetic origin, constitute the body of Islamic law. It has been suggested that the *sharī'a* in this context is a remote ideal, unrealizable and therefore, in the banal sense, utopian. Recently the proposition has been put forward that it was the ideal of the caliphate, as overseer of the *sharī'a* and vicar of prophecy, that constitutes the utopianism of Islamic political theory.[12] It was proposed in addition that so unrealizable was this that it left ample space for the social and political opportunism of the elaborators of this utopianism, the politically quietist '*ulamā*': the ideal caliphate can not be denied in principle, nor affirmed in reality.

The essential distinction that is being made here is between the caliphal ideal and political reality, be this reality associated with the caliphate as under the Abbasids, or with a non-caliphal form of royal sovereignty, as that under, say, the Mamluks. The distinction is not novel, though the imputation of utopianism is. It corresponds to the traditional theses of Orientalist studies, and these are based less on a proper consideration of historical realities than on the selective incorporation of these realities within the *topoi* and rhetorical conventions which constitute the fundamental working material of these studies in the form which still predominates today – though I must stress that this predominance has not been without serious challenge in the past decade or two. Axial among the presuppositions of this tradition of scholarship is that the *sharī'a* is an unambiguous body of rulings, at one and the same time all-embracing and definitively normative and, above all, a moment of divinity. It is, for Tilman Nagel, 'die in Buchstaben geronnene Form' of the divinely willed order.[13] For him, collective life in Islam is the divinely ordained form of human society.[14] Louis Gardet calls this fantasy 'the Islamic city', which he describes as an ideal type which has no existence.[15] The same is repeated by other works. Thomas Arnold[16] imagined that theories of government had their consummate beginnings very early on, in the Medinan period at the very beginning of Islam, naturally enough with no reference to reality.

It is this presumed divorce from reality, this gratuitous, dreamy quality, which is underlined. The *sharī'a* in its political and social moment is, according to the these under discussion, the sole legitimate regulator of mundane life for extra-mundane ends. By the same token, it is utopian. There is little merit in this supposition. In the first place, the *sharī'a* is the nominal umbrella of a variety of different things and is by no means univocal. The majority of its rulings do not have the finality attributed to them by modern studies. With few exceptions, Islamic law is a body of differences and of general rulings. The great works of public law and governmental statutes, such as those of Māwardī and Abū Ya'lā (d. 1066),[17] are themselves with few exceptions highly multivocal. On the various points they elaborate they adduce a multiplicity of conflicting precedents, rulings, deductions, all of which are considered equally legitimate, and the caliph is called upon to pronounce legal preference, in much the same way as jurists do – and a precondition for the caliphate is juristic competence. Ultimately, the supposition I am contesting here is inscribed in the *topos* of decline according to which Islamic history is imagined in standard textbooks and which holds, among other things, that the untenable ideals of the beginning give way to reality until the former, according to Gibb and Rosenthal,[18] give way completely to the latter, with which it is by definition, almost by a force of nature, in contradiction and dissonance. The essentially flawed utopian ideal is refuted, but in their inveterate folly Muslims somehow keep on cherishing it, as a dreamy utopia, making it the object of curiosity rather than of historical, political or ideological analysis.

This same idea is also pitched at another level. Laroui maintains that the application of the *sharī'a* that is, the institution of *siyāsa shar'iyya* denotes the legality of the state, but is not sufficient for this state to be legitimate.[19] This distinction is an adaptation of a Khaidūnian distinction between kingship and the true caliphate. According to this precept, the true caliphate was a miraculous irruption which was perverted and degenerated into mere kingship. This distinction, incidentally, derived less from the tradition of Sunni political or historical thought than from the cyclism of chiliastic sufism current in the Maghreb and the Andalus in the Middle Ages.[20] It is premised by Laroui on the unobjectionable proposition that a legal state is nothing but a natural state, a mundane, profane creature, which adopts the *sharī'a* as its legal system.[21] Also adapting Ibn Khaldūn, who in this case rehearses a thesis which was then well established, though it was not as constant a refrain as one would expect from modern commentaries, Laroui maintains that the only political order which is legitimate as well as legal is the pristine caliphate – the regime at Medina, whose appearance was miraculous and which, by the nature of things, was of short duration.[22] It was also in the nature of a regime such as this, and of society whose instrument it is, to teach the individual member, whose duty it is to transcend himself and his natural condition, in order to become akin to the ideal man whose perfect example is the Prophet Mu ammad: the aim of this state is therefore beyond society, and 'l'Islam ne quitte pas . . . le royaume des fins'. It is herein that utopia lies.[23]

This point will, however, be pursued without reference to either the term or the notion of legitimacy, for it is one which is ill-fitting in relation to Islamic political thought: legitimacy is a notion relating, in distinct ways, to dynastic and other forms of agnatic integrity, and to representative government. It is hence at best peripheral in Sunni Islamic political thought, which as we saw is concerned with the administration and violent regulation of an order whose hinge is a pre-established power, although the identity of imperfection and illegitimacy can be imputed to some strands of Shi'ite dogma. The following account will therefore join the almost universal consensus of Muslim scholars and regard all political regimes to be legitimate as long as they do not actually foster systematic hostility to Islamic law.

Ibn Taimiyya, who is always direct and explicit in the statement of his assumptions as well as those of others, excavates and brings forth a position often stated by others but left unvalorized and in an emblematic isolation: that a *milla*, a community of believers, is not simply one form of polity among others. Ibn Taimiyya emphasizes this in order to reject a correlated proposition, that prophecy is merely a form of just *siyāsa* granted to mankind for the proper conduct of mundane life.[24] This holds without regard to the nature of a regime based on the *shar'* and whether it be caliphal or sultanic. Whereas Māwardī[25] and Ibn al-Jawzī (d. 1201),[26] for instance, reflecting general consensus, asserted that the *shar'ī* order guaranteed and managed by the caliphate is instituted for the good order of the world and of religion, Ibn Taimiyya assimilates the former to the latter: he establishes an exclusive primacy of divine purpose which leads to the identity of the mundane order with it – if this order be based on *shar'*.

The key to this reduction is a specific form of traditionalism, *salafiyya* – the contemporary term is fundamentalism, or *intégrisme* in France: the one term derived from the traditions of Protestantism, the other of Catholicism. In *salafī* traditionalism the ultimate in exemplary tradition and utopian model is that which can be attributed to the prophetic example and that of his associates and some of their early successors, in addition to some central figures of universal recognition and exemplitude, such as A mad b. anbal (d. 855). Though neither holy nor divine, this body of exemplars, conveniently called the Medinan regime, is in some way – by miracle or by direct communion – evidence of the transitivity of the divinity. It is in full conformity with divine purpose and ordinance – it is indeed the manifestation of this purpose and ordinance. It is an instance of unalloyed perfection; the literary critic Northrop Frye, writing two decades before *glasnost*, described utopian discourse as one in which the utopian location is inspected under the guidance of a sort of Intourist guide.[27] Indeed, writings on prophetic biography as on the Medinan regime have this quality to a very appreciable degree, and it is this history which constitutes the material of *salafī* utopia. This is utopia in the strict sense of something which exists elsewhere, rather than an atopia which exists nowhere – and I say 'elsewhere' mindful of the anachronism which this may bring to mind – yet temporality is not an element of the primitivist traditionalism which is *salafiyya*, for this is really premised on the denial of temporality, or at least of its cumulativeness, and is equally premised on the reversibility of time.

Of course, *salafī* traditionalism is not confined to what it is convenient to call fundamentalism (I define fundamentalism as that moment in all religions which gives primitivism and primevalism precedence over history, which seeks to eliminate history and regard it as, at best, an illegitimate accretion onto the pristine beginning, and as such regard the present condition and its immediate precedents as corrupt, or at best as corruptions of an abiding beginning): this notion is, of course, shared with all other movements with claims to revivification, notably nationalism and populism. The primitivist vitalism of these tendencies is reflected in the names they have taken, and of these I need mention only the *Risorgimento* and the Baath. I think this is a crucial point to bear in mind when thinking of contemporary Muslim radicalism. In terms of this traditionalism, history is the history of corruption and of decay. Primitivism and utopia here are one; the ideal is historically concrete and always immanent, and the task is for its restoration or re-enactment.

But for historical as distinct from fundamentalist Islam, for the Islam that was and is lived as distinct from that of fantasy both medieval and modern, for the Islam that took account of the work of time, the Islam of *ijmā'* (consensus) and *ikhtilāf* (difference with mutual recognition), whose legal theory regards its own judgements as only probable regardless of their practical necessity and compulsion[28] – in other words, for the Islam that represents the experience of the overwhelming majority of Muslim peoples, terrains and histories, the consequences of the corruptive influence of time are not drawn with any consistency. Primitivism here is ideologically piecemeal and whimsical, with a moralistic rather than a political valorization. Exemplary history, the history of the Medinan regime, is a quarry of precedents elaborated within the body of legislation and of legal discourse concerning public affairs.[29] The Medinan regime is the true Golden Age which should be approximated in so far as this is possible in an imperfect world, and a situation which is only repeatable under determinate circumstances to which I will address myself in due course. This is not a totalitarian utopia, therefore, in any consummate sense, but a utopia in terms of the here and now: an elsewhere, some examples from which can be made into legal statutes for the here and now; a moral, didactic utopia, with practical use in jurisprudence, but not repeatable in its totality, and therefore not involving political engagement. In other words, in historical Islam the primitivist moment is a myth, in the classic sense of the charter of a ritual in which the status quo is dramatized, not overturned; accomplished, not sought.

Utopia in the fuller sense emerges in the fundamentalist moment: the Medinan regime may well be a unique phenomenon, but its purity and integrality can be re-established, and its institutes constitute a programme of political and social action whose actuality, though not palpable, is yet possible. Indeed, Ernst Bloch quite rightly stated that utopian ideas, which might be likened to a child's dream about presents, induce a rhapsodic enthusiasm which carries the dreamer beyond considerations of means. This same condition can keep its holder restless and expectant, full of life and striving. Otherwise put, again following Bloch but with some adaptation this time, utopia in this instance is not only a device for voyeuristic palliation, but a vital stimulus.[30]

The Medinan Caliphate can thus be regarded, with Laroui, as a utopia. What Laroui omits is an important complement without which consideration of this matter would remain incomplete: this is eschatology. Unlike activist, fundamentalist utopia, this finalist state of felicity and rectitude associated with the future reigns of the Mahdī (the Messiah) and of 'Īsā b. Maryam (Jesus Christ) is not the result of voluntaristic action. Like the Medinan regime and the prophetic example, it is a miraculous irruption by divine command onto the face of history, although it will be announced for the believers by many cosmic and other signs. Not only is the End a recovery of the Muslim prophetic experience, it is also the recovery of the primordial Adamic order, of the line of Abel, of every divine mission like those of Noah, Abraham, Moses, David, Solomon, Jesus and Mu ammad, who incorporates, transcends and consummates them all in the most definitive form of primeval religiosity, Islam. The End, like the beginning and like the periodic irruptions of prophecy, is really against nature; it is the calque of the beginning so often repeated in history, and is the ultimate primitivism.[31]

Eschatology and past example become utopia when they become activist, when they become a chiliasm, with a sense of total imminence. They become utopia when legalism and moralism give way to total political contestation. This occurs when the fundamentalist moment as distinct from historical Islam is ascendant among particular groups in society. Islamic political and social ideals based on primitivist models become utopian when these models are activated and valorized, when fundamentalism ceases to be a cliché and takes on programmatic specifications and, as a precondition of this specification, acquires a social and political constituency. Historically, this has taken two main forms. In the Islamic Middle Ages, radical fundamentalism was, as far as I know, invariably chiliastic, associated with the complex of ideas generically known as Mahdism. North African history is especially replete with Mahdism both Sunnite and Shi'ite: the Idrīsids, the Fātimids, the Almohads, Sufī politics like that of Ibn Qasī (d. 1151), a thaumaturge who established a short-lived state in the Algarve, and countless others. These have already been mentioned briefly, and associated with Ibn Khaldūn's theory of kingship.

The second form of activist utopianism is contemporary Islamic radicalism, for which there is no precedent in Islamic history. Like chiliasm, it relies on the specification of fundamentalism, that is to say, on the precise and imminent interpretation of the pristine model, be that divine pronouncement or utopian example. This is quite natural in all utopias, for by their very nature these have to establish a constituency by affirming the univocality of texts and examples which are, in themselves, naturally multivocal:[32] Plato specified his Republic in the *Laws*, Rousseau his Contract with his projected Corsican constitution.

Similarly, Islamic radicalism, a very recent phenomenon indeed and the illegitimate offspring of Islamic reformism and Wahhabite-Mawdudian fundamentalism, was born of a particular specification. It specified *jāhilīyya*, the non-Islam that is to be converted into Islamic order, as an actual presence. Of course each movement in this fundamentalism produced particular specifications consonant with its social, political and cultural import. Wahhabite fundamentalism in Arabia, from the beginning until the definitive establishment of utopia by the Imam (later King) 'Abd al-Azīz (the foundation of Saudi Arabia) and the suppression of the Ikhwān Wahhabite militia in 1927, decreed all territory identified for absorption by the expanding Saudi polity as *jāhilīyya* – and by territory I mean geographical territory to be subjugated, sociopolitical territory to be linked to the House of Saud in a tributary fashion, and of course religious territory defined by the diversity of local cults whose centralization and homogenization under the title of *Sharī'a* was a cultural precondition for political centralization.[33] *Sharī'a* here is of course in the main Hanbalite, characterized by a moralistic rigour which homogenizes public life on the one hand, and an economic liberalism on the other, much like some early Protestant polities.

Yet the suppression of the Ikhwān in Saudi Arabia was not the end of the story. Once the *jāhilīyya* was overcome, the utopian motif did manage to sustain itself in roughly the same way as it had over many centuries – as somewhat fulfilled in the institutes of government, in the uncontested circus games occasionally on offer in main squares of Saudi cities after Friday prayers, in the motifs of the state cultural and educational system. Each of these was a glimpse into the utopian beyond daily forced into the imagination, most especially of theology students. Yet in contrast to previous times of activism, the utopian model in Saudi Arabia, and especially the anti-utopia, was hardly specified: it referred to remote matters like communism and the Soviet threat, more of pertinence to the US perspective in the Cold War than to Arabian matters. It is a remarkable though typical fact that fundamentalist texts – the works of Mu ammad b. 'Abd al-Wahhāb and of his commentators, for instance – are highly unspecific: they speak of *jāhilīyya*, of *shirk*, of unbelief, of various iniquities, not in terms of contemporary indication but of events, personalities, conditions and sayings which purportedly took place in early Islamic times. Reality as perceived today is an implicit gloss, a parallel register of examples and anti-examples, each singly reducible to precedents of both rectitude and iniquity, each an expression, in code, of the other. They are, in a technical sense, tokens of each other.[34] Once the one is formally assimilated to the other, a practical activist programme emerges.

In this context there exists no difference between the general fundamentalist outlook of the chief official cleric in Saudi Arabia, the Sheikh 'Abd al-'Azīz b. Bāz, and Juhaymān b. Mu ammad al-'Utaibī, the leader of the chiliastic group which took over the enclosure of the Ka 'ba in 1979. In his writings, Juhaimān b. Mu ammad often refers, with great respect, to Ibn Bāz, and records that the cleric had seen and approved his writings. The only difference arose over specification: the utopia and its anti-type was for Ibn Bāz a textual outline at once abstract and hyperconcrete. He refused to join Juhaimān and his comrades in specifying the anti-type as the House of Saud, and in specifying the eschatological signs with which Saudi Arabia abounded as the actual occurrences that are referred to in Juhaimān's writings.[35] He was a signatory to the *fatwā* obtained to execute the survivors after the holy enclosure was stormed.

It was perhaps not unnatural that utopia in Saudi Arabia took on a messianic form; it reflects the relatively low level of cultural and political development of the country – though we must speak of backwardness with humility, in the light of the abiding irrationalism of political life in the West, evident in the currency of Nostradamus's prophecies of the apocalyptic political fantasy animating the American right and much foreign policy under the Reagan presidency, not to speak of the influence of Mrs Quigley on the White House. Elsewhere radical Islamism – as in Egypt, for instance, under the influence of thinkers like Sayyid Qu b (d. 1965) and Abul-A'lā al-Mawdūdī (d. 1979) – displays utopia and the anti-utopia with a similar traditionalist literary mode. But the range of external references is of course much wider and denser, is far more concrete, and has absorbed much of the social and economic programmes of leftwing movements. When, for instance, Khālid al-Islambūlī and his associates assassinated Sadat, indications are that they were expecting to precipitate an uprising in order to locate utopia in Egypt, not the announcement of the advent of the Messiah. This represents the response of specific social, economic and cultural groups in Egypt to particular public circumstances which have been much discussed, and under the leadership of what I like to call the lumpenitelligentsia.[36]

The difference between Arabian and, say, Egyptian Muslim utopianism arises from distinct historical worlds to which they belong. Arabian utopianism imagines the chiliastic order in terms of miracle and without necessary political reference to the state; this is very much in keeping with medieval Islamic habits. Egyptian utopianism, on the other hand, regards its relation to the state as fundamental. It seeks immediately to take the state by force, as with the radicals professing notions like *takfīr*. It also seeks, as with the Muslim Brothers in their fundamentalist mode, to work a rhetorical reconciliation of the notion of *shūra* (a form of Medinan consultation) and of liberal political notions with the aim of gaining power. A similarly primitivist Islamism has gripped some sectors of the Middle Eastern intelligentsia, some of them of a Marxist background – the best known are perhaps Jalāl Al-ī Ahmad of Iran, and Mu ammad 'Umāra in Egypt. But what we have here is a very modern phenomenon – just as European evolutionism in the Enlightenment and the nineteenth century wedded utopia and natural law to produce evolutionism, these intellectuals have wedded theories of dependency with a Muslim primitivist utopia to produce what they call 'the Muslim left'. But I am of the firm opinion that what we have here is not an Islamic primitivism but shades of a hypernationalism, a different story altogether.

# Notes

1. For instance, E.I.J. Rosenthal, *Political Thought in Medieval Islam*, Cambridge 1958; A.K.S. Lambton, *State and Government in Medieval Islam. An Introduction to the Study of Islamic Political Theory: The Jurists*, Oxford 1981.

2. A. Al-Azmeh, *Ibn Khaldūn: An Essay in Reinterpretation*, London 1982, pp. 26ff.

3. A. Al-Azmeh, *Al-Kītaba al-tārīkhīya wa'l ma'rifa al-tārīkhīya* [Historical Writing and Historical Knowledge], Beirut 1983, pp. 71ff.

4. W. Sharāra, 'Al-Mulk/al-'āmma, al-tabī'a, al-mawt' [Kingship/Commoners, Nature and Death], *Dirāsāt 'Arabiyya*, XVI/12, 1980, pp. 19–47; Al-Azmeh, *Al-Turāth, bayn as-sultān wa't-tārīkh*, Beirut and Casablanca, 1989, pp. 41ff.

5. Ibn Jamā'a, 'Ta rīr al-Ahkām', ed. H. Kofler, *Islamica*, VI, 1934, p. 365.

6. Al-Azmeh, *Ibn Khaldūn*, pp. 51–2, 155.

7. Ibn al-Muqaffa', *Al-Adab al-Kabīr wa'l adab al- aghīr* [The Greater and Lesser Disciplines], Beirut, n.d., p. 11.

8. Al-Azmeh, 'Al-Siyāsa', p. 284; in general, see Rosenthal, *Political Thought*, ch. 3.

9. E.A. Havelock, *Preface to Plato*, Oxford 1963; E. Le Roy Ladurie, *Montaillou*, transl. B. Bray, Harmondsworth 1978, ch. XV.

10. Rosenthal, *Political Thought*, pp. 28 and passim; T.W. Arnold, *The Caliphate*, London 1924, pp. 67 and passim; H.A.R. Gibb, *Studies in the Civilization of Islam*, ed. S.J. Shaw and W.R. Polk, London 1962, pp. 143 and passim.

11. H. Laoust, 'La Pensée et l'action politiques d'Al-Māwardī (364/450–974/1058)', *Pluralismes dans l'Islam*, Paris 1983, pp. 190, 192 and passim.

12. A. Laroui, *Islam et modernité*, Paris 1987, ch. 1.

13. T. Nagel, *Staat und Glaubensgemeinschaft im Islam*, Zürich and Munich 1981, vol. 1, p. 13.

14. Ibid.

15. L. Gardet, *La Cité musulmane*, 2nd edn, Paris 1961, preface.

16. Arnold, *The Caliphate*, p. 25.

17. Māwardi, *Les Statuts governmentaux*, transl. E. Fagnan, Algiers 1915, repr. Paris 1982; Abu Ya 'lā, *Al-A kām al-Sultānīya* [Statutes of Government], ed. M.F. Fiqi, Cairo 1966.

18. Rosenthal, *Political Theory*, pp. 28, 33; Gibb, *Studies*, pp. 142, 151ff., 162.

19. Laroui, *Islam*, p. 26.

20. Ibn Khaldūn, *Les Prolégomènes*, ed. E. Quatremère, Paris 1858, vol. 1, pp. 375–6 and passim.

21. Laroui, *Islam*, pp. 21ff; Ibn Khaldūn, *Prolégomènes*, vol. 1, p. 344.

22. Laroui, *Islam*, pp. 26–7; Ibn Khaldūn, *Prolégomènes*, vol. 2, p. 249.

23. Laroui, *Islam*, p. 19.

24. Ibn Taimiyya, *Minhāj al-sunna al-nabawiyya fī naqd kalām al-Shī'a wa'l-Qadariyya* [Critique of Shia'a and Qa arite Doctrines According to Prophetic Pronouncements and Actions], Cairo AH 1322, vol. 1, p. 3.

25. Māwardi, *Al-A kam al-sultaniyya* [Statues of Government], Cairo 1973, pp. 3, 5.

26. Ibn al-Jawzī, *Al-Mi bāh al-mu ī' fī khilāfat al-Musta ī*, [The Brilliant Lamp on the Caliphate of Al-Musta ī] ed. N.A. Ibrāhīm, Baghdad 1976–77, vol. 1, pp. 93–4.

27. N. Frye, 'Varieties of Literary Utopia', in *Utopias and Utopian Thought*, ed. F.E. Mannell, Cambridge, MA 1966, p. 20.

28. H. Hanafi, *Les Méthodes d'exégèse*, Cairo 1965, pp. 165ff., 272ff; A. Al-Azmeh, *Arabic Thought and Islamic Societies*, London 1986, pp. 71ff.

29. An inventory of some of these is conveniently assembled in M.I. Faruqi, 'Early Islamic History as a Model for the Development of Some Islamic Legal Categories', unpublished PhD thesis, University of Exeter, 1988.

30. E. Bloch, *A Philosophy of the Future*, transl. J. Cumming, New York 1970, p. 87.

31. Al-Azmeh, *Al-Kitāba al-tārīkhīya*, pp. 107ff.

32. Cf. M. Le Doeuff, 'Dualité et polysémie du texte utopique', *Le Discours utopique. Colloque de Cérisy*, Paris 1978, p. 333.

33. W. Sharāra, *Al-Ahl wa'l Ghanīma*; Al-Azmeh, 'Wahhabite Polity', this volume, ch. 7.

34. Al-Azmeh, 'Wahhabite Polity', this volume p. 154.

35. Below, pp. 155–6.

36. There are many works on radical Islamism, most of which are unreliable. For a judicious overview, see B. Johansen, *Islam und Staat, Abhängige Entwicklung, Verwaltung des Elends und religiöser Antiimperialismus*, Berlin 1982.

# 8

# Wahhabite Polity

An Iraqi opponent of the Wahhabite movement[1] in the early part of the present century could not comprehend why the Wahhabites were bent on inverting the correct order of things, as he understood it, in terms of which the ijāz and Najd were connected. Whereas the Najdī Wahhabites had considered the ijāz to be territory to be conquered, subjugated and corrected, being technically *dār al-arb*, it was in fact Najd (or rather the southern parts of it) which, in the early years of Islam, was the abode of the anti-prophet Musaylima, and was thus accursed territory that could in no way figure as *dār alhijra*, as the Wahhabites claimed.[2] The repudiation of the irenical character of the mutually recognized and validated schools of Sunni law was one of the charges most often levelled against the Wahhabites. Stress was laid on their radical intolerance of all but their own adepts to the extent of ascribing unbelief (*takfīr*) to all others, a feature that was often compared to the original position of the universally proscribed Kharijites,[3] and such stress was the substance of the very earliest critical pronouncements against the Wahhabites.[4] Mu ammad b. 'Abd al-Wahhāb himself devoted a lengthy epistle to refuting, among other charges, the charge that he was seeking to transcend the four schools of Sunnī law,[5] and this charge seems to have been quite persistent, having been repeated in a threatening letter sent by the then Pasha of Damascus to Su 'ūd b. 'Abd al-'Azīz in 1808, in which the Ottoman official stated that the Wahhabites were ignorant bedouins without instruction in the fundamentals of the four schools.[6] There was indeed much confusion pertaining to the articles of Wahhabite belief, not to speak of events inside Najd; Mu ammad b. 'Abd al-Wahhāb was accused of sorcery,[7] and the fable according to which he fled 'Uyayna as a result of having murdered its ruler, Ibn Mu 'ammar, in the mosque became a fact to a contemporary British consular report.[8] The incomprehension and misinformation in which Wahhabism was and is still engulfed is due to more than the fact that its works were little known outside Arabia (with the exception of India) until well into this century,[9] and certainly to more than the undoubted intellectual poverty and aridity of such works or to the relative isolation of Najd. The anti-Wahhabite polemic[10] was due principally to a primary and original trait of the Wahhabite movement and its concomitant ideology: that of making an absolute demarcation between an expanding polity and all its surroundings.

The social and political dimension of Wahhabite ideology is the setting of strict limits of exclusivity to a particular 'a abiyya (tribal power group), thus rendering all that is external to this expanding 'a abiyya social, political and geographical territory whose plunder and subjugation are legitimate, indeed incumbent upon members of this exclusive group.[11] Kufr (unbelief) is an attribute of others and, in the accentuated Wahhabite form, of otherness tout court. It is an attribute which makes conquest and subjugation incumbent, under the banner of jihād, both as the political act of an expanding polity and as a legal–religious obligation. This exterior of kufr comprises not only idolatrous religions, nor is it confined to non-Islamic monotheism, but describes non-Wahhabite co-religionists as well. Ibn 'Abd al-Wahhāb himself emphasized this, justifying it on the analogy of Muhammad himself having fought believers in the one God.[12] The hallowed principle of Sunnī Islam, according to which all those who profess the shahāda are Muslims, is rejected in favour of the assertion often made by Wahhabite divines that even reserve towards the necessity of pronouncing non-Wahhabites (generically dubbed mushrikūn) to be kuffār (unbelievers) and of fighting them in itself constitutes kufr.[13] Sulayman b. 'Abdillāh b. Mu ammad b. 'Abd al-Wahhāb, a prominent descendant of the movement's founder, banned not only alliance with the kuffār, but also their employment, consultation, trust, visiting, advice, friendship, emulation, cordiality and affability towards them.[14] Needless to say, the full rigour of these principles was not always brought to bear; this was dependent on the political and social conditions of the time. The third Saudi Imām, Su 'ud b. 'Abd al-'Azīz b. Mu ammad, was particularly noted for his severity,[15] while the population of Qa īm in the north of Najd and their local divines were known for their relative leniency and considered neither the Ottomans nor other Muslims generally to be kuffār.

In the first instance, the concrete manifestation of otherness to be suppressed was the particular Najdī forms of shirk. This comprised such matters as the idol Dhā 'I-Khil a, destroyed very early in the history of

Wahhabism,[16] against which apparently infertile women rubbed their buttocks in the hope of fertility[17] – Dha 'l-Khil a was the name of an idol destroyed in early Islamic times in Najd; it is not clear if what was involved in the eighteenth century was more than some sort of ritual re-enactment of this, made possible by the metonymical conflation of past and present in which fundamentalist discourse is grounded. Najdī *shirk* also involved the sanctification of the dead and supplication and sacrifice at their shrines, such as that of Zaynab bint al-Kha āb at Jubayla, where people sought success in business, or the cult of the male palm tree, at Bulaydat al-Fi a and elsewhere, to which spinsters flocked praying for matrimony, and much else.[18] The felling of sacred trees and the destruction of shrines (not the obliteration of graves or their desecration) were some of the very first acts of Ibn 'Abd al-Wahhāb, who was particularly vehement in his condemnation of devotional acts directed towards any objects of sanctity other than God; these included supplication to the *jinn*, the celebration of feasts connected with the birth of persons of sacred attributes (including that of the Prophet himself), the use of talismans and of sorcery, and similar actions imputing potency to mere creatures.[19] Some of the first acts of the Wahhabite forces of Su 'ūd b. 'Abd al-Azīz upon the invasions of Mecca in 1803 and Medina in 1805 were the destruction of sacred domes designating shrines.[20] Over a century later, the Saudi government destroyed the dome of a shrine in Jidda supposedly containing the remains of Eve, and banned popular devotions at the site.[21] To these local iniquities were added others derived from conditions farther afield. One prominent Wahhabite divine in 1808 included among iniquitous practices in Syria the drinking of alcohol, the smoking of tobacco, the playing of cards and listening to popular story-tellers.[22] Finally, Shi'ite Muslims throughout the history of Wahhabism and until the establishment of Saudi Arabia have been a favoured target of unremitting Wahhābī ferocity, ideological as well as military; the Ismā 'īlī Shi'ites of the Banū Yām in 'Asīr were eventually converted.

There can be little doubt that the Wahhabite assault on popular practices and on other manifestations of devotional and doctrinal difference was directed not only against dogmatic and devotional aberrations, but was also the counterpart of the fact that these were not only aberrant, but also and decidedly local. This acted to fragment religious authority in this world as well as in others, and militated against the emergence of a political authority which, busily devouring and incorporating social and geographical territory into a unifying vortex, was sustained

by the Saudi-Wahhabite alliance.[23] Prior to the emergence of the Wahhabite state of the Su'ūd family, scholarly activity in Najd was scanty,
although it was on the increase along with the growth in population
in general, and urbanized habitation in particular, during the seventeenth century.[24] Much of this learning was cultivated in the context
of connections with Damascus and (to a smaller degree) other centres
where Hanbalism was in currency; indeed, the *adhān* in Burayda in the
early part of this century was described by one observer as having been
delivered in the tones of Syria.[25] Ibn 'Abd al-Wahhāb himself belonged
to a prominent scholarly family, and his twenty or so marriages,[26] some
to members of the princely families of Mu 'ammar and Su'ūd, indicate social alliances concomitant with the politico-religious alliance in
which his career and those of his descendants find their bearings.[27]

The role of Wahhābī divines is inseparable from the role of Wahhabite doctrine and its emphasis on the application of Islamic law;
aspects of this will be analysed further below. The most direct aspect of
the social alliance between divines and Saudi princes is the direct political role of the former. Though it may be true that the original compact
between Mu ammad b. 'Abd al-Wahhāb and Mu ammad b. Su'ūd at
Dir'iyya, the first Saudi capital, was one in which the divine was 'the
senior partner',[28] this is only so in the sense that it was he who was in
charge of the legal system. Yet the pre-eminence of the Āl al-Shaykh,
the descendants of Ibn 'Abd al-Wahhāb, in the legal and religious institutions of successive Saudi states is a factor connected both with their
position in family alliances and their capacity formally to charter trans-
fers of power.[29] Acting upon the hallowed principle repeated by Ibn
'Abd al-Wahhāb, that power is legitimate however it may have been
seized, and that obedience to whoever wields this power is incumbent
upon all his subjects – so much so that the prerogatives of the Imamate
belong to the holder of power irrespective of his own status[30] – the senior ranks of the Wahhabite devotional and legal institutions have acted
as legitimizers of the successive transitions of power within the House
of Su 'ūd, both peaceful and seditious. It appears that, in all cases, such
legitimation, *bay'a*, was always undertaken at the behest or command
of the effective ruler.[31] In the period of turmoil and internecine Saudi
struggle in the 1860s and 1870s which saw eight changes of supreme
Saudi authority in Riyadh between the death of Faysal b. Turkī in 1865
and 1877, the position of the Wahhabite hierarchy embodied in Āl al-
Shaykh was one of attempts to reconcile, followed by the recognition
of the victorious party.[32]

The Āl al-Shaykh have therefore been rather like the house clerics of the Saudi clan, to whom their loyalty never wavered even in the worst days of Egyptian occupation in the early nineteenth century or during the ascendancy of the Āl Rashīd of ā'il. For leadership in the desert polity, which the Saudi states were, was the prerogative of a particular clan within a possible wider federation, and this polity was based on the absolute pre-eminence of a particular family combined with the political peripheralization of others. As always, desert polity is based on the patrimonial ascendancy of a particular clan – here the Su'ūds – which holds in tow an alliance of other clans which are by definition tributary and excluded from power. And whereas the leading clan – the only one, strictly speaking, which can arrogate to itself a political role – does not base its emergence to leadership on the extraction of public surplus but derives its wealth from private property and trade, its role as political leader, and the geographical expansion of this role, is based on systematic utilization of public surplus, a fact which is made possible by the tributarization of subject populations.[33] A similar situation, that of the Rashīdī state at ā'il, has been described in an excellent account as a trade state at the core, and a tribute state at the periphery,[34] and one could well say the same about the successive Saudi states. Built upon the settled population of al-'Āri (the early Islamic Yamāma), it came to command and extract surplus from the trade of Qa īm, whose rival towns of Burayda and 'Unayza sat astride the important Ba ra–Medina route and held one of the key routes to Kuwait; others to Kuwait and Bahrain passed in more southerly territory. These territories were early incorporated into the Saudi state, although they seem to have been prepared readily to turn against it in times of crisis, as during the Egyptian intervention.[35] From the Gulf Najdī trade reached as far as India, and 'Unayza traders had a stake in a pearling trade whose main buying organization was, in the early part of this century, represented by a M. Rosenthal of Paris, known locally as abib.[36] Besides trade in necessities, the export of horses was sometimes significant and sometimes in decline.[37] Also in the territorial core of Wahhabite polity was an erratic, but sometimes flourishing, agriculture.[38]

The bedouin tribes, however, were connected with this system only in so far as trade routes passed through their territory, *dīra*, and from this passage they extracted protection fees and offered guidance services. The 'Ajmān, for instance, controlled routes between Najd and both Kuwait and asā. Similarly, other tribes of the surrounding territories, such as 'Utayba, Āl Murra, Mu ayr, 'Aniza (to which the House of Suʿūd 'belong'), Shammar, and others, controlled routes leading to other territories, the ijāz, Syria, and elsewhere. But for these tribes to come to be considered as anything other than idolators, they had to be incorporated into the political system whose core was (and still is) the Saudi clan. This entailed these tribes becoming tributaries to the centre of power in southern Najd, and this, in its turn, entailed not only their subjection to taxation (in kind such as camels), but also their exclusion from the political sphere. The centralization in the extraction of surplus and the elimination of the role of these nomadic tribes in the extraction of surplus for their own benefit, as they did from protection fees (*khuwwa*) paid by agriculturalists and by traders passing through tribal territories, implied more than the technical reorganization of such extraction in general by relegating this task to a central authority which then redistributed to every group its proper due. It also implied political eradication, that is, the abrogation of tribal right for the benefit of a political right exclusively exercised by the centre. This new political right erected over the debris of tribal right is itself derived from an eminently tribal concept, that of protection, *imāya*, exercised by the central authority,[39] in exactly the same way as the nomadic tribes had hitherto offered protection and thus politically neutralized settled and trading groups in return for taxation. The relation of power expressed in its exercise, and thus the exercise of politics, by certain groups, and the exclusion of others from it, is the means by which tribal society is stratified. This selfsame process is repeated, in reverse, in the subjugation of nomadic tribes to the centre.[40]

Martial nomadism is thus emasculated by its reduction to the same vulnerability and susceptibility to fiscal subjugation, with its concomitant political obliteration, that had been the lot of the weaker agricultural settlements. In the religious terms of Wahhabite divines and of the principles of government they imparted to the House of Suʿūd, this reduction of nomads, agriculturalists and townspeople equally into subjects of the Saudi polity, this compact of protection and allegiance, was expressed in terms of the canonical alms tax, the *zakāt*.[41] Religious ordinances advocated by reformists are never disembodied, and their practical translation in the Wahhabite instance is a compact of protection between unequal parties modelled on tribal relations. The one is unthinkable without the other. It appears that the Saudi clan, by means of the military forces it could muster from the ʿĀriī population and its own domestic militia (*fidāwiyya, zghurtiyya*), and by skilful manipulation of desert and international diplomacy, not to speak of the use of vast wealth accruing from agriculture, trade, and various forms of tribute, was capable of turning itself into the only unit in the territory of faith which plays the role hitherto performed by martial nomadic tribes; the erstwhile masters of the desert are thus transformed into tribal tributaries connected to the House of Suʿūd by ties of obligation brought about by unequal power. That is why the founder of Saudi Arabia invoked ties of kinship with tribal groups way out of his areas of control to express his bid for expansion.[42]

With the *zakāt* the criterion of inclusion within the exclusive group is indicated; the group comprises the parties to a compact of unequal power, sharing a common exterior which exists for the purpose of expansion. The incursions of Wahhabite forces in Iraq, Syria, the ijāz, the Yemen and Oman in the early nineteenth and early twentieth centuries are instances of this. War being one vital manner in which tribal groups cohere, it is clearly impossible effectively to detribalize tribes and to atomize tribesmen by means of subjection to *zakât* and simultaneously to have them as tribal units with a tributary status; the only effective solution to this was agricultural settlement and the physical obliteration of tribal military force, both of which ʿAbd al-ʾAzīz was to attempt in the first third of this century, succeeding in the second.[43]

Zakāt is only one manifestation, albeit one of great importance, of the tendency of Wahhabism to homogenize that society subject to the control of the House of Suʿūd. *Shar ʾ*, of which *zakāt* is an instance, is certainly the method whereby society is homogenized, rid of its irregularity and reconstituted so that it becomes more amenable to central direction. *Lex talionis* was one thing that the *shar ʾ* imposed by Wahhabism on both nomads and townspeople abolished; it prescribed the substitution of money for blood, but this worked imperfectly,[44] indicating an as yet unconsummated project. The prohibition of usury, widely used amongst the bedouin,[45] is a similar issue. Customary marriage not involving a proper Muslim contract, and the customary division of inheritance whereby women were deprived of canonical shares, were common practice, particularly among bedouins,[46] who in some cases favoured the marriage of women who were already married but whose husbands were in captivity.[47] It was not until Saudi power was consolidated by means of *zakāt*-collecting local agents that the *shar*ʿ and precepts derived from it were applied by the legal authorities answerable to the Wahhabite divines.[48] Just as local devotions detracted from the authority of the centre, so did local customs for which there was the possibility of a central provision that could be enforced by the corps of

Wahhabite *'ulamā'*. In all cases, Wahhabism in its devotional as well as its legal aspects seems an element for the homogenization of society.

But his homogenization had limits that we have already touched upon, namely, the fact that domination of the tributary type exercised by tribal polity based on the absolute monopoly of power by one particular clan requires the maintenance of tribal particularism and of the social system of stratification prevalent in the desert. Homogenization is a political, not necessarily a social, process. It is thus not surprising that, despite the vehemence of Wahhabite proselytism, the ulubba were untouched by it, although they did not dwell *in partibus infidelium* but nevertheless revered the stars and held beliefs akin to heathens.[49] But this finds its explanation in their caste-like social inferiority and occupational stratification. Conversely, status and political necessity were allowed to override the requirements of the *shar'* in cases of personal status touching princely or royal personalities. The frequent marriages of members of the Su 'ūd clan, in some instances for no more than one or two nights, are sometimes reminiscent of Shi'ite *mut'a* marriage, proscribed by all legal schools of Sunnī Islam.[50] Particularity could not be eliminated as totally as Wahhabite doctrine might require, and it is undoubtedly true that the ethos of Wahhabism, with its embeddedness in tribal society, militated against the very homogenization it prescribed and required for its total practical consummation. This is why the administration of legal as opposed to customary justice, especially the attempts to eliminate the right of asylum and blood revenge, was at best very imperfect and had to await the modern Saudi state for its serious implementation.[51] It is according to this contextual condition, or reality principle, of Wahhabite fundamentalism that Wahhabite polity, with the definitive establishment of the state in the first quarter of the twentieth century, becomes strictly Saudi polity. Saudi polity tributarizes other clan groups no longer nomadic, and ties them as clans stratified according to a particular pecking order to the redistribution of Saudi wealth; for plunder is substituted subsidy and the privileges of citizenship, such as the legal sponsorship of foreign business (*kafāla*), akin in many ways to the exaction of protection money (*khuwwa*). Thus tribalism becomes ascendant, not merely a *modus vivendi* or a traditional structure of society. For its part, Wahhabism abstains willy-nilly from ordering society, and becomes a state ideology in the most common acceptation of 'ideology'. Wahhabism remains pervasive not only in the educational system, the media, and public discourse in general, but also in international proselytizing and other activities, not to speak of its spectacular performances in the shape of the public punishment of errants and criminals, much reminiscent of the Roman circus. Indeed, the Saudi–Wahhabite alliance reminds one of one Roman principle of statecraft, *panis et circenses*.

Yet Wahhabism preserves its integrity entire. For despite complications of unwieldy reality, Wahhabism sought the abstraction of society according to a utopian model whose current name is 'fundamentalism', denoting the attempt to fashion society according to a fundamental model already accomplished. Like all fundamentalism, Wahhabite doctrine[52] is cast in the mode of revivification. It purports to detail the exemplary behaviour of the Prophet and his contemporaries, and to utilize this register of exemplaries as a charter for reform. The fundamentals of rectitude are contained in this register, and the history that intervenes between the occurrence of exemplary acts and today is an accident that no more than sullies and corrupts its origin, and which therefore can be eliminated, as history is the mere passage of time, not the work of social, political and cultural transformations. It is not chance or an act of incomprehensible blindness to the facts of history that causes the fundamental doctrinal texts of the Wahhabite movement – Ibn 'Abd al-Wahhāb's *Kitāb al-Taw īd* and its main commentaries and glosses[53] – to contain little concrete reference to contemporary reality, but to be rather like commentaries on this reality in a different medium, that of detailing exemplary acts and sayings culled from historical and scriptural knowledge. The two are set in parallel registers and are expressed in terms of today's fundamentally right bearings, making the iniquities of today less historical realities than supervening mistakes which can be eliminated by reference to exemplary precedent.

History is therefore reversible; alternatively, that history which interjects itself between the fundamental examples of the past and today is liable to elimination. Wahhabite doctrine not being historical scholarship, this position finds its bearings in the social and political being of this doctrine. For the import of fundamentalism is to require is (willing or unwilling) adherents to become subject to its requirements, that is, to lay Wahhabite territory open to the authority of Wahhabism, and therefore subject to the Saudi polity. By requiring subjection in principle to the authority whose voice is Wahhabism, this doctrine simultaneously renders these subjects open to the dictation of cultural and societal relations whose ground and condition are this authority. In short, Wahhabite fundamentalism puts forward a model whose task is to subject local societies with their customs, authorities, devotions, and other particularities to a general process of acculturation[54] which prepares them for membership in the commonwealth whose linchpin and exclusive *raison d'être* is the absolute dominance of the House of Su'ūd.

Such is the import of the abstraction from contemporary reality which marks all fundamentalism: an absence is engendered, which is filled by interpretations provided by those with the means of enforcing an interpretation. It leaves the way open for the social and political contexts of fundamentalist doctrine to weave themselves into the terms of fundamentalist discourse, and by so doing to translate the terms of this discourse into contemporary facts and realities. The abstract reference of Wahhabite ideology has its counterpart also in the infinite possibilities for endowing it with meaning by those capable of enforcing a particular interpretation. The major one in this context is the abstract exterior, open for correction and demanding of struggle: instead of local and other infidels, the spectre of communism is posited by the Saudi state, autonomously and in tandem with its almost utter dependence on the United States, as the primary evil and manifestation of *kufr* and *shirk*. Fact and fantasy become tokens of each other. Wahhabism thus seeks to flatten the contours of societies under its authority and to prepare them for the receipt of new form by those powers who wield the ultimate authority and the ultimate sanction of force – the House of Su'ūd. Thus the definition of the interior in terms dictated by political authorities is the counterpart of the iniquitous exterior defined by the divines of Wahhabite doctrine.

The definition of this interior is based on the fundamentalist mode of perceiving this interior, in the sense that presentation of the present in terms of scriptural and historical examples eliminates its reality and transforms it into a *tabula rasa* on which the authoritarian writ can be inscribed. This is the import of the execration of *taqlīd* from the days of Ibn 'Abd al-Wahhāb,[55] in line with a long Hanbalite tradition. And since law perhaps best reflects the transformations of reality, it is there that the encounter between Wahhabite doctrine and the political and social reality for which it is the charter is best regarded; the legal system of the Saudi state is based on the twin pillars of devotional severity, whose ultimate authority is the Koran and the *sunna* as mediated by the authority of Wahhabism and its professionals (imams, *mu awwi'* corps), and of legal liberalism, one of whose most important categories is that of public welfare or the common weal, *ma la a*.[56] The liberalism of the Saudi legal system is not only manifested in the wide use of discretionary legislation based on the notion of *ma la a*, in line with Hanbalite tradition, but in a strong tendency towards doctrinal eclecticism, and the wise use of non-Hanbalite law,[57] particularly after 1961.[58] All in all, economic legislation in Saudi Arabia has been consonant with conditions prevalent there. 'Islamic banking', for instance, is consonant with conditions of speculative capitalism such as exist in Arabia today, and is in many ways reminiscent of European banking practices in the early nineteenth century.

*Ma la a* and devotional puritanism therefore become the twin pillars of the construction of the Wahhabite interior,[59] and both have the sanction of Wahhabism and its professionals. The king's prerogative as imam in the conduct of politics according to the *shar'* becomes referred to as *ijtihād*.[60] Thus when a *fatwā* pronounced the insurance of commercial goods to be illegal, King 'Abd al-'Azīz reversed the ruling on the grounds of public interest.[61] And when the Wahhabite divines wanted to abolish the commercial codes of the ijāz which had been modelled on the Ottoman *Mecelle*, 'Abd al-'Azīz desisted and, when this code was overhauled in 1931, it was simply purged of reference to interest and was still modelled on the Ottoman code of 1850.[62] The king's position was clear from the outset. He declared publicly that he would abide by the judgements of Ibn 'Abd al-Wahhāb and others only if they were demonstrable with reference to the scriptures;[63] direct reference to scriptures with the elimination of intervening authorities implies *ipso facto* a call for reinterpretation. Such is the real import of the rejection of *taqlīd* and the injunction to *ijtihād*.

The Saudi-Wahhabite alliance therefore subjected populations to legal abstraction, cleared the way for legislation in line with the discretionary requirements of what is habitually termed 'development', and inflicted upon these populations a constant social invigilation and control undertaken by the corps of *mu awwi'ūn* who assure adherence to standard devotions and precepts of public puritanism. This last function assures the control over social relations that obtain in the tribal society which Saudi polity has always considered to be its natural domain, relations that entail the strict exclusion of women, the observance of very conservative attitudes, and other means of severe social control, in addition to rituals of inwardness, such as public punishments. Such puritanism has often been the counterpart of economic liberalism, and Saudi Arabia is no exception. Yet the constraints on tribalism as well as on the consummation of a strict and integral Wahhabite order, both the results of practical Wahhabism, have resulted in two major episodes that have disturbed the Saudi-Wahhabite order.

The first was the series of events which led to the final military elimination of the Ikhwān during the late 1920s. These were irregular forces levied from settlements of bedouin populations known as the *hujar*, modelled on the *hijra* of Mu ammad and designed as places of exemplary life and repositories of military manpower at the disposal of the Saudi state, and established from about 1908 onwards at various strategic locations in Najd on tribal territories belonging to the clans.[64] They were therefore tribal-military settlements, extensively subsidized by 'Abd al-'Azīz,[65] and marked by the observance of strict codes of fundamentalist morality, including a vestimentary code.[66]

'Abd al-'Azīz did not construct a civic militia in the *hujar* – he had his townsmen for this purpose – but constructed tribal abodes with definable boundaries. We have seen that the Wahhabite-Saudi alliance deprives social collectivities of a political constitution, but preserves them as social units. This applies especially to nomadic tribal groups, which sustained their social being by raids into infidel territory, not only for booty, but for the maintenance of desert social stratification, as has already been suggested. When the borders of present-day Saudi Arabia were solidifying as a result of agreements and treaties, mainly with Great Britain, the checks put on bedouin raiding activity led to a situation expressed by one of the leaders of the Ikhwān revolt, Fay al al-Duwaysh, chief of the Mu ayr and of the Ar awiyya *hijra*, as one in which 'we are neither Moslems fighting the unbelievers nor are we Arabs and Bedouins raiding each other and living on what we get from each other'.[67] The Ikhwān had indeed 'worked themselves out of a job',[68] and a conflagration was inevitable and was predicted by a discerning ethnologist.[69]

The exterior was no longer to be territory open to conquest and subjection, as it should be with Wahhabite doctrine, and the revolt of the Ikhwān might have turned into a general rebellion had it not been for the fact that an analogue of external plunder was found: oil, the wealth accruing from which is redistributed after a patrimonial manner according to the pecking order required by, and conducive to, the maintenance of tribal structures and status. The distinctions brought about by wealth and privilege, the correlatives of the tribal structure, define a novel exterior, that of expatriates employed in Saudi Arabia, over and above the local exterior, women.

So much for the disturbing social consequences of Wahhabite polity. As for the ideological consequences of this polity, that is, of the Wahhabite-Saudi alliance, these have taken a form unchanged since 1927 when the Ikhwān, in full rebellion, charged 'Abd al-'Azīz with violating the relationship of interior and exterior by sending his son Su'ūd to Egypt (occupied by a Christian power and inhabited by infidel Muslims), using wireless telegraphy and other works of the devil, not compelling the Shi'ites of  asā to adopt the Wahhabite creed, and so forth.[70] Indeed, the Ikhwān had been suspicious of 'Abd al-'Azīz's dealings with infidels from a much earlier date; in 1918 they were not enthusiastic about the campaign against the Wahhabite  ā'il, on the assumption that they were playing a British political game.[71] Very much the same sort of objection to the political power of the Saudi state was voiced by the participants in the seizure of the Great Mosque with the Ka 'ba at Mecca in November 1979 – the second episode to disturb the Saudi-Wahhabite order. One chief iniquity and manifestation of *kufr* is the constant contact and co-operation with Christians; and the state which pretends to *taw īd*, the technical name of Wahhabism, in fact performed the unification, *taw īd*, between Muslims, Christians and polytheists, confirmed Sh'ites in their heresies, and, while it combated fetishism, instituted the fetish of money.[72] The facts of today, in perfectly fundamentalist manner, are assimilated to scripturalist models and are made to translate them, and the prime motif of the group which precipitated the events of 1979 was the assimilation of contemporary events to eschatological events,[73] which justified their messianic revolt.

The Wahhabite divines who condemned the 1979 rebels to death[74] are truer representatives of Wahhabism than the dead puritans. The grand Muftī of Saudi Arabia, Shaykh 'Abd al-'Azīz b. Bāz, a signatory to the death sentence,[75] did not seem to disagree with the theses of the rebels who had read some of their treatises to him, but simply declined to specify the object of criticism as the present Saudi state.[76] The secret of fundamentalism resides in the absence of specification, in the very tokenism of the letter, in the parallelism but never in the identity of the scriptural and the real registers. The latter can therefore be the meaning of the former through the imputation of such meaning by the agency that has the power and authority to posit, consolidate, and enforce meaning. The impossibility of utopia derives from the impossibility of conflating the two registers and contexts of reference, the scriptural and the real. Juhaymān al-'Utaybī and his followers conflated the two registers and identified them. They consequently read the eschatological script as an immanent chiliasm, precipitating their mundane perdition. Without the distinction between the registers which allows the powers that be to penetrate the script and infuse it with their power, fundamentalism becomes redundant, an idle chiliasm without a chance in this world.

# Notes

1. I use this term in preference to *Muwa idun* used by the Wahhabites because it is common and because the latter is confusing, being used by the Druze and, indeed, by all Muslims, to designate themselves.

2. M.Sh. Alūsī, *Tārīkh Najd* [History of Najd], ed. M.B. Atharī, Cairo, AH 1343; AD 1924, p. 50.

3. Ibid., pp. 50ff.

4. For instance, Al-Jabartī, *Min Akhbār al-Hijāz wa Najd fī Tārīkh al-Jabartī* [Narratives on Hijaz and Najd from the History of Jabartī], ed. M.A. Ghalib, n.p. 1975, p. 97.

5. H. Khalaf al-Shaykh Khaz 'al, *Hayāt al-Shaykh Mu ammad b. 'Abd al-Wahhāb* [The Life of Ibn 'Abd al-Wahhāb], Beirut 1968, pp. 119ff.

6. Fleischer (transl.), 'Briefwechsel zwischen den Anführenden Wahhabiten und dem Paşa von Damascus', *Zeitschrift der Deutschen Morgenländischen Gesellschaft*, xi, 1857, p. 441.

7. Ibn Bishr, *'Unwān al-Majd fī Tārīkh Najd* [Summits of Glory in the History of Najd], 2 vols, Riyadh AH 1385, 1388; AD 1965, 1968, vol. 1, p. 18.

8. M.A. Khan, 'A Diplomat's Report on Wahhabism in Arabia', *Islamic Studies*, 7, 1968, p. 40.

9. M. Kurd 'Alī, *Al-Qadīm wa 'l- adīth* [The Classical and the Modern], Cairo 1925, p. 157.

10. See M.R. Ri ā, *Al-Wahhābiyya wa 'l- ijāz* [Wahhabism and the ijāz], Cairo AH 1344; AD 1925, for a critical exposition, and see in general Z.I. Karout, 'Anti-wahhabitische Polemik im XIX. Jahrhundert', unpublished doctoral dissertation, University of Bonn, 1978.

11. The best account of the social and political bearings of Wahhabite ideology and of the overall history of the movement is that of W. Sharāra, *Al-Ahl wa 'l-Ghanīma: Muqawwimāt al-Siyāsa fī 'l-Mamlaka al-'Arabiyya al-Su'ūdiyya* [Clansmen and Booty: The Principles of Politics in the Saudi Arabian Kingdom], Beirut 1981.

12. *Majmu'at al-Taw īd*, Saudi Arabia n.d., p. 52 and passim.

13. Ibid., pp. 284 and passim.

14. Ibid., pp. 121–2 and cf. pp. 251ff., 288–9, 292.

15. Alūsī, *Tārīkh Najd*, p. 94.

16. H. Wahba, *Arabian Days*, London 1964, pp. 99 and 112.

17. Ibn Bishr, *'Unwān al-Majd*, vol. 1, p. 6.

18. Wahba, *Arabian Days*, p. 87.

19. For instance, Ibn 'Abd al-Wahhāb, in *Majmū'at al-Taw īd* [The Tawhid Collection], pp. 9–10, 58, 66 and passim.

20. Jabartī, *Akhbār al- ijāz*, pp. 92,104.

21. H. Wahba, *Jazīrat al-'Arab fī' l-Quarn al-'Ishrīn* [The Arabian Peninsula in the Twentieth Century], Cairo 1967, p. 31. For practices of talismans and magical healing in today's ījaz, see M. Katakura, *Bedouin Village. A Study of a Saudi Arabian People in Transition*, Tokyo 1977, pp. 68–9

22. Fleischer, 'Briefwechsel', p. 438.

23. Sharāra, *Al-Ahl wa'l-Ghanīma*, p. 91.

24. U.M. Al-Juhany, 'The History of Najd prior to the Wahhabis. A Study of the Social, Political and Religious Conditions in Najd during Three Centuries', unpublished PhD Thesis, University of Washington, 1983, pp. 250ff. On population, see pp. 165ff. It must be stressed that Juhany's conclusions are based on sketchy source material and that they should be treated with some caution as indicating general trends rather than anything else.

25. H. St. John B. Philby, *Arabia of the Wahhabis*, London 1977, repr. from 1928 edn, p. 195.

26. Khalaf al-Shaykh Khaz 'al,   *ayāt al-Shaykh Mu ammad b. 'Abd al-Wahhāb*, p. 341.

27. Ibn 'Abd al-Wahhāb's sworn and active enemy was his own brother (ibid., pp. 250ff).

28. M.J. Crawford, 'Wahhābi *'ulamā'* and the Law, 1745–1932', unpublished M.Phil thesis, University of Oxford, 1980, p. 38.

29. Ibid., pp. 42ff., 52.

30. Khalaf al-Shaykh Khaz 'al,   *ayāt al-Shaykh Mu ammad b. 'Abd al-Wahhāb*, p. 140.

31. For instance, Ibn Bishr, *'Unwān al-Majd*, vol. 1, pp. 96, 101, 203; vol. 2, p. 60.

32. See the discussion of this by M.J. Crawford, 'Civil War, Foreign Intervention and the Question of Political Legitimacy: A Nineteenth-Century Sa 'ūdi Qā ī's Dilemma', *International Journal of Middle East Studies*, 14, 1982, pp. 227ff.

33. For the stratification of Najdī society, see Juhany, 'History of Najd', pp. 173ff.

34. H. Rosenthal, 'The Social Composition of the Military in the Process of State Formation in the Arabian Desert', *Journal of the Royal Anthropological Institute*, 95, 1965, pp. 184ff and passim.

35. Ibn Bishr, *'Unwān al-Majd*, vol. 1, p. 240.

36. Philby, *Arabia of the Wahhabis*, p. 285.

37. For instance, R.B. Winder, *Saudi Arabia in the Nineteenth Century*, London 1965, p. 214; J.G. Lorimer, *Gazetteer of the Persian Gulf, 'Oman and Central Arabia*, 6 vols, Calcutta 1908–15, vol. 1, pt. 2, pp. 2335ff; Philby, *Arabia of the Wahhabis*, p. 216.

38. For a full description of the earlier period, see Juhany, 'History of Najd', pp. 182ff.

39. Cf. Sharāra, *Al-Ahl wa 'l-Ghanima*, p. 67.

40. On the Saudi taxation system, see, for instance, Winder, *Saudi Arabia*, pp. 211ff.

41. Cf. C.M. Helms, *The Cohesion of Saudi Arabia*, London 1981, pp. 152ff.

42. Kh. Ziriklī, *Shibh Jazirat al-'Arab fī 'Ahd al-Malik 'Abd al-'Azīz* [The Arabian Peninsula under King Abd al-'Azīz], Beirut 1970, p. 290; and A. Rihani, *Maker of Modern Arabia*, Boston and New York 1928, pp. 60–61.

43. See the detailed account of J.S. Habib, *Ibn Saud's Warriors of Islam. The Ikhwan of Najd and their Role in the Creation of the Sa 'udi Kingdom, 1910–1930*, Leiden 1978.

44. For instance, Winder, *Saudi Arabia*, pp. 158–9.

45.  J.L. Burckhardt, *Notes on the Bedouins and the Wahábys*, London 1831, vol. 2, p. 150.

46.  Ibid., vol. 1, pp. 107, 131; J. Chelhod, *Le Droit dans la société bedouine*, Paris 1971, pp. 70–71, 134; J. Henninger, 'Das Eigentumsrecht bei den heutigen Beduinen Arabiens', *Zeitschrift für vergleichende Rechtswissenschaft*, 61, 1959, p. 29.

47.  Ziriklī, *Shibh Jazīrat al'Arab*, p. 464.

48.  For instance, Burckhardt, *Bedouins and the Wahábys*, vol. 1, pp. 99, 101, 120; vol. 2, pp. 136–9.

49.  For a description, see Lewis Pelly, *Journal of a Journey from Persia to India through Herat and Candahar. By Lieut. Colonel Lewis Pelly . . . also Report of a Journey to the Wahabee Capital of Riyadh in Central Arabia*. Bombay 1866, pp. 189ff.

50.  One could also cite as evidence of animist manifestations (or survivals) the *wasm* with which 'Abd al-'Azīz branded his camels, described by Philby, *Arabia of the Wahhabis*, p. 53, and sketched in H.R.P. Dickson, *The Arab of the Desert*, London 1949, p. 420.

51.  Cf. for instance Winder, *Saudi Arabia*, p. 208.

52.  A thorough sketch can be found in H. Laoust, *Essai sur les doctrines morales et politiques de Takī-d-Dīn A mad b. Taimīya*, Cairo 1939, bk 3, ch. 2.

53.  Sulaymān b. 'Abdillāh b. Mu ammad b. 'Abd al-Wahhāb's *Taysīr al-'Azīz al- amīd fī Shar Kitāb al-Taw īd*, Damascus n.d. [1962], is a detailed linguistic and historical commentary; *Fat al-Majīd* by 'Abd al-Ra mān b. asan Āl al-Shaykh, Riyadh n.d., is in many ways a summary of its predecessor, while the same author's *Qurrat 'Uyūn al-Muwa idīn fī Ta qīq Da'wat al-Anbiā' al-Mursalīn*, Riyadh n.d., is a collection of glosses on the original.

54.  Cf. Sharāra, *Al-Ahl wa'l-Ghanīma*, p. 101.

55.  Text in *Majmū'at al-Taw īd*, p. 60.

56.  See, for instance, Crawford, 'Wahhābī "*ulamā*" ', pp. 68, 110.

57.  For instance, ibid., pp. 70–71.

58.  A.W.I. Abu Sulaiman, *The Role of Ibn Qudāma in anbalī Jurisprudence*, unpublished PhD thesis, University of London, 1970, p. 248.

59.  Cf. O. Carré, 'Idéologie et pouvoir en Arabie Saoudite et dans son entourage', in P. Bonnenfant, ed., *La Péninsule arabique d'aujourdhui*, Paris 1982, vol. 1, pp. 242–3 and passim.

60.  Crawford, 'Wahhābī "*ulamā*" ', p. 111.

61.  Wahba, *Arabian Days*, p. 94.

62.  Crawford, 'Wahhābī "*ulamā*" ', p. 97; Wahba, *Jazīrat al-'Arab*, pp. 319ff.

63.  A. Rī ānī, *Tārīkh Najd al- adīth* [The Modern History of Najd], vol. 5 of Rī ānī, *Al-A'māl al-'Arabiyya al-Kāmila* [Complete Arabic Works], Beirut 1980, p. 374.

64.  A. Musil, *Northern Neğd. A Topographical Itinerary*, Oriental Explorations and Studies, no. 4, New York 1928, p. 283.

65.  Habib, *Ibn Saud's Warriors*, p. 143.

66.  Ibid., pp. 33ff.

67.  Ibid., p. 136.

68.  Ibid., p. 119.

69. Musil, *Northern Neğd*, p. 303.

70. Habib, *Ibn Saud's Warriors*, pp. 122, 135. On the curious controversy over telegraphy, see Wahba, *Arabian Days*, pp. 57–8.

71. Philby, *Arabia of the Wahhabis*, p. 102.

72. Juhaymān b. Mu ammad b. Sayf al-'Utaybī, *Da'wat al-Ikhwān: Kayfa Bada'at wa ilā ayn Tasïr* [The Call of the Ikhwān: How it Started and Where it is Heading], n.d., pp. 32–3; and *Al-Imāra wa'l-Bay'a wa'l- ā'a wa Kashf Talbīs al-ukkām 'alā alabat al-'Ilm wa 'l-'Awāmm* [Rulership and Delegation of Power and Obedience and the Unveiling of Rulers' Snares against Commoners and Scholars] (n.p., n.d.), p. 28.

73. `Utaybī, *Al-Fitan wa Akhbār al-Mahdī wa 'l-Dajjāl wa Nuzūl 'Īsā b. Maryam wa Ashrā al-Sā'a* [Eschatological Disturbances and Narratives of the Messiah and Antichrist and the Descent of Jesus and Signs of the Apocalypse], n.d., passim; and *Al-Imāra*, pp. 20–21.

74. The text of this *fatwā* and other documentation is contained in 'A. Ma i 'nī, *Jarīmat al-'A r. Qi at I tilāl al-Masjid al- arām* [The Crime of the Epoch. The Story of the Occupation of the Holy Mosque], Cairo 1980, pp. 43–4.

75. Ibid., p. 45.

76. `Utaybī, *Da'wat al-Ikhwān*, p. 8.

# 9

# Islamic Studies and
# the European Imagination

... quasi tota natura cum ipsis insaniret

Spinoza

It was customary for medieval Muslim scholars and divines to deliver a public lecture marking the translation to a professorship. The purpose of this rite of passage was not entirely ritual nor necessarily frivolous, and need not be so today. It gave the incumbent the chance publicly to announce the provenance of his learning, to declare the direction of his scholarship, to inventorize his stock-in-trade, and to scrutinize the state of his field. Such formal statement of scholarly patrimony and intent is salutary. Reflection is always creditable; and taking up a chair, like the mid-life crisis, is a good vantage point for reflection, and I am perhaps fortunate in that the two do not coincide in my case. Without reflection, scholarship will become and remain captive to the unaided native intelligence, the truest companion error, and of course prejudice: prejudice shared with one's fellow-professionals and with society at large.

I wish to continue this tradition; but I am acutely aware that an antique tradition such as this can only persist if subjected to change. So I shall invert the venerable order of things. I shall not assert the antiquity of my scientific pedigree. Neither do I propose to underline my faithfulness to my profession of orientalist, nor do I wish to celebrate what commonplace prejudices I might share with this profession and tradition. What I intend my reflections to do is to scrutinize the condition of my orientalist profession and patrimony, and perhaps to perform a metaphorical act of parricide. I will take up two interconnected matters. I shall first discuss the way in which a particular notion of Islam is conjured up by the European orientalist imagination and how this has provided and still provides Islamic studies as a scholarly discipline within orientalism with conceptual and categorical baggage which I re-

174

pudiate.[1] Let me add here a word about orientalism: I understand by orientalism the deliberate apprehension and knowledge of the orient; I see orientalism as an ideological trope, an aesthetic, normative and ultimately political designation of things as oriental in opposition to occidental. It endows such things with changeless, 'oriental' properties, some repellent and others charming, that go beyond history, that violate the changing nature of things, and that confirm them in a distant and irreducible specificity transcending the bounds of reason and forever valorizing common fantasy and folklore. To complement this first line of reflection, I shall briefly indicate major orientations for the dissolution of this orientalist category of Islam, and for the reconstitution of the study of Islam on the solid grounds of modern historical scholarship.

Let me first recall a predecessor, who to my knowledge was the first orientalist at Exeter. In 1704, Messrs Philip Bishop and Edward Score, of the High Street in Exeter, published a book entitled *A True and Faithful Account of the Religion and Manners of the Mohammedans*. The author, one Joseph Pitts, was born in Exeter. In 1678 at the age of seventeen, he fell victim to his king's rapacious activities in the Mediterranean, when the ship on which he served his apprenticeship was overwhelmed by Algerian corsairs. Nobody thought him worthy of a ransom, and he spent the next fifteen years in slavery, during which time he converted to Islam and made the pilgrimage to Mecca, but finally escaped and returned to spend the rest of his days in Exeter.

The book was quite a success; it went into at least four editions, and was reprinted in London as late as 1774; and this success was fully deserved, as the book almost completely confirmed the expectations of its readers, and there are strong indications that it was actually written according to printers' specifications. With the exception of such fantasies as could be falsified by tangible observation – such as the assertion of countless generations of Europeans that Mu ammad's tomb in Medina was suspended in mid-air – the book rehearsed the usual repertoire of folkloristic absurdities current for centuries, absurdities which arise from a fundamental structure of all orientalist discourse: namely, that observations, and judgements without reference to observation, constitute two separate registers, with hardly any means of contact between the one and the other except for the possibility of the latter (judgements) given the guise of the former. Such are, of course, the possibilities of fantasy. Thus Islam was still for Pitts, as for medieval Europeans and a number of young orientalists today, 'a miscellany of popery, Judaism, and the gentilism of the Arabs'. The Turks – the quintessence of Islam for Pitts and his contemporaries – are so much given to sodomy that 'they loath the Natural Use of the Woman' and Mu ammad could be nothing but 'a vile and debauch'd imposter'. The Koran for Pitts, needless to say, is but 'a Legend of Falsities, and abominable Follies and Absurdities'.[2]

That observation is incapable of correcting prejudice was not a matter confined to semi-literate personalities such as Joseph Pitts. A still more staggering contrast is observable between Voltaire's nearly modern and historical view of Islam in his *Essai sur les moeurs*, and the dark medievalism of his tragedy, *Le Fanatisme ou Mahomet le Prophète*. That Mu ammad was an imposter dominated by ambition and lust, and that he was therefore a worthy inspiration for Islam, is a medieval view which was shared by Edward Gibbon as by many until very recently. This medieval canon on Islam was fully formed by the end of the twelfth century, the offspring of two independent but remarkably parallel traditions of anti-Islamic polemic, the one Byzantine and the other Mozarabic. This canon, both theological and literary, was remarkably impervious to observation. Marco Polo's descriptions are largely based on literary and theological conventions which were astonishingly resistant to the observation of reality or to the reading of original Arabic sources, although these had already been available in translation from the time of the Cluniac collection in the middle of the twelfth century. And replete with factual information as they were, the medieval romances, the *histoire chanté* of the time, were yet unremitting in their subordination of fact to propaganda and literary convention. It appears that Crusaders and others who were in direct contact with Muslims learnt nothing about them, and only borrowed the arts of gracious living. For the rest, the Islamic orient was a source of fantasy, the Land of Cockaigne, and the source of military antagonism. It is not the individual contents of knowledge that matter, but the conformation of contents, and this was orientated to a specific warring fantasy. In this, the truth of individual statements is incidental.

The overriding need was to speak ill, and knowledge of Islam was a kind of defensive ignorance. Referring to Islam, Guibert de Nogent said in the twelfth century, 'It is safe to speak evil of one whose malignity exceeds whatever ill can be spoken.' Such evil as was and still is spoken in very tangible survivals of medievalism, is not purely arbitrary. It belongs to a repertoire of images and aesthetic judgements – judgements of value. Every culture thrives on establishing difference from others, and pursues this establishment of savage difference with particular energy in situations of serious external conflict or internal flux and uncertainty. It is often repeated that Jews in Europe were considered tokens of evil and scapegoats for issues with which they had no connection. Yet it is Islam and other orientals in this tokenist mode which have been most pervasively construed as an emblem of repellent otherness – it is not for nothing that Moses Hess, an early Zionist, took offence from the remark made by Bruno Bauer that the Jews were orientals.[3] For a person such as myself, whose vision of history is one of radical mutations, it is a strange matter indeed to observe such instances of an archetypal collective memory, of a dark area of cultural life alive with continuing folkloristic emblems – a study of recent Spanish clinical psychology, for instance, has revealed the pervasive and obsessive presence of the abominable Moor in Spanish fantasies.[4] This of course involves a process very commonly met with in psychological and ideological phenomena, the process of displacement, where one image stands for another to which it has a certain normative contiguity, or where one image or name is substituted for another with which it shares a certain property – in this case, unspeakable evil and horror. It is in this same emblematic mode that hysterical reactions are almost automatically triggered off today by such virtually inter-changeable tokens of evil as communism, Shi'ism, Islam, terrorism, Arabism, Qadhafi, the PLO and a host of other phantasms nightly brought to our attention on television and in the other media, not to speak of fundamentalist Christians and media firebrands. Witness, for instance, the so-called prophecies of Nostradamus now in currency, where a dark apocalypse is constructed from Qadhafi, the Soviet Union and anti-Zionism.[5]

These persistent images are really less in direct continuity with the medieval image of the Saracen than mutant restatements of political and cultural antagonism. In the Middle Ages, they were born of the conflict between Islamic lands and Christendom – both before and after the Crusades, when Christendom became a unit of political thought, of geographical demarcation, and of cultural self-consciousness: the salient dates are the conquest of Sicily in 1060, the fall of Toledo in 1085 and the occupation of Jerusalem in 1099. Of this conflict were born the categories of Saracen and Moor. They, the observable instances of Islam, became the indices of a class of phenomena which are different, negative, fearsome. Orientalism, as a cultural mood and a component in a negative aesthetic repertoire, naturally had to be expressed in the prevailing literate cultural idiom of the times, and it is therefore not surprising that medieval orientalism represented Islam in terms of re-

ligious polemic, as religious idiom was the terrain where both antagonism and concord were encoded.

The Saracens thus were explained in terms of biblical legend as being
of Hagarene descent, and Mu ammad was thought of as a cardinal with
frustrated papal ambitions; earlier, he had been thought of as one god
among others worshipped by the Saracens; these included Mars, Plato,
Apollo and what was termed Alkaron. In the plays and romances of the
Middle Ages, Saracens came to be regarded as an index of repellent difference pure and simple. The term 'Saracen' was applied indifferently
to Muslims as to north European heathens, to Roman emperors, and to
various disagreeable personalities in the Bible. William the Conqueror
seems to have thought that he was engaged in battle with the Saracens
of Britain.[6] It is not surprising, in the light of this general indexical function that shaped the categories of orientalism, that Mu ammad should
be endowed with sweeping evil universality. In Canto 28 of Dante's
*Inferno*, he is relegated to the eighth of the nine circles of Hell, as a
sower of schism and scandal, outdone in this by only Judas and Brutus.

Dante was a scholar; scholarship, in the Middle Ages as today, is
inseparable from the cultural politics of its day, and knowledge never
was, and will never be, an innocent endeavour, but was, and is, utterly
sullied. Scholarship is the enunciation, in specialized terms for a specialized audience, of certain current principles which are, in scholarship, identified, concretized, categorized, ordered and concatenated.
Medieval scholars of Islam conceived it as a form of Arianism; most
notably, it was thought of in terms of biblical prophecy. Eulogius and
Alvarus, not to speak of Nicetas, saw it as the preparation for the final
appearance of the Antichrist, and such a view has been peculiarly resistant to time, change, rationality or progress. Duncan Black Macdonald,
a jewel among orientalists, could still state in 1933 that Islam was a
second-hand Arian heresy.[7] In 1597, an English Catholic exiled to the
Continent spoke of Calvino-Turkism, in response to which the Angli-
can Matthew Sutcliffe spoke of Turko-Papism. Such attitudes had noble
precedents. John Wycliffe had already seen Islam as the name for evil
within the Church, and Luther himself, in a foreword to the 1543 edition of William of Ketton's Latin Koran, had declared that, whereas the
pope was the head of the Antichrist, Islam was his body. Throughout the
Reformation and well into the nineteenth century, Islam was seen as the
lesser of the two horns of the ram made famous by the eighth chapter
of the Book of Daniel, the greater horn being identified with the Pope.
I myself witnessed such anti-Arab apocalyptic propaganda in Britain

during the 1967 war. Hopeful crusading clerics even took heart from the appearance of Genghis Khan and his attack on Islamic domains; they saw in him a new David destined to fulfill the prophecies of Ezekiel.[8]

Let me remind you again that these conceptions existed among the learned public despite exact scholarship. In the shadow of the defeated Crusades, the Council of Vienne had, in 1312, ratified ideas previously canvassed by Roger Bacon and Raymond Lulle, which called for the learning of Arabic – this was in keeping with the times, as the receding Crusades were giving way to another way of carrying on the war, by missionary effort. These attitudes persisted despite the fact that chairs of Arabic were established in Paris and Oxford in 1539 and 1638; that the language was taught in Leiden from 1593; that the Arabic grammar of the Dutchman Erpenius and the dictionary of his student Golius, existed from the early seventeenth century.

We are not talking of two separate types and domains of knowledge about Islam, one for the scholarly elect and another for the rude masses, but of the coexistence within orientalism of two substantially concordant registers, one of which – the scholarly – has greater access to observation, as I have already indicated, and which looks all the more abject for this. Regardless of access to real or specious facts, facts are always constructed and their construction is invariably culture-specific. Orientalist scholarship is a cultural mood born of a mythological classificatory lore, a visceral, savage division of the world, much like such partisanship as animates support for football clubs. As in all myth and in primitive logic, difference gives way to antithesis in a play of binary structures. All cultures operate in terms of antithetical typologies of culture and savagery, of normalcy and disnature. It is in terms of these structures that Islam and things Islamic are construed, categorized, divided and connected, and it is such parameters that dictate the terms of discourse on things Islamic. It is quite inevitable that one's own culture is taken for the norm whose terms and whose language become the metalanguage of a cultural typology in which other cultures appear not merely as other, but as contrary. What happened during the long emergence of the bourgeois-capitalist order which Christendom became was that the evil which was Islam gradually became a want, a deficiency in the natural order of things which was this order itself seen, from the Enlightenment onwards, as the culmination of universal history. Islam, once evil vying with good, thus became an anachronism, a primitive stage in an emergent historicist notion of things.

This was certainly a derogation, and it was a derogation in terms of might. It was made possible by the actual superiority in terms of political, economic and technical power, which the bourgeois-capitalist order came to feel as a result of its universal expansion. Fear of the Saracen, of the Moor, of the Turk, once 'the terrible scourge of the world', gave way to contempt, and the Ottoman Empire was soon to become the Sick Man of Europe. But it also gave way to enjoyment, which had become politically and culturally possible. Let me indicate, though, that European collective representations were not all nightmarish – a prurient fascination with things Islamic had titillated the libido of medieval monks no less than that of Lady Mary Montagu and of Alexander Pope.

Exoticism, frivolous or aesthetic admiration, is of course premised on an unreflected notion of utter otherness; it is a mode of consuming an object, of employing it for decorative and other purposes, in a context other than its own. Exoticism is a pleasant way of subjugating one's contrary, and ran closely parallel to the changing fortunes in the power relations between Europe and the domains of Islam. As early as 1454, at a banquet in Lille, a centrepiece of the entertainment was a tower carried on the back of an elephant led by a gigantic Turk.[9] An art historian has spoken of the 'oriental mode' in the work of Dürer, Bellini and others,[10] and indeed this persists today in illustrated editions of the Bible. Turkish and Persian carpets were in great vogue in the sixteenth and seventeenth centuries. Later, Charles II of England adopted Persian dress in court, in order to stop imitating French courtly costume. Samuel Pepys recorded that the new garment was quickly discarded as the king of France promptly ordered his footmen to be similarly dressed. There were more durable results of this exoticism, this containment and enjoyment of the bizarre; Islamist orientalism was to have a great artistic impact – I mention, at random, Marlowe's *Tamburlaine*, Goethe's *West-Östlicher Diwan*, Mozart's *Entführung aus dem Serail*, the art of Delacroix and Ingres, and the Brighton Pavilion. At close quarters, exoticism ceases to amuse and gives way to the barbarism that underpins it. Take for example the village of 'Ain Hud in occupied Palestine. It is a village for Israeli artists, and its title to special exotic privilege is one of characteristic grossness: it is the fact that its colourful houses in which the artists live have been left as they were when their owners and inhabitants were driven out in 1948.

Decorativeness is thus superimposed on subordination, one that is premised on eradicating the reality of the exotic. There is hardly anything Moorish about Othello but for the fatal magic handkerchief given to his mother by a witch, who was, incidentally, only Egyptian. Corneille criticized Racine for putting common Frenchmen in Turkish dress. This list can be extended at will. Otherness is always the context of deploying one's own concerns. Such was the admiration for Islam, however sullied and ambiguous, of, say, Condorcet, who considered it to be a natural religion in contradistinction to superstitious Christianity. Such is also the substance of artistic exoticism. For Dürer or Bellini, oriental themes and images were no more than visual frames for the depiction of biblical themes. The languid odalisques of Ingres are really derived from an antique sculpture, and they are given an oriental context and texture by motifs derived from the writings of Lady Mary Montagu and Montesquieu. Ingres had never been further south than Italy, and the same schematization in terms of genre and fancy is evident in nineteenth-century 'ethnographic' painting of the Middle East.[11]

By the Enlightenment, therefore, Islam was no longer invariably and necessarily evil. It had also become something bizarre, distant, occasionally ridiculous. It had become a deficient order of things, and an order of deficient things. Deficiency is, of course, a polemical notion. It implies a requisite completeness, a consummate plenitude, in relation to which deficiency is measured. But this involves not only measurement: the correct order of things causes others to be seen and judged in its terms and on it own terms. The discourse involved is one of contrasts, very much like the primitive logic that underlay medieval and early modern conceptions. Alongside the continuing contrast of good with evil, orthodoxy with heresy, moral probity with libertinism and sodomy, the Enlightenment scheme of things required the presence of other players in this game, which it could call its own. These were reason, freedom and perfectibility, the three inclusive categories of the present epoch. Along with this, the birth of modern orientalist scholarship in the Enlightenment was accompanied by the secularization of the profession. Clerics gave way to traders, dilettantes, gentlemen of leisure, and to consuls. In the course of the nineteenth and twentieth centuries, journalists took the place of the dilettantes, salaried academics that of gentlemen of leisure, while colonialists and sundry spies joined the ranks of all categories. As scholarship always follows the flag, Napoleon's invasion of Egypt was accompanied by an army of scholars who produced the monumental *Description de l'Egypte*, and the French invasion by Algeria led to a prodigious scholarly effort. The *Journal Asiatique* was founded in 1823, the *Journal of the Royal Asiatic Society* in 1834, and the *Zeitschrift der deutschen morgenländischen Gesellschaft* in 1849.

The polemical structure of modern orientalist discourse is precisely premised on the definition of things Islamic in terms of contrasts of reason, freedom and perfectibility.[12] These yielded three major characteristics of things Islamic and from the topical clusters thus generated can be derived all the topics of orientalism and of Islamic studies, in an essential form complete and hardly altered since the mid nineteenth century. Those of you who are familiar with orientalist Islamic scholarship will readily recognize these topics. To reason corresponded enthusiastic unreason, politically translated as fanaticism, a major concern of nineteenth-century scholars and colonialists as of today's television commentators. This notion provided an explanation for political and social antagonism to colonial and post-colonial rule, by reducing political and social movements to motivations humans share with animals. Montesquieu, Hegel and many others saw Muslim politics as life in the whirlwind of fortune, an intensely sensuous life in which passion, that low manifestation of nature, reigns supreme. Such passion according to this paradigm has two outlets: fractious and predatory politics, or else vice. In both, we have an abstract enthusiasm. Energy in the secular world is geared towards negative purposes only and is incapable of setting up a mature political order. Thus politics of communities designated as Muslim are amorphous and infinitely pliable. Muslim cities are seen to be formless and fissiparous, and Muslim conquests and movements directionless and utterly wild. Muslim history is an absurd succession of events, time without duration, described by dynasties which Hegel said were 'destitute of organic firmness', which belong 'to mere space'.[13] The corollary of this is a wretchedly dogmacentric life, a total abandonment of individuality to the exclusive worship of an abstract God. Another corollary to this, and the political analogue of this abject subjection of mind, will and person to God, is the subjection of individuality to collectivity, the oriental mirror image of freedom and its antithesis. From the eighteenth century, this topic was designated as oriental despotism, the irredeemable, immediate and unbridgeable gap between total tyrannical power on the one hand, and anarchy on the other. This theme,[14] developed by major thinkers like Montesquieu, has been applied by minor intellects to the study of Arabic and Islamic polities and political theory.

These two primary categories for the apprehension of things Islamic – unreason and servitude – posit Islam as a creature in diremption, as the unlikely coexistence of sheer animality on the one hand, and an abstract, hence forever forced and repressive, principle of order on the other. Nothing mediates the relation between the war of all against all on the one hand, and the Leviathan on the other; nothing mediates God and the world; one of them only is triumphant at a given moment. Civil society, the realm where individual needs are rationally co-ordinated, and that which brings forth the state, is unthinkable. It is little wonder that a variation of this theme has come increasingly to prominence. This is a characteristically dismal orientalist adaptation of the social sciences, one which views clan, tribe, locality, sect or ethnic group as a natural entity, one whose sole determinant is virtually a seminal predetermination. It is at once a natural entity which refuses to be subdued by a higher principle of order such as the state, and a unit whose connection to its members is irrationally obligatory, and therefore despotic. Social groups, rather than being regarded as properly sociological categories, are looked upon as no more than involutions upon some infra-historical essence which does not admit of historical study except in the most banal sense, an infra-historical order which is ever present and which explains present-day events. These groups – sects, ethnic groups and other *dramatis personae* which populate orientalist discourse, which fill the pronouncements of experts and which come to us nightly on our television screens in stories of irrational carnage and outrage – such groups are seen as irreducibly specific, hence naturally antagonistic, endowed with a congenital propensity to factionalism. Thus communalism, which is a very recent phenomenon, is thought to be primordial. The title under which this animal existence is officiated is 'identity', a hugely mystifying notion of great incidence and preference in expert opinion. It is this pathetic notion which is responsible for much of the nonsense one hears about the supposedly primordial antagonisms of Lebanon, about the conflict between Arabs and Berbers or between sedentary and tribal folk which animated French colonial historiography of North Africa.

The third category out of which things Islamic were identified and categorized is perfectibility. In the course of the nineteenth century this term, though not its meaning, fell out of use and was absorbed in the wider senses of evolutionism and historicism. And, indeed, the evolutionary schemata of world history, be they that of Condorcet, of Auguste Comte, of Hegel, Marx or Herbert Spencer, as of such theories as underlie development theory and the disastrous policies of the World Bank – all these theories can accommodate accounts of the specific differences which distinguish the oriental-Islamic from the occidental-normative. Normative and terminative correspond to one another in the evolutionist-historicist Eurocentric scheme: Islam, as anomaly, as a flaw, is seen to be an anachronism. Its characteristics – despotism, unreason, belief, stagnation, medievalism – belong to stages of history whose inferiority takes on a temporal dimension.

It is quite striking how the antithetical structures in terms of which Islam is apprehended run parallel to the manner in which feudalism has traditionally been regarded, and indeed the notion of primitivism shares many features with both the orient and feudalism. But over and above the explicit insertion of Islamic history within evolutionist schemes, such as the unusual position it occupies in Hegel's *Philosophy of History* or the peripheral position to which it is relegated in terms of the Asiatic mode of production, the historicity of Islam in terms of the philosophy of progress has been dubious. No properties of things Islamic were seen as contributory to the topical thematics of progress and evolution. Islamic history was and is still regarded as, at best, an accidental vehicle for the transmission of Greek learning to the West. As for its proper historicity, it is regarded in terms not of progress, but of decline; it is seen as an irrational irruption on to the canvas of history, an irruption which, for those of a generous disposition, carried a number of creditable principles. But it could only decline. Its original irrationality is implicitly seen in terms of either a doctrinal or a racial inadequacy. On assuming power, on founding a frenetically expanding empire, and sponging the wares of superior civilizations, this unworthy beginning can only realize its nemesis by very rapid corruption, senescence and atrophy. And this rapid fall is implicitly reducible to the discordance between the loftiness which some generous scholars ascribe to Islam's original impulse, and the dead weight of the Muslims' original irrationalism, their animal enthusiasm, the abstractness of their power, the formlessness of their societies. Whatever is construed as itself rational never goes beyond the bounds of the singular event to which it relates. Islamic history thus becomes, at best, a ponderous tragedy, at worst a soap opera, and in all cases a misadventure. Decline thus becomes not a fact of the historical order, but a predictable event of the metaphysical order. Decline is here not essentially a historical fact, but is natural given the antithetical conception of Islam employed: the antithesis of normalcy and nature is anomaly and disnature. Decline becomes metaphysically necessary, a foregone conclusion underlined by an actual disparity in might. That racist stereotypes and historical justification are concordant comes as no surprise.

Such are the schemata according to which modern orientalism conceives things Islamic. They should be recognizable to anyone studying the standard textbooks. They did not, and still do not, appear as simply the products of a collective imagination steeled with colonialism. On the contrary, they appeared, and still appear, as the result of direct observation and of scholarly endeavour. What gave them this prerogative was another result of the Enlightenment, and the backbone of Islamic studies: philology. Let us not forget how this philology grew, what fecund intellects worked for its establishment, and to what simplistic degradations it was subjected by orientalist Arabic philology. It was not only an outgrowth of antiquarian research; its beginnings were a rich web of antiquarian learning, and of criticism of the biblical text – Richard Simon's unconsummated work stands out, as does the more comprehensive albeit historically less influential work of Spinoza. Philological work on Sanskrit, and its later development into comparative Indo-European philology by Bopp are also crucial, as are the momentous later developments of biblical criticism and textual hermeneutics by the likes of Schleiermacher and (in a different direction) of Friedrich Strauss. The luxuriant writings of German Romantic historians, are also germane. In general, philology sought, with Spinoza, the separation between the sense of a text and its truth,[15] a truth which had been typologically or otherwise pre-given in traditional biblical exegesis. Philology rested in its decipherment of the world in the example of Vico, for instance, not on irreducible difference, but in similarity, hence accessibility to understanding on the basis of a humanity commonly shared by the philologist and by his charges.[16]

But altogether, orientalist philology in its Islamic-studies mode retained from this revolution in the historical sciences only two rudimentary elements. The first is the positivism of incipient philology – and I use 'positivism' in the generic epistemological sense, without reference to evolutionist doctrine. Positivist philology was and is a discipline with a decidedly moralizing stance, a somewhat devotional sanctimoniousness, one which was described by one of the greatest classical philologists of the nineteenth century[17] in terms of asceticism and self-denial, which he contrasted with Nietzsche's *Birth of Tragedy*, a text which provoked the outburst I am referring to. Let us not forget that morality has no business in a world devoid of infamy, and that consequently the other side of this technicalist purity is technically accomplished fraud: in fact, the eighteenth and nineteenth centuries were the golden age of scientifically authenticated fraud. I need only remind you of Macpherson's Ossian, of Chatterton's medieval poetry and of the Chronicle of Richard of Cirencester. These textual contrivances are of the same type as taxidermy, also perfected in the nineteenth century, and both taxidermy and positivist philology aspire to an ideal of the same order.[18]

This pedantic aspect of positivist philology was not infrequently the object of ridicule; the original Larousse dictionary, for instance,[19] stressed this matter, but equally underlined the value of the discipline. This value resided, and still resides, in its pursuit of the sense of a text; it is a sort of ethnography of the past. In the field of Arabic, the tone was set by Antoine Isaac Sylvestre de Sacy, the father of Arabic philology in the West, who brought the full burden of his Jansenism to bear on his material. In his work as in that of his numerous students and of subsequent generations, somewhat critical editions of Arabic works have been established, lexica produced, the main factual outlines of Islamic history sketched in Western languages, the manuscript holdings of various European libraries inventorized – a process which was, incidentally, accompanied by the plunder of libraries in Muslim lands. Positivist philology aims for the 'scientific' study of texts, of the meanings of their words and sentences, of the referents to which the text belongs: these are, according to a standard nineteenth-century textbook, historical facts, cultural life, religion, law and society.[20]

This exactitude of information and of designation which fired whatever spirit positivist philologists may have had, was animated by a typical Enlightenment motif, and was aimed at the seizure of the Real without the intervention of Passion. It is a form of vernacular realism. This realism does not yield the truth; it only yields discrete items of information, factoids, according to implicit criteria of selection which are fundamentally inhibitory, which work by a sort of censor principle not unlike that of the naturalistic novel.[21] Naturalism is fundamentally a censor, a defence against passion, and positivist realism is essentially antiseptic. In the field of philology it is the scholarly counterpart of bureaucratic rationality. It produces a disorganized array of these factoids according to a rudimentary principle of positivist epistemology, that the linguistic sign and the real signified can be made directly to correspond without any mediation – this view is contradicted, of course, by linguistic science, by congnitive psychology and by the history of art. Semantics thus gives way to an abstract lexicalism, and the unfounded supposition is made that the meanings of words, of terms, of beliefs, of doctrines, no less than of dogmas, of texts and of statements, are univocal and can therefore be uncovered once their origin has been exposed. The cardinal principle in the face of which postivist philology flies is an ancient principle of rhetoric, now brought back to prominence by linguistics and discourse analysis; namely, that all things involving words have to deal with the technical problems of words. And the key to these is neither the lexicon nor the grammatical compendium, but the properties and rules of semantics, the structure of text, the construction of discourse, the infinite resources of language, the rhetoric of meaning and reality, the boundless ambiguity of the text. No text has an intrinsic and univocal objectivity of meaning; it is always context-specific, internally and externally, and thus open only to structural analyses.

What positivism thus seeks to establish is not scientific knowledge, but naturalistic apprehension. Its entire project is based on the notion of verisimilitude which is ultimately a visual metaphor, and vision is, of course, the most primitive of cognitive means. Knowledge is modelled on a sensuous paradigm of immediacy, as a mimetic rendition of 'reality' full of the concreteness of immediate life. Such a project in fact is far from a consummated naturalism, and is closer to the Romantic notion of poetry, albeit unspeakably inferior to it.

Thus positivist philology is a genetic mode of study, an indication by a term of its origin. I do not call it historical because it lacks the totalizing orientation of modern historical scholarship. It seeks to describe past events – words, occurrences, dogmas, or whatever – according to the famous but unremarkable and not very profound aphorism of Leopold van Ranke, that he wrote history 'wie es eigentlich gewesenn', a teasing phrase which, with or without justification, has come to embody the historiographical utopia of the nineteenth century. This genetic investigation seeks the explanation of things in terms of their origins, and produces inventories of correspondence which are then served up as causal chains: texts fragmented and their parts reduced to other texts, events explained by single antecedents, fragments of dogmas explained by scriptural fragments, totally without respect to the fact that, even if, let us say, dogmas are explicitly set out in terms of scriptures, this does not mean they are derived from them except in the banal sense that a scripture, like any other text, is almost infinitely interpretable, and universally deferred to. The true meaning of a text, by contrast, is historical; a text has no sense outside the various and contradictory traditions that appropriate it. Even fundamentalists invoke the original text to the exclusion of commentary in order to substitute their own novel glosses. No end is really prefigured in its beginning. The resulting picture is of scholarship which is almost entirely enumerative, enumerating instances of an origin and variations therefrom, a very extreme form of philosophical realism totally oblivious to the fact that, even if it were possible to identify origins – and this is a very dubious proposition – it is surely impossible to make an exhaustive inventory of beginnings and thus arrive at an approximation of the Truth, genetically conceived, of course. The event and the explanation of the event are therefore of the same order: the order of narrative is at the same time the order of explanation and comprehension; vision and reason are united in a poetic reverie in the guise of an exacting philological severity.

Thus orientalist scholarship piles fact upon fact and date upon date in an order ostensibly blind to all but real succession. But this research is always geared towards the discovery of origin. It is not at all surprising that the overwhelming volume of orientalist research into Islamic matters has investigated beginnings, historical beginnings and Koranic textual beginnings. It has claimed to find in these beginnings the fount, origin and explanation of the whole sad story of Islamic history, institutions, societies and thought. From the Koran this scholarship has derived the principles of economic life and the supposed failure of capitalism. From the same text it seeks to explain the actual source of history. From the principle of *jihād*, holy war, one of the most eminent orientalists in Britain today derived all political activity in India, Turkey, the Levant, Iran, Spain and the Sudan over 1,200 years.[22] From the conflict of 'Alī and Mu'āwiya, orientalist scholarship seeks to explain the war between Iran and Iraq. If you looked at the 'explanations' of the Iranian revolution and of the Iran–Iraq war, you would find yourselves in the company of much discussion of the so-called 'martyrdom complex' of Shi'ism, of the death, nearly 1,400 years ago, of Husain. You will find hardly any discussion of Iranian history over the past hundred years or so. Islamic studies is thus a cluster of pseudo-causal chains. These chains are meant eventually to be reducible to the irreducible essence of Islam, which really performs an explanatory function very much akin to that of Phlogiston in eighteenth-century chemistry. The result is that elusive origins are sought, and the actual course, outcome, institutions and processes of Islamic history and culture are ignored, except under the metaphysical auspices of the study of 'decline'.

This is of course a retrospective construction, a casting of the origin in the light of subsequent events, which flies in the face of the most elementary principles of historical scholarship. Scholars working in this field have always sanctimoniously claimed 'objectivity'; yet their procedure is imbued with a vast meta-historical principle, an origin of origins, the pseudo-cause of other pseudo-causes, which is presupposed in Islamic studies. An irreducible substance is posited, one to which all occurrences in Islamic history are reducible – other occurrences are decreed anomalous and of non-Islamic origin. What we witness is not a genuinely barren agnosticism, in which many orientalists take pride, except seldom; what we find is not literally a display of what Croce called the 'sumptuous ignorance' of philological history, nor simply what Lord Acton praised as 'colourless' writing. What are at play in the naturalism of Islamic studies, in the censor principle mentioned, are enunciations which are not formless, nor simply polemical and directed outwards, nor again devoid of passion. Islamist discourse is thoroughly and irredeemably structured by implicit ideological notions, notions which identify things as Islamic, as original, and which organize the world of things Islamic in terms of the European imagination, and of the colonialist and neo-colonialist management of the world. It is not only that the unreflected and uncritical assortment of factoids must be the victim of implicit ideologies, folkloristic images and racist stereotypes. These facts have to be identified as relevant, others have to be rejected as irrelevant, sequences of putative influence have to be judged as plausible, others are unthinkable, all in the name of the naturalistic mode.

History is thus captive to meta-historical schemata; it is structured by a poetics, according to the terms of Hegel's analysis of history, epic and poetry in the third book of his *Aesthetics*. It is structured by the three meta-historical notions I spoke of: unreason, despotism and backwardness. Each is in fact a class of topics, of criteria of selection and of relevance, and together they set the boundaries of that which is thinkable. It is assumed that there are a number of intrinsic substantive qualities which characterized a changeless, or only superficially changeable *homo islamicus*: a creature born of distance, not only of the antithetical distance I have spoken of, but of the accompanying political distance established by colonialism.

I have already spoken about the character of this *homo islamicus*, of how he is defined by the inversion of the three cardinal notions through which the bourgeois-capitalist epoch conceives itself: reason, freedom and perfectibility. To this schematization of the self corresponds the schematism of the other. Each of these schemata is a topic which is invariably called forth to schematize things that are observed Islamic. Thus there are 'Islamic cities' unlike all other cities, 'Islamic economies' to which economic reason is inapplicable, 'Islamic polities' impenetrable to social sciences and political sense, Islamic history' to which the normal equipment of historical research is not applied. Facts are disassociated from their historical, social, cultural and other contexts, and reduced to this substantive Islamism of the European imagination. Accurate detail becomes local colour, a mere enhancement of naturalism, 'reality-effect'.[23] This is why orientalism in its Islamist mode is a mode of perception and apprehension, not of knowledge. It identifies things as Islamic, and does not know them as historical. It names things as Islamic, and at the same stroke endows them with the changeless and age-less characteristics of the *homo islamicus*. This is another reason why Islamic studies is, as I have already said, exhaustively enumerative: the identification of things as Islamic by their reduction to a textual Islamic origin is what it considers to be its proper task. Things Islamic, when identified with a beginning, add nothing to their origin. They have no specificity defined in terms of their historical circumstances and apart from the meta-historical specificity of their origin. This accounts, incidentally, for the dull repetitiveness which many scholars believe they see in Islamic history; it accounts even more so for the implicit uneventfulness and lack of real change in which is premised this genetic study, this degraded form of historicism. All in all, things Islamic are uniform, indistinct, isomorphous. This is of course a thoroughly unhistorical view. Revolutionary Iran is as far from Saudi Arabia as tenth-century Islam in Spain is distinct from contemporary Iran. One needs to substitute 'Christianity' for 'Islam' to see how ridiculous the picture will look. It is true that Bantu messianism and revolutionary Nicaraguan Jesuitism are both Christian. But this is a far cry from assuming their essential identity, or from assuming their indistinctness except in appearance from say, atavistic Catholicism in Poland or the politics of the Reverand Ian Paisley, or, for that matter, from Maronitist politics in Lebanon. Anyone who asserts the essential identity of Cathars, Flagellants, Rasputin and the Dutch Reformed Church will surely be pronounced mad. European scholars of Islam are in a strange league with Muslim fundamentalism. Both espouse a savage essentialism, a changeless ahistorical irreducibility, a mythical 'real' Islam independent of time and existent only at the beginning of things Islamic and at its pristine fount. Both insist that a rigourist form of religiosity is the characteristic, the real, of which Islam in places as different as twentieth-century Turkey and tenth-century Canton are mere avatars, any difference between these two Islams, or between aspects of them and the supposed pristine condition, is relegated to mere incidentals. Both fundamentalism and orientalism therefore eliminate the major part of history: rigourist fundamentalism was only very seldom espoused, and always by very small minorities, and the historical reality of Islam, as of other religions, is the normal course of events in which fundamentalist moments are incidental. One cannot use the brand of Christianity propagated by the Reverend Jerry Falwell as an explanatory principle with which to unravel the reality of Philip II's Most Catholic dominions. Fundamentalists realize the wildest fantasies of orientalism; for the former, as for the latter, the striving is for a myth of origin.

Yet the Islamism of things Islamic is only convincing because it is a classificatory token upon which scholarship is superimposed, a token of political and cultural otherness. In this otherness, things are levelled for ideological convenience. Things Islamic therefore duplicate each other. Studies have shown[24] how this takes place, how the structures of society duplicate those of theology, how theology structurally duplicates the essential features of despotic devotions, how these themselves duplicate the structures of power and of morality, how the whole of history is deployed to show the changeless integrity of the *homo islamicus*. Orientalist discourse on Islam indeed presents it through 'a set of representative figures',[25] a vocabulary and a repertoire of plastic images which are invariably encountered – much like the repertoire of plots, textual units and their permutations which account for the repetitiveness of science fiction, folk tales and pornography. All that cannot be made liable to reduction to these topics and notions of orientalist Islam is denied to Islam: thus Arab–Islamic philosophy is seen as only nominally so; Sufism, spiritually rich, is forced into the modes of heresy and non-Islamic provenance; the celebrated Ibn Khaldūn was made into a precursor of positivism and other European doctrines, or, in extreme cases, a representative of the Berbero-European anti-Arab spirit, all by virtue of his supposed modernity.[26] Indeed, virtually the whole of Muslim intellectual history is written in terms of a supposed conflict between Reason and Belief, the one foreign and the other native. This is not really very different from certain medieval processes of thought: some of you might know that medieval writers, in awe of and in admiration for Saladin, explained his excellence by asserting that his mother was one Countess of Pontieu.

In effect, the orientalist rendition of Islam is only putatively historical. The rejection by traditional orientalist scholarship, as by nineteenth-century historical and philological scholarship, of what it termed 'speculation' is really the counterpart of this. It was only natural that emergent disciplines should distance themselves from others; the nineteenth century saw the professionalization of history, and the attempt to suppress its rhetorical status. Chairs of history were established in Berlin in 1810 and in Paris in 1812, but in Britain it was only in 1866 that a chair of history was established at Oxford. Great historians like Guizot and Michelet were dismissed for teaching 'ideas' rather than facts. But one can clearly see that the rejection of positivism, idealism and Romanticism in nineteenth-century historiography and orientalist philology was nominal and institutional, not conceptual. Orientalist philology, as I have tried to show, is nothing but thoroughly structured by positivist epistemology and an essential category of Islam. Instead of the antiquarianist ideal, the result of this is the enemy of antiquarianism, what is derisively termed *histoire romanesque*.

Thus in the orientalist study of Islam are aborted both the full possibilities of positivism and of historical study. The possibilities of positivism are aborted because the field of relevant facts is severely circumscribed, and the facts themselves severely schematized. The possibilities of historical study are aborted because of the genuinely ahistorical character of the genetic reductionism I have spoken of. Historicism is used antithetically; it does not seek to look for genuine changes and transformations, to chart the course of history, but to fix distance, to affirm the Islamism of Islamic history, that is, to reduce it to its schematized meta-historical components, which affirm the antithetical difference of things Islamic from things normal. This is why orientalist Islamic studies have been so peculiarly resistant to the acquisitions and advances of the modern historical, including the social, sciences and to the normal procedures of philological and historical study today. This is also why many of my fellow-professionals in this field work on history in total oblivion of historical methodology, or literature in total innocence of critical theory (or even any inclination to literature), on grammar with hardly any awareness of linguistics. This is so much the case that there is hardly any perceptible change in the essential categorical, thematic and conceptual baggage of Islamic studies in more than a century; works supersede one another only by the addition of detail. But the features I have outlined, and the profound anti-intellectualism which animates the profession of Islamic studies, are essential for the survival of Islam as a category of orientalist discourse. The profession lumbers on with the disquieting confidence of its anti-intellectualism. It is still not unusual to take such library skills as are requisite in the editing of manuscripts and the collating of sources to be adequate indications of consummate scholarship. It is equally common in view of this involuted cultural homeliness to regard some form of contact with

Muslim countries to be adequate for intellectual mastery of the area, and thus to hold 'experience' as an adequate substitute for study and lived exposure to 'Islam' as perfect substitutes for scholarship.

Not at all unlike sympathetic magic, contagion is seen as the cause of effectiveness, and partial contiguity in space is taken for mastery of the whole. Again not unlike magic, this is a technique of control. Expertise in Islamic or Middle Eastern matters is thus unrelated to learning; learning is one thing, and expertise is quite another matter, connected less with knowledge than with belonging to particular circles which politicians and businessmen endow with oracular qualities, less because of reliability than because of a unity of practical purpose – diplomacy, war, subversion and profit, with the occasional tinge of romanticism. The context of practical expertise in which studies of Islam and of the Middle East find themselves is premised on the protean quality of Islam I have spoken of, and can only be preserved with the systematic resistance of the discipline to the present conditions and requirements of historical and sociological scholarship. The Islam of Islamic studies is not 'out there', but is a politico-cultural cannon. Without it, many people would find themselves out of a job.

Thus abandoned to the native intelligence, to folkloristic images, to a spurious notion of objectivity, the very premises of Islamic studies are radically and thoroughly unsound; their very foundation, the identification and the construal of relevant facts, is based upon a political and cultural imagination. This corresponds to what has been called the 'intoxicating Orient of the mind', a 'state between dreaming and walking where there is no logic . . . to keep the elements of our memory from attracting each other into their natural combinations'.[27] Thus the only possible attitude for historical scholarship towards the entire tradition of European Islamic studies is one of a very radical scepticism. One may be prepared to accept some bibliographical and textual-critical results of this tradition. But any proper writing of Islamic history has to rest on the dissolution of Islam as an orientalist category. It will have to start with putting into question the very notion of objectivity itself – or rather, to regard it as a historical category and as a historical and discursive problem. It will have to come to terms with the prodigious intellectual revolution inaugurated by Marx. It will have to take account of the fact that narrative, born out of fiction, myth and epic,[28] is on the wane in the study of history, and that not reality but intelligibility is the cornerstone of modern historical scholarship. It will have to take full account of the discovery of historical discontinuity and bear out the full consequences thereof, as of the rejection of 'origin'.[29] Full account has, moreover, to be taken of modern philology and rhetoric, and the simplifications of notions such as 'influence',[30] and gear itself towards 'fields of sense' and associated categories[31] and towards the acquisitions of modern critical theory as in the work of Benjamin, Frye, Barthes and others and the theory of discursive formations. It has to liberate itself from Islam, and scrutinize Islamic histories, societies, economies, temporalities, cultures and sciences with the aid of history, of economics, of sociology, critical theory and anthropology. Only then will Islam be disassociated, and reconstituted as historical categories amenable to historical study. In this, positivist philological research is axial. But this is only in the sense that it is to be presupposed; like literacy, it is the elementary beginning, not the end of research and study.

## Notes

1. In what follows I have drawn on the following: J. Fück, *Die arabischen Studien in Europa*, Leipzig 1955; N. Daniel, *Islam and the West*, Edinburgh 1960; R.W. Southern, *Western Views of Islam in the Middle Ages*, Cambridge, MA 1962; J. Kritzeck, *Peter the Venerable and Islam*, Princeton 1964; N. Daniel, *Islam, Europe, and Empire*, Edinburgh 1966; A.-T. Khoury, *Polémique byzantine contre l'Islam (VIII–XIIIe)*, Leiden 1972; D. Metlitzki, *The Matter of Araby in Medieval England*, New Haven and London 1977; B.P. Smith, *Islam in English Literature*, 2nd edn, New York 1977; E.W. Said, *Orientalism*, London 1978; E.W. Said, *Covering Islam*, London 1981; A. Abdel-Malek, 'L'Orientalisme en crise', *Diogène*, 44, 1963, pp. 109–42; M. Rodinson, 'The Western Image and Western Studies of Islam', in J. Schacht and E. Bosworth, eds, *The Legacy of Islam*, Oxford 1974, pp. 9–62; A. Laroui, 'The Arabs and Cultural Anthropology: Notes on the Method of Gustave von Grunebaum', in *The Crisis of the Arab Intellectual*, Berkeley and Los Angeles 1976, pp. 44–80; A. Al-Azmeh, 'If ā al-Istishrāq', *Al-Mustaqbal al-'Arabi*, 4/32, 1981, pp. 43–62 and the shortened version published as A. Al-Azmeh, 'The Articulation of Orientalism', *Arab Studies Quarterly*, 3, 1981, pp. 384–402.

2. *A True and Faithful Account*, preface, pp. 13, 18, 21. On printers' requirements, see Daniel, *Islam, Europe and Empire*, p. 14.

3. J. Carlebach, *Karl Marx and the Radical Critique of Judaism*, London 1978, p. 140.

4. T.F. Glick, *Islamic and Christian Spain in the Early Middle Ages*, Princeton 1979, pp. 3, 317 n. 1.

5. J.-C. de Fontbrune, *Nosterdamus. Historien et prophète*, Paris 1981, pp. 352ff, 381ff.

6. Metlitzki, *The Matter of Araby*, p. 119.

7. D.B. Macdonald, 'Whither Islam?', *Muslim World*, 23, 1933, p. 2.

8. M. Eliade, *The Myth of Eternal Return*, transl. W.R. Trask, London 1955, p. 142.

9. J. Huizinga, *The Waning of the Middle Ages*, transl. F. Hopman, Harmondsworth 1972, p. 241.

10. J. Raby, Venice, *Dürer and the Oriental Mode (Hans Huth Memorial Studies, 1)*, London 1982.

11. M. Steven, 'Western Art and its Encounter with the Islamic World, 1798–1914', in M.A. Stevens, ed., *The Orientalists: Dalacroix to Matisse*, London 1984, pp. 17, 21.

12. Al-Azmeh, 'If ā al-Istishrāq'.

13. G.W.F. Hegel, *The Philosophy of History*, transl. J. Sibtree, New York 1956, p. 105.

14. For the despotism theme, see A. Grosrichard, *Structure du sérail. La fiction du déspotisme asiatique dan l'Occident classique*, Paris 1979; and the observations on Montesquieu by L. Althusser, *Politics and History*, transl. B. Brewster, London 1972, pp. 75ff.

15. T. Todorov, *Symbolisme et interpretation*, Paris 1978, pp. 128ff.

16. E. Auerbach, 'Giambattista Vico and die Idee der Philologie', in *Hometange a Antonio Rubio i Lluch*, Barcelona 1936, vol. 1, pp. 293–304.

17. U. von Wilamowitz-Möllendorf, *Zukunftsphilologie. Eine Erwiderung auf Friedrich Nietzsches 'Geburt der Tragödie'*, Berlin 1872, p. 32.

18. See the discussion of S. Bann, *The Clothing of Clio*, Cambridge 1984, pp. 16ff.

19. Paris 1866, vol. 12, p. 823, col. 4.

20. A. Gercke and E. Norden, eds, *Einleitung in die Altertumswissen-schaften*, Berlin and Leipzig 1910–12, vol. 1, pp. 35–6.

21. N. Frye, *The Anatomy of Criticism*, Princeton 1971, pp. 51–2.

22. Said, *Covering Islam*, p. 108.

23. R. Barthes, 'L'Effet du réel', *Communications*, 11, 1968, pp. 84–9.

24. See Al-Azmeh, 'If ā al-Istishrāq'; and Laroui, 'The Arabs and Cultural Anthology'.

25. Said, *Orientalism*, p. 71.

26. See A. Al-Azmeh, *Ibn Khaldūn in Modern Scholarship*, London 1981.

27. P. Valéry, 'Orientem Versus', in P. Valéry, *History and Politics*, transl. D. Folliot and J. Mathews, New York 1962, p. 381.

28. R. Barthes, 'Historical Discourse', in *Structuralism. A Reader*, ed. M. Lane, London 1970, p. 155.

29. M. Foucault, *The Archaeology of Knowledge*, transl. A.M. Sheridan Smith, London 1972, pp. 3ff, 141ff.

30. For a statement of classical philology, see E. Auerbach, *Introduction aux études de philologie romane*, Frankfurt 1949, p. 27.

31. For instance, J. Trier, *Der Deutsche Wortschatz im Sinnbezirk des Verstandes*, Heidelberg 1931; and P. Ricoeur, *The Rule of Metaphor*, transl. R. Czerny et al., London 1978, p. 103.

32. G. Dumézil, *L'Héritage indo-européen à Rome*, Paris 1949, pp. 34–6, 42.

# 10

# Postmodern Obscurantism and 'The Muslim Question'

ihm doch schien, als ob irgendwo inmitten zwischen den strittigen Unleidlichkeit, zwischen rednerischem Humanismus und analphabetischer Barbarei das gelegen sein müsse, was man als das Menschliche oder Humane . . . ansprechen durfte

Thomas Mann

je voulais, moi, occuper les Français à la gloire . . . les mener à la réalité par les mensonges

Chateaubriand

I would not be in the least surprised if some readers felt a little vexed by the title of this chapter. What might it conceivably be that relates postmodernism to obscurantism, and specifically to religious obscurantism, which for many, I am sure, must automatically come to mind when the full title is recalled? Might I be referring to obscurantism in postmodern times, or might I be deliberately invoking paradox, or indeed charging postmodernism with being obscurantist in certain of its instances?

I hope that, in what follows, I might persuasively show that I am doing all these things at once, except for the invocation of paradox, and that my assertions will carry some conviction. But let me start by stating in a preliminary way that by 'The Muslim Question' – the name is derived from an analogy with the Eastern Question which bedevilled statesmen of the great powers in the nineteenth century, and has several elements in common with it – I mean that bundle of matters concerning political Islamism on which minds have been universally concentrated after September 11, matters that may be summed up by the existence of movements and sentiments that pursue relentlessly the quest for an unattainable absolute that is regarded by their holders as a pietist Shangri-La divinely commanded. In other words, 'The Muslim

Question' refers to regarding a particular inflection of political Islamism – one which might be compared to the Anabaptists and other radical groups among Protestants in relation to mainstream Lutheranism – as not only central but eminently characteristic of both the broader phenomenon of political Islamism as of Islam *tout court*.[1] This is of course a standard mechanism of stereotyping, in which an ethnological fragment is overdetermined and read as a total ethnological type, much like regarding all Germans as either skinheads or Bavarian rustics; every Hungarian male as a melancholy Atilla or Arpad; every Hungarian woman as Zsazsa Gabor. In order to understand this 'Muslim Question', I will argue that it be made to stand on its feet rather than on its head, as it does in the common imagination, and that for this to be done, the name Islam must be taken apart and its referent re-constituted.

Some may well ask how one should have the temerity to question the solidity, the fastness and indeed the self-evidence of this monolith, Islam – represented today in the form of 'The Muslim Question' – let alone talk of its re-constitution. How could one conceivably disassociate the constituent elements of an entity which has for years now been reiterating its ubiquity, its exotic fastness, the pride and prejudice of its singularity, its massive presence: a presence constantly displaying an elemental force, claiming an authentic atavism, enforcing this claim with the spectacular display of sheer energy and senseless violence, all the while asserting its inevitability as the post-colonial, albeit pre-existent destiny of an entire host of nations, of territories, almost of entire continents, all of them termed Islamic? How might one question this fastness of Muslim peoples, this primal condition of pre-colonial innocence, this inevitable post-colonial destiny?

Let me first of all dispose quickly of the easiest of relevant issues, that of the 'war of civilizations', the common cant expressed in scenarios proposed most famously by Professor Huntington and by his double, Mr. Bin Laden, the two locked in a fevered mutual demonization unmitigated by the primitive political language of President Bush and of much of his constituency: quite simply, civilizations do not go to war; what go to war are societies, armies and institutions. Civilizations are not societies, though some societal forms may in certain instances be symbolically sustained by appeal to fictitious genealogies, which might be called civilizations; civilizations are rather hyper-social systems. They are not entities but performative categories, now active, now not. And in any case, speaking of entities, though there are indeed many Muslims in the world and Muslim religious sub-cultures, there is no longer in existence something that might remotely be called an 'Islamic civilization' – like Hellenism and Romanity, this is a bookish memory no matter how much it might inflame the imagination and the aspirations of partisans and adversaries alike.

I think that we could go some considerable way together if we were to curb the fascination in which the imposing visibility of 'Islamic' matters and their associated political stakes ensnare the imagination. Fascination is none other than beholding an object as if it were a marvel, as the spectacle of marvels suspends the normal operations of the human understanding. It is precisely this suspension of the understanding for which Paul Valéry was the spokesman in a pithy and moody contribution of his *fin-de-siècle* spirit of disbelief and artifice, of modernism in the opium den, albeit in a celebratory rather than a melancholy or hostile spirit: he relished the intoxicating Orient of the mind, delighted in this reverie of the 'least exact knowledge', this 'disorder of names and imaginable things', to which neither logic nor chronology was available to keep the elements of this imaginary from falling together into 'their natural combinations'.[2]

I will be party here at least to those spoilers of imagination transfixed by fascination, and I shall not make my case in the customary manner of an oriental sage. I shall appeal to history, and will start by recalling recent memories: these will tell us that the imposing visibility and amplitude of mass political and social Islamism is a new phenomenon which dates back a mere thirty or so years, beguiling as it may equally be to its detractors, its adherents, and its admirers. Yet the all-too-human proclivity to short-sightedness colludes with political perspectives of the moment, to project a fragmentary image of the present instant into the essence of eternity, and to postulate Islam as the trans-historical protoplasm in the life of all Muslims.

A vast culture, and indeed a vast industry of misrecognition is in place, all the more firmly after September 11, by advocates of Islamism as by Western opinion (both expert and inexpert) purporting to read over and above the complex and multiple histories and present conditions of Muslim peoples a homogeneous and timeless Islam, construed as a culture beyond society and history, as a repository of 'meaning'. This, it is maintained, informs essentially all significant thoughts and actions of real or putative Muslims at all times and places, unless these be anomalous. Thus these super-Islamized beings are made to yield Islamic economies unlike all economies; Islamic political systems with bizarre and irrational principles; Islamic forms of knowledge whose anachronism lends them charm or revulsion, according to taste; Islamic sensibilities in pronounced distemper; Islamic dress and coiffure; Islamic law as clear, univocal, and barbarous as it is Levitically strict[3] – in short, a total and totalizing culture which overrides the inconvenient complexity of economy, society and history.

Islam thus becomes fully a 'culture' in the most inchoate, yet most comprehensive and determinative of senses: it is thus reviled, but also long patronized in many circles in an altogether preservationist spirit, in the spirit of an ethnological Greenpeace much beloved by multi-culturalists, as entirely *sui generis*, and in need of recognition in its own terms and indeed of empowerment and the recognition of agency. Islam becomes impermeable to all but its own unreason, utterly exotic, thoroughly exceptional, fully outside, frightfully different – or alternatively and correlatively, it becomes fully an affective subject with prodigious internal coherence. In this capacity, the religion of Islam becomes a term that at once fully describes and adequately explains peoples, histories, and countries that are made to fall under its taxonomic sway.

In the practice of everyday discourse, such implicit notions as I have just referred to take the form of the proposition that, in some way, Muslims have in the past three decades been *returning* to matters that constitute them essentially; that they are reverting to type, rejoining a transhistorical nature prior to their modern history; and that integralist or fundamentalist Islam is a strident and bloody yet adequate expression of this inherent nature. Impermeable to the normal equipment of the human and social sciences, the *phenomena islamica* – 'The Muslim Question' since September 11 – thus comes to acquire more than a radical exoticism, and I use the term 'exoticism' in a fairly rigorous sense deriving from its etymology. Their study comes consequently to require a particular effort of distantiation and estrangement, officiated under the signature of sympathetic understanding – the *Verstehen* of alien cultural meanings, a hermeneutical procedure whereby the observer is spiritually translocated and in a sense transubstantiated into the recesses of this Muslim other, or indeed by the two meeting at a conversational site (a 'dialogue of civilizations') in an ethereal in-between so beloved of postmodern anthropologists and perplexed politicians and strategists in non-governmental organizations, and increasingly by official instances of many states and international organizations, including the UN. This accounts to a large extent for the recent tendency towards a radical relativism regarding the study of matters Islamic, under the title of cultural specificity which, like other forms of exoticism, I take to be a grid of misrecognition.

I am truly galled by this extraordinary revival of nineteenth century procedures of ethnological classification in the guise of social-scientific innovation, even after all the fertile debates on orientalism in the past two decades, and after history and professional ethnography had seriously – albeit unevenly – contested its conceptual equipment. Let me remind you that, whereas ethnography carries no necessary classificatory agendas or loyalties, ethnology is above all else a theory of racial and cultural types, and is in practice never free from an implicit or explicit normative ranking. It is apt at this juncture to indicate an unfortunate by-product of the use now ordinarily made of Edward Said's critique of orientalism: while this use, under the rather grandiose title of post-colonial discourse, tapped a certain libertarian impulse, its excess of zeal – most characteristically in the United States – has led to a reverse orientalism grounded in an ahistorical notion of the West and its various others.

The late capitalist, postmodern emphasis on self-referentiality and self-representation; the drift towards conceiving difference as incommensurability; the cognitive nihilism associated with post-modernism; the dissolution of objects of ethnographic study into 'voices' – all this, to my mind, leads to the implicit, though in most cases inadvertent and unreflective, ejection of historical and social sciences tools in favour of an irrationalist and anti-historicist sympathetic sociology of singularity, and of an instinctivist theory of culture. This latter tends, with its vitalist metaphysics, to collapse knowledge into being by relating it not to cognition but to *re*cognition – particularly recognition of the collective self, such that what mediates being and representation is life as Will, and such that social knowledge, represented as culture, becomes but a moment of Being itself. All this is undertaken in the name of restituting marginalized voices and histories. Such a sociology of meaning and such valorization of the voice devolves in practice to substituting associative prolixity, self-referentiality, and political posturing for scientific practice. And such advocacy of singularity invariably results in the essentialization of identity through the irreducibility of difference, and consequently in confinement to unassailable clichés; the vogue in recent years of the theme of 'memory' is premised in this context on obscuring the fact that collective memory itself has a history.

Thus emerges a vicious circle, in which anti-orientalism leads directly, in its claims for authenticity and singularity, to the re-orientalization of orientals – much as this is denied, this denial remains rhetorical and discursively ineffectual. And thus arose a traffic in mirror-images between re-orientalizing orientals speaking for authenticity, and orientalizing neo-orientalists, now working with social rather than philological materials, speaking for difference. This takes on particularly deleterious forms in the social sciences when the claim is made that categories of ostensibly Western provenance, like religion and class, are intransitive, incommensurable, entirely collapsible into their origins, as if ontologically so fated and therefore applicable to Muslim peoples neither as descriptive nor as explanatory categories.

I will leave this matter for the time being, and I shall propose to you that this construal of Islam as a culture which in itself explains the affairs of Muslim collectivities and overdetermines their economies, societies, and non-religious cultures, is the fundamental element in the culture of misrecognition that I am addressing – the condition of possibility for valorizing the trope of return. It is a culture of misrecognition with two main protagonists who provide mirror-images of one another: the one is the Islamist revivalist and politician; the other, the western writer or actor who shares the essentialist culturalism of the former, and who elevates his obscurantist discourse on the present, the past, and the future of Muslims to the status of indisputable knowledge: I mean here the all-too-common procedure, taken as self-evident, by which the essentialist reading of past, present, and future, propounded by Islamist political or otherwise apologetic discourse, is taken for an adequate reading of the past, diagnosis of the present, and blueprint for the future of Muslims.

This reading is, of course, summed up in a number of basic propositions ceaselessly repeated and formulaically reiterated: that the history of Muslims is constituted essentially by religion, that the past two centuries of their histories are the story of usurpation and disnature by 'westernizing elites' unrepresentative of 'civil society', that the future can be no more than, with minor adjustments, a restoration of this prelapsarian condition of cultural innocence which modernity has not altered but only held, somewhat ravaged, in abeyance.

I can at this stage offer some elements of an answer to the question of what is meant by re-constituting Islam: if 'The Muslim Question' – if phenomena termed 'Islamic' or reclaiming a certain interpretation of Islamism – are to be understood, the first step to be taken is to critically decompose the notion of Islam, and to look instead at the conditions of its recent emergence: social forces, historical mutations and developments, political conflicts, intellectual and ideological realities, and devotional and theological styles and institutions, in addition to local ethnographic detail – it being clearly understood that ethnographic detail is to be regarded for what it is, and not simply as an instance or merely a concrete figure of a pervasive Islamism of life. Without this decomposition, the totalizing category of Islam will continue performing its phantasmatic role of calling things into being simply by naming them. Once this decomposition has been performed, once the reality of history has been disengaged from wanton fancy, we might be able properly to understand what is meant by Islam and by the appeal to this name: thus will Islam – and the carriers of this name – be subject to one manner of re-constitution, among many others that will emerge in the course of my talk.

I should like to comment immediately on the timing of the extraordinary visibility of what today appears as 'The Muslim Question'. The conjunctural element is crucially important, and the trope of return cannot be understood without it. As we know them (and I will confine my comments largely to the Arab World), political Muslim phenomena developed out of marginal pietistic and proto-fascist youth militias and sporting club movements in the 1920s and 1930s, some in brown shirts and others in grey, mainly active in Egypt but also in Syria broadly conceived. In the 1950s and 1960s, these were nurtured and provided with extraordinary financial largesse, mainly through petro-Islamic agencies and their obscurantist systems of public education (of which Mr. Bin Laden and his cavemen are sterling, unalloyed later products), by means of which they built local and international cultural, educational, and organizational structures animated by hostility to Arab nationalism in a conception of Muslim extraterritorialism that was commensurate with conditions in countries with sub-national political structures (Saudi Arabia, Pakistan). This took place, initially, in the context of an international climate dominated by the Truman Doctrine, but was later to have a wider reach. The containment of Communism had a spectacular career, and in the Arab World, developed into a policy applied to counter secular Arab nationalist, socialist and arguably pro-Soviet regimes. Those familiar with works on Arab politics published in the 1950s and 1960s will find very clear statements of the theory of Islam as a bulwark against Communism, and that the main cultural and ideological plank in pursuing the Cold War in the Arab World (and also in Indonesia and Malaysia) was the encouragement of social conservatism and of political Islamism. Later, in Afghanistan, this same policy was to have messier, bloodier, and more immediately dramatic effects, well illustrated by *Rambo III*, American champion of the leonine tribesmen of Afghanistan – a film some readers may have had to endure.

Yet these movements, particularly in the Arab World (though not in Southeast Asia) had little initial success, and only came conspicuously and strongly to the fore in the mid- and late 1970s, in a specific conjuncture marked by two elements. The first of these elements is the continuing trend towards a minimalization of state action in economy and society, under the impact of new international structural conditions. This is characterized by the correlative elements of deregulation and the ascendancy of finance, and complemented by a natural theology of the free market. In social terms, this entailed the break-down of the post-Second-World-War Keynesian consensus, with its emphasis on social and cultural (no less than on economic) progress. This breakdown led, in the West, to structural unemployment and attendant results, like the rise in influence of extreme right-wing ideologies, and the counter-racism of various brown European and North American groups – some of which define themselves as Muslim. Let me add that attendant upon these trends was the growing incidence of cult phenomena with bizarre cosmic beliefs. Correlatively, unremitting structural disorientation and various forms of deracination in some Muslim communities – such as the so-called Arab Afghans – under present conditions of globalization took to a virulent xenophobia as an antidote to anomie and to national frustration, and produced nihilistic political phenomena which, with the sustenance of certain Islamist political forces, conjure up and pursue an apocalyptic 'war of civilizations' waged against a spectral enemy. And please note that, though I shall be addressing a general mood permeating Islamist movements, I will also be addressing one of their specific sub-cultures – represented by Bin Laden – that arises from very specific circumstances: networks that determinedly wage a 'war of civilizations' are marked by a metapolitical rather than a political calculation, in which the criteria of efficacy is extra-mundane, even when they are not declared to be eschatological.

In the Arab World, as elsewhere in the South, these new conditions, under titles like 'structural adjustment', have been exacting a very heavy social price, correlative with the breakdown of both the will and the capacity to carry out policies of development. States were increasingly reduced to functions of pure administration and policing the effects of global deregulation. Correlating to economic deregulation were also social and cultural deregulation, ideologized by communalist, anti-state paternalism on the part of western non-governmental organizations and their local analogues, which became not only distributors of aid, but also loci for the production of culturalist knowledge and social practice in the name of Difference – a sort of gentrification of backwardness. Mass social and economic marginalization in the South produced results analogous to those in the North. Among these is the strong appeal of the ultra-conservative hyper-nationalist populism, with a chiliastic flavour, which we call radical Islamism, or which in India is associated with movements like the RSS (Rashtriya Swayamsevak Sangh). Both political Islam and the RSS – and indeed also the Revisionist Zionism so undeniably central in Israel today – followed the rhythm of modern world history: first in their simultaneous emergence with Fascism in the 1920s and 1930s under al-Banna, Golwalkar and Jabotinsky, and then in their simultaneous revival with the retreat of modernism, with the spurning and denigration of the Enlightenment, and the correlative revival in the West of conservative ideologies, religious and secular. This revival was officiated under a benign signature as well as a malignant one – the one xenophobic and the other xenophilic – both premised on a culturalist differentialism which has recently become hegemonic, and both of which, in two different spirits, speak of 'cultural specificity' that, towards the end of the twentieth century, came to perform the same conceptual functions as race had earlier.[4] Racial, national and religious 'profiling' as practiced since September 11 – most hysterical in the US where it is accentuated by the stridency of Republicanist Protestantism – is unthinkable without the differentialism to which I refer.

So much for the singular rhythm of political Islam. But before I widen my purview, let me add this: the Islam of militant and conspicuous Islamism repudiates the lived Islam of its milieu in its attempt to 'return' to the atopian Islam presumed to have been out there before the Fall and imagined to be still seething below the surfaces of falsehood and inauthenticity. This accounts for the extraordinary violence it has always needed to deploy in the quest for authenticity. It constructs an imagined Muslim past using symbolic materials derived from Muslim canonical and quasi-canonical texts, but cast in ideological moulds common throughout the history of international conservative populism, as well as anti-Enlightenment motifs associated with a ferocious subalternism, making it somehow adorably postmodern. These moulds and motifs use vitalist and fiercely social-Darwinist figures of history and of society, a romantic notion of politics as restorative Will and direct action, an organistic conception of culture and of law – all of them reminiscent not of Muhammad and the Koran, but rather of Herder, Savigny and Spengler; of de Bonald, Gobineau and Le Bon; and perhaps most pertinently in present circumstances, of Nechaev, Osinsky and Morozov. Two of the most influential works of revolutionary Islamism in Arabic and Persian (by Sayyid Qutb and `Ali Shariati) both specifically and most enthusiastically esteem the work of Alexis Carrel: a Frenchman who, as some may know, started his highly distinguished medical career in New York, where he developed highly elaborate social-eugenic theories (for which he was crowned with the Nobel Prize), and then went on to become the cultural and scientific oracle of the Maréchal Pétain at Vichy. His works are now standard reading material in youth summer camps run by the Front National in France. Carrel's emphasis on the creative salvational minority and his strictures against cultural and racial degeneration were, of course, not as systematic in spirit, broad in reach, and sophisticated in approach and conceptual wealth as those of German thinkers such as Nordau, Klages, Nietzsche, and Jünger.[5] Let me say parenthetically that it is too early to predict how postmoderns, with their reclamations of obscurantism and their predilection for the backward in the name of post-coloniality, will react to September 11, and whether they will feel the waves of disorientation, dislocation, and terminal menace that have started seriously to beset Islamist political movements of all shades. What is certain is that I have not yet seen the destruction of the World Trade Center described quite simply as a performative speech-act,[6] nor anything comparable to Baudrillard's playful characterization of the Second Gulf War as an irreal, virtual happening[7] – although, I must say, feminist descriptions of the events as an act of supreme phallicism have indeed been voiced.

Be that as it may, the point is that this notion of degeneration and decadence, which is sometimes but not always hankering after a pre-capitalist arcadia, has generic affinities of an ideological and conceptual nature with the Islamist critique of contemporary society: both are the products of times of considerable commotion and disorientation, and both are anchored in a vitalist conception of society. But whereas the Germans (and Americans like Albert Freeman and Henry Ford) blamed the proletariat and the massification of society and the polity for this degeneration, Muslim thinkers like Mawdudi and Qutb blamed what they termed *jahiliyya* – un-Islamicity pure and simple – or 'Occidentosis' or 'Westtoxification', according to the English translators of the Iranian priest of authenticity, Jalal Al-i Ahmad. I might add that all the European figures I mentioned are of prime importance for political life and thought in modern European history. The fact that they are not so very well-known today, or that they have until recently been relegated to minor positions in textbooks of political and social theory, can only be read as a rather hopeful collective amnesia organized by liberal regimes following the Second World War. The postmodernist adulation of difference is not often sufficiently aware of its own ideological and conceptual provenance.

And to round out the picture, I must also add that there is an affinity between the parties I mentioned – Islamists and representatives of European political irrationalism – that is far more than subliminally elective: a respect for the mystique of death and sacrifice as the morbid edges of life and antidotes to a vision of decay, and the glorification of blood, fire and steel as direct forms of political action beyond the world of daily life. One might mention here, by way of example, Ernst Jünger's memoir of the First World War and the notion of *jihad* according to radical Muslims.[8] It is just as pertinent to cite the Russian Narodnovoltsy and certain fringes of European anarchism, particularly in Russia and Spain: Morozov's immortalization of the revolutionary; Nechaev's Cathechism; more generally, the metaphysical rather than immediately functional status given to the insurrectionary act of terror; the cult of self-sacrifice that includes death, regardless by whose hand it might come; and the 'absolute present' (Karl Mannheim's term[9]) through which insurrection is conceptualized, rendering the present moment an instance in an indistinct eternity.[10] I am not suggesting that Mr. Bin Laden might have heard of Mikhailovsky or Morozov, or that he might have read Carl Schmitt, but rather that all of these and many others were possessed by an apocalyptic language of ultimate war and of death as the ultimate affirmation of life, and that all of them belong to a modern world in which the distinctiveness of political violence, unlike the Middle Ages, correlates to the emergence of the notion of 'the people' who might, through acts of exemplary violence, be made to rise up[11] to precipitate a predetermined outcome. They all belong equally to a modern world in which it is possible, in vitalist terms, to think of war as the ultimate manifestation of collective energy, acting as an antidote to decadence and degeneration; to believe that the world will rise again from the ashes of the *Götzerdämmerung* they intend to precipitate,[12] with an *amor fati* and a spirit of Dionysian nihilism that characterizes the Absolute Subject. In this picture, life and death are seen to be interchangeable, with the latter being proof of the former and its supreme testament. It is the nihilism of a transcendental Narcissus which, in its defiant reversal of degenerate values, generates the heady sense of freedom I believe energized the perpetrators of 'September 11' – who were also clearly possessed of a keen sense for the postmodern mediatic aesthetic of the absolute event in real time. In a sense, these matters might be analyzed as instances of what Hegel termed Absolute Freedom and Terror, where freedom 'ascends the throne of the world', albeit one without real antitheses. They are like throwbacks to a previous moment of consciousness, in which the normal dialectical movement of a self-referential subject in a struggle of master and slave is condemned to remain unconsummated, in which individuality is condemned to remain an instance of ahistorical, pure, perpetual and singular negativity[13] outside historical time, and without the labour of the negative.

I think it is crucial that one resist the habit of looking at these acts as entirely inspired by the promise of a tumescent Paradise, for what we have is a cult of martyrdom and of war in which self-sacrifice is a rite of passage and an act of intense socialization – and radical Islamic political movements do subject their members to intense resocialization.[14] Goebbels, we may recall, declared that war was the most elementary form of love for life,[15] an attitude which to my mind provides the fundamental affective element of Carl Schmitt's theory of the state. That Bin Laden warned what he termed Jews and Crusaders that he and his people loved death more than their enemies loved life, belongs to the same trope of militaristic nihilism, and this is a matter that may be approached, and sense made out of apparent senselessness, in terms of anthropological theories of sacrifice and of the feast.[16]

Such analogies as I am drawing may appear improbable and indeed inflated. But they are very suggestive, and the analogy I am making between religious zealotry and romantic anarchism and nihilism is – imperfect as its definition might be – premised on their shared repertoire of vitalist notions, which were not available before the era of modernity, or, better stated, their emergence from the same conditions of possibility, which allows for convergence and comparability. Thus I would also add that radical Islamists use much the same political language and make similar use of archaic political iconography as do vitalist romantics everywhere, for all atavism harbours a primitivist aesthetic which appeals to a concrete image of a prelapsarian, arcadian nature to be restored. This was evident in the Balkans recently, among other places. The penultimate televisual appearance of Mr. Bin Ladin took place before a cave, recalling the Cave of Hira`, where Muhammad first received his divine inspiration. This is all reminiscent of certain colourful fringe phenomena in the Vienna of Hitler's youth, with the revaluation of racial purity and of ancient Germanic myths by Guido von List, who adopted the swastika as the emblem for his Aryan fraternities, and particularly of Georg Schönerer's folkishness.[17] Thus Bin Laden and his associates adopted a medievalizing coiffure, manners of dress, holy relics, and private forms of behaviour and affected turns of phrase not very much out of keeping with the lurid and exhibitionistic culture of bad taste evident in analogous cult groups, in a sort of dandyism-in-reverse. They acted according to a notion of authenticity analogous to the Hindutva of the communalist Right in India, and they combined the political mysticism of the secular Zionist Right with a mild form of the doctrine of divine election propounded by Jewish fundamentalists

It is important to note that the rhetoric of authenticity and the trope of return, according to which matters I mentioned have been cast by religio-political revivalists, are not the unmediated voice of the natural history of a culture or of a race, but rather a *recherché* self-representation of some particular social force presuming normative hegemony. It is precisely such a process that people commonly call an identity – a word much overused and abused in current public debate. Authenticity, in this perspective, is highly inauthentic and indeed a counterfeit identity, for identity is a performative category, not one of indication; it instead presents, as described by Adorno in another (aesthetic) context, a *für andere* masquerading as an *an-sich*. Such is the case of the wholesale invention of vestimentary and intellectual traditions by Islamist movements, and the simultaneous assertion that these correspond to social practice; the deification of the Buddha in the atheistic religion of Buddhism; and similarly, the elevation of the Ram to divine status, on account of its primacy, by Hindu communalists, in what has been termed the 'Semitization of Hinduism'.

In all these and other cases, we witness a traditionalization as distinct from traditionalism; we witness the folklorization of classicism, in which elements from the remote past are presumed to constitute the lived present, which often results in varying degrees of Disney-fied psychodramatic self-parody – it might be appropriate here to mention the great yet now seldom-read anthropologist, Edward Tyler, who asserted that 'the serious business of ancient society may be seen to sink into the sport of later generations, and its serious belief to linger on in folk tales'.[18] In this way, tangible tokens or icons of authenticity are produced – such as a particular manner of dress or of punishment – along with virtual collective memories exhumed from old books and made into elements of a populist rhetoric, by asserting them to be actual memories. Through these virtual memories, an historical romance is construed and then offered as an utopian social programme meant to construct a finalist and definitive Shangri-La. Here, everyone and everything might be authentic, whether it be called an Islamic state, a *tausendjäriger* Reich, life in the Ramrajya according to the Sanskritik *dharma*, or indeed the arrival of the Messianic age (once the impeccable red heifer has been genetically engineered by Jewish Ayatollahs in the occupied territories). Therefore, under such conditions, life most frequently devolves to performance: the performance of a socially and politically disembodied psychodrama, which might indeed gather social momentum and come to constitute a facet of social reality. But this constructed facet is a measure of the distance between the past itself and its iconographic monumentalization or bloody memorialization. I might add by way of clarification that, though this primitivism has become standard fare in Islamist movements, the radical primitivism that came to the fore in the figure of Bin Laden goes even further. It relentlessly abstracts itself from both its conditions of genesis and its present state, and lodges itself in perpetual psychodramatic performance – enforced by tropes of extraterritoriality and exile made possible through the social and physical topographies of provincial Saudi Arabia and Yemen (from whence many members of al-Qaeda came) and Afghanistan (to which they moved); the potential for self-alienation in the United States, and under conditions of multiculturalist placelessness resulting from ethnic cantonment in various European countries (not unlike the Hasidic cantonment at Borough Park, Brooklyn, for instance, or in Finsbury Park in London, where the Hasidim coexist with an equally insular Muslim community, with whom they cooperate over matters concerning public morals and multicultural educational demands). It is from such conditions that al-Qaeda and the Jewish Defense League recruit their membership.

Not so, of course, are the suicide bombers active in Israel and the occupied territories in past months. There we witness acts carried out within a very specific political situation and with discernible and specific antagonists, perpetrated in a situation of near-absolute national disempowerment where the embryonic structures of Palestinian self-determination were being systematically destroyed. This occurred through unspeakable acts that are radically counter to all norms aside from primitive tribalism: the destruction of civil service records, cultural institutions, security forces, water and power resources, and the physical liquidation of all political cadres – the latter according to a savage political doctrine that echoes some that have been taken up above and has been eloquently expressed by Ariel Sharon: it was an 'iron law' of history 'that he who won't kill will be destroyed by others', and that it was 'better a live Judeo-Nazi than a dead saint'.[19]

In the same instance, Sharon stated: 'We shall start another war, kill and destroy more and more, until they have had enough. And do you know why it is worth it? Because it seems that this war has made us more unpopular among the so-called civilized nations'. Quite apart from the mass psychopathological condition underlying the need to be feared rather than admired, this unfinished 'dirty work of Zionism'[20] takes on an aspect of sub-political, biological, vitalist predation (comparable to the notion of *Lebensraum*). The unspeakably savage (the words are chosen deliberately to convey the sub-political and sub-civil) character of this political genocide provoked a response that was equally blind to language and reason. Thus the young woman who exploded herself in Jerusalem on 12 April 2002 declared on video that she was intending to 'state with her body' what the Arabs had not said with words: where the means of resistance and national self-determination had been depoliticized and transformed into Darwinist predation, a vitalist counterpoint appears eminently purposive.

Here martyrdom becomes not an apocalyptic cult, as with al-Qaeda, but a nationalist act of resistance that is rather akin in its mechanisms and conceptions to Sorel's myth of the general strike. In past months (these lines are being written towards the end of April 2002), the religious character of the discourse surrounding suicide bombers has gradually receded in favour of more decidedly and sometimes unmitigatedly nationalist language, not only on the part of suicide bombers belonging to the secular al-Aqsa Brigades (the al-Aqsa mosque being a national symbol), but also by bombers belonging to Hamas. This is not too dissimilar to the suicide bombers of the Communist Party and the Syrian Nationalist Party in South Lebanon, whose actions had more consequential effects.

Having made a very specific and important distinction, I will return to the main argument of this chapter and state my conclusion that, over and above iconography, there is precious little that is generically distinctive about Muslim integralism and fundamentalism, beyond the specific way that the tissue of its different times and places is created by its various conjunctural and structural elements. The 'return' to Islam is in fact a return to a newly created place. Its different components are generated from romantic and vitalist ideological elements present in a repertoire of political ideas that are universally available, no matter how much rhetoriticians of identity and of authenticity might deny this; they are constructed from a social material which requires for its understanding a sociology of structural marginality; a sociology of elite competition; a social psychology of middle and upper class radical youths in situations of normative schizophrenia and structural closure (not an ethnology of pre-colonial Arcadia); and, last but not least, a sociology of subcultures and cults. The understanding of Islamic political phenomena requires the normal tools of the social and human sciences, not their denial.[21] Let us not forget in this context an extremely important and novel feature that has supervened onto the international legal order since the collapse of the Socialist Bloc, namely the fact that the indeterminate fluidity evident in regimes of extra-legality and extra-territoriality is, under a normative signature, overdetermined by hegemonic military capacity deploying the 'power of exception' as a novel legal norm.[22] It renders formerly prevalent modes of legality (including notions of national sovereignty) virtually irrelevant – the best examples of this being the embargo against Iraq and Israeli policies in the Occupied Territories. That lawlessness in a situation of normative legal fluidity is seen to be legitimate is unsurprising: this is the lawlessness in international relations as in economies structurally beset by illegal transactions. It requires precise analysis and cannot be understood through moralist condemnation alone.

Nor is Muslim revivalism today itself generically specific. The construal of the utopia desired as a re-enactment of supposed origins or beginnings, and the trope of return to authentic beginnings, is a constant feature of all religious discourse and of nationalist and indeed much conservative discourse. In the Christian religious traditions it is termed typology, where present and putative origins are organized as type and reenactment, as beginning and manifestation, as original and figure, and where Reformation announces itself as no more than fidelity to origins. Thus, many Christian kings were described as the New David and as *typus christi*; Byzantine emperors were likewise regarded as instances of *Christomimesis* and their capital the New Jerusalem. All this forms a standard component of a broad sweep of *Heilsgeschichte* (salvation history) which is foreign to no monotheistic religion. That this also occurs in Islam is entirely unremarkable, and is a matter to be investigated in the context, not of an unreconstructed ethnology of the *homo islamicus*, but of the history of religions, which has much to say about beginnings as types and mythological charters, of stereotypical reproduction, of mythopraxis (in Sahlins' expression), and of the relation of these to ritual.

Before I go any further, I shall briefly try to dispel any surprise toward the notion of Islamism as an offspring of modernity rather than of tradition. Let me remind you that the Arab world, like all parts of the globe, was variously and unevenly incorporated from the mid-19th century, into an international order of ideology and culture, in which discursive forms and ideas circulated. Though these were of Western European origin, they became universal and came to be produced and reproduced locally, being inracinated in the cultural, legal, and educational apparatus of Bonapartist states (states that actively sought hegemony in the cultural and legal spheres). These states spread throughout the world from the early nineteenth century onward: by Napoleon himself, in Spain, Italy, and Poland; by direct Napoleonic example, as in the states created by Simon Bolívar and his example in Latin America; and in the Ottoman Reformed state, which is particularly relevant to the Arab World. This was a state of extraordinary innovativeness, incorporating into its reforms some of the most advanced ideas of the age, such as non-sectarian education, which in their countries of origin were thought to be dangerously avant-garde. The reformed Ottoman state of the mid-nineteenth century was almost a veritable laboratory for Comtean ideas and of positivist social engineering – Auguste Comte was quite aware of this, and his delight was evident in the open letter to Reshid Pasha that he printed at the beginning of the first volume of his *Système de politique positive*. We could actually say that the history of the Arab world in the past century and a half is an accelerated history of acculturation, in which major changes occurred very rapidly, much like the cultural history of England in the seventeenth century, including the absorption of irrationalist ideological motifs and concepts.

Of the new cultural forms were the journalistic article, the pamphlet and evolving forms of the novel, all of which utilized a new form of Arabic that was generated in the mid-nineteenth century and incorporated substantial lexical, some syntactic and extensive stylistic developments. Of the ideas, one might cite ideas of the nation, of the economy (which was born as a determinate conceptual field only in the eighteenth century), of society itself (which in the early nineteenth century superseded the notion of estates), of the body-social as the assembly of individuals that we mostly inherited from English philosophy, and the related idea of an abstract assembly of rights that we find in natural right theories. It goes without saying that the ideas of progress, of popular will, of romantic notions of the organic continuity of history and the homogeneity of society, among others, are of the same order.

None of these has precedents in Muslim traditions; all belong to the universal regime of modernity, which in one of its aspects constituted an exclusive repertoire of the conceptual apparatus by which peoples world-wide thought and wrote on public affairs. These imperative global forms of cultural expression are analogous to what were called 'modules' in an influential book on nationalism. I do not deny the pervasive existence of archaism in the political and social aspirations of Islamists and other conservative populists elsewhere. What constitutes the specificity of Islamist groups is their appeal to a particular historical experience and its symbols, construed as a foundational myth, and what I wish to insist upon is that this is not some explosion of a long-repressed ethnological force but a very *recherché* primitivism deliberately crafted from the universal modularity of modern ideologies. This discourse of inwardness, of authenticity and of particularity expresses a political sentimentalism, formulated in a language and by means of concepts that are entirely heteronomous: sentiments of what is called identity are not immediately translatable into politics, but need to be sensualized in emblematic or iconographic form which then acts as a node of ideological interpellation, then parsed in the form ideological propositions. When such sentiments do explode immediately, they take the form of direct action: as melancholic musings normally associated with the romantic sensibility, but also, when wrath in unbridled, sentiment pours forth as inarticulate terror.

The broader current in which religious sentimentalism was thus ideologically articulated was not the work of theologians, but of a group that emerged from the new public educational system, which marginalized the public role of the Muslim priestly establishment (and I am not here speaking of the peculiar conditions of Saudi Arabia[23]), and which was analogous in its purpose and some of its effect to the role played by the *lycée* system in France or the *Gymnasium* system in Germany. A new class of intellectuals arose, analogous (according to a poor man's analogy) to that which some German scholars refer to – with some dread in describing their own history – as the *Bildungsbürgertum*. It is this same class of the intelligentsia that sustained secularist and otherwise secular ideologies, in concert with and by participation in the state. But it is the subaltern components of this intelligentsia that produced Islamism: reformist Islamism at the end of the nineteenth century, and political revivalism at the end of the twentieth. In both cases, effective secularization led to the possibility of defining religion separately from the social realities within which it had previously been embedded, and of giving it the internal homogeneity, coherence and consistency of a total social and political programme. [24]

None of the matters I have highlighted are particularly mysterious or inaccessible to the understanding. The socio-economic conditions, the birth of Islamism from the interstices of universal modernity, the virtual reality of particularity which uses universal modules to construct itself, the multiple causalities that work to produce – amongst some Muslims as well as others – projects of involution and interiorization: all these, and many other collateral matters, are well-documented, and in some instances well-studied in published work, and they alone, unlike the postmodern mood, can help us clarify 'The Muslim Question' – quite apart from Valéry's relish in the 'disorder of names'. What is particularly striking is that there is so much resistance to perceiving the realities of the situation, and so much insistence upon misrecognition.

I do not intend to review from the start the debates concerning orientalism, nor do I wish to dwell now on the fetid alleyways of the collective European memories of historical antagonisms – clearly but not always articulately evident in Bosnia, Iraq, and Palestine in the last few years. I do not wish to mention more than in passing and by way of reminder, the systematic and fevered demonization, under the title of terrorism, of various Muslim peoples, or the never-ending story of immediate political interests and the interests of arms manufacturers.[25]

What I intend to do is to return to the present point in time, and to try and understand why it is that misrecognition is so passionately willed; to probe the conditions for the exceptionalism attributed to Muslim peoples, which places them outside the remit of the historical and sociological understanding and relegates them to ethnological folklore; and to consider why it is that I – like many others – have to waste so much of your time on matters that ought to be taken for granted.

To a considerable extent, this has to do with the social and political organization, in western countries, of knowledge concerning Islam, of the production and circulation of this knowledge, of its criteria of public validation, and of the position that rigorous research (as distinct from what is publicly claimed as expertise) occupies in this organization – quite apart from the spectacular newsworthiness of similar reclamations emanating from Islamist political movements in the quest for normative hegemony in their lands of origin. It is manifestly the case that expert knowledge – institutionally known as orientalism and as area studies – on these matters is marginal; it has no social authority to arbitrate knowledge on Islam; members of the public and persons in positions of authority seem free to make all manner of whimsical or irresponsible statements and assumptions concerning Islamic matters, without serious fear of disgrace or even of definitive correction. There is hardly a body of exact knowledge concerning Islam which is publicly authoritative and self-perpetuating, and this also applies, *grosso modo*, to the organization of university faculties, in which studies of Islam occupy a marginal and rather slight position. Though some scholars of Islam regard this as a rather seraphic blessing, this explains to a large extent not only the manifest conceptual retardation of this field and its vulnerability to common cant, but also the virtual absence of Islamic materials in the context of other disciplines, for instance, including the history of religions.

This marginality is evident in many other ways: the substantial though scattered advances in the study of Muslim societies in the past two decades have not come into general circulation; the excellent contemporary studies published in Arabic remain unread, for lack of linguistic competence of western experts no less than from their contempt for Arabic scholarship; and above all the public primacy that is generally given to forms of expression and discourse with higher ideological density, authority and of wider reach than orientalist or area expertise. This is not new, of course: perhaps most glaringly but by no means uncharacteristically, we find that the public authority on Islamic matters in nineteenth century Germany, for instance, was none other than Otto von Ranke. Some may recall that Ranke wrote what was then regarded as the definitive history of the Ottoman and Spanish empires in the sixteenth and seventeenth centuries, in which he paid scant attention to the results of orientalist scholarship or to Ottoman sources, and preferred to rely instead on Venetian archives.

At present, such authority is assumed most specifically by mediatic forms of representation and their pre-literate techniques of semiosis, to whose conditions and categories university experts frequently succumb, not necessarily because of dishonesty, but rather because of conceptual vulnerability and disorientation, rendered all the more acute by the constraints of the medium. This general situation applies also to scholarship in general public circulation and with a public credibility far exceeding that of more careful research.

I would cite as an example the work of Ernest Gellner, which theorizes the demotic notions of Islam in common currency and shares with this demotic notion one of its constitutive features, that of overinterpreting an ethnographic fragment (or, more traditionally, textual fragment) as a total ethnological type. Gellner studied a village in the Moroccan Atlas in the 1950s, then came to conclude that the bird's-eye view from these panoptical heights revealed an apparition or indeed an integral epiphany of Islam as history, society, culture – a view which at once exemplifies it and sums it up. The general and the particular correspond to one another absolutely in this totalizing vision, just as concrete and abstract classifiers are mutually convertible in myth.[26] Thus Islam is fully representative of Muslims and can indeed be substituted for them: you will recall my earlier mention that naming is conjuring, and this is a very good case in point.

Briefly stated, present discourse on Islamic matters is characterized, broadly and in its publicly-broadcast form, by what we might call a neo-Renanism (the reference being, of course, to Ernest Renan's famous theories about the congenital incapacity of the Semitic mind to produce science and philosophy, but to excel nevertheless in the realm of poetry), or a discourse based on taxonomic antitheses. We have a politilogical neo-Renanism which speaks, among other things, of the essential inappropriateness of democracy for countries characterized as Muslim, because democracy goes against the grain; as a corollary, we have the proposition, propounded in many circles, that democracy for such countries is best achieved through rule by groups which best correspond to the society's authentic nature, which in this case is Islam. Correlatively, we also have a neo-Renanist pseudo-sociology, which takes the populist declamations of authenticity for accurate descriptions of social reality and which denies the realities of secularism in Arab life on grounds of congenital incapacity, served up under the title of 'revivalism' and the trope of return. This discourse has as its Leitmotif a culturalist differentialism, that is to say, a culturalist ethnology which supposes 'cultural meaning', including the trope of return, to determine at once action as well as its interpretation. This is a matter to which I have given considerable thought and I have concluded not only that culturalism uses the same figures and tropes that had previously been employed in racialist discourses, but that like racialism it operates in a rather simple manner, which consists of selecting visible tokens of ethnographic distinctiveness – which could be the colour of the skin, a certain manner of dress, or certain propositions concerning the organization of gender relations – then proceeding to give these the status of iconic markers or of stigmata of otherness – or correlatively of inwardness, as nodes of ideological interpellation (as I indicated earlier).

These are finally served up as totalizing criteria of ethnological classification broadly conceived, constituting Muslims by analogy with ethnotypes or what older American anthropology referred to as 'patterns of culture' – though I must say that Ruth Benedict was far more conscious of her appropriate intellectual genealogy than present-day proponents of the postmodern version of this conception, citing few anthropologists but appealing rather to German vitalist thinkers like Dilthey and Spengler. This is not unlike regarding Lederhosen and skinheads as the iconic markers of Germanity, for instance, or of cowboys and mobsters as markers of the North American identity, corresponding to its inner nature and constituting its cultural genetic capital, and proceeding to construct an ethnic type based on the associations of these images.

I think it will be clear to all of you that this procedure partakes of all the characteristics of polemical rather than of scientific discourse, notwithstanding copious footnotes. It would be highly instructive to compare narrative features of this commonplace discourse on Islam with the tropes of polemical discourse generally, including anti-Masonic, anti-Arab, anti-Communist, anti-Semitic and other writing and other forms of propaganda designed in antagonism. One might well compare Muslim history conceived in this fashion with left-wing histories of the Society of Jesus written in nineteenth century France, in terms of structure, imagery, and argumentation, in which the record of Jesuit history was read as a symptomology of the Jesuit spirit, and in which links between events had mythical rather than causal significance.[27] All polemical discourse is, like religious discourse, typological: a history of beginnings and re-enactments, in which change is illusory and where every particular is a mere illustration of the general, and in which the primacy of mythical signification is undisputed.

Yet all this has in the recent past been expressed in terms of a disarming condition of innocence, often described as a postmodern concern for diversity, individuality, the empowerment of the marginal and a whole host of other propositions, on which there is a concurrence between xenophobes, liberals, and Third World communalists and integralists, all of whom speak the rhetoric of diversity, of difference, of particularity, a rhetoric which conflates the banal realities of diversity and of particularity with the *topoi* of culturalist and ethnographic classification. All in all, the kitsch and the spectacular are taken for the authentic and invariant, and this procedure is often freely encouraged not only by spokesmen for authenticity, but by various other native informants, some of them professional, who play to an eager gallery, although this is not often noticed by anthropologists, journalists or other experts.[28]

This postmodernist delight in the pre-modernity of others is all the rage; what it subtends really is a vigorous and triumphalist postmodernism, premised on post-Communism, and bereft of the normative, aesthetic and cognitive attributes of modernism. It is hence captive to the relativistic drift inherent in the use, by history and sociology, of the metaphor of the organism to describe identities as absolute subjects. This, I have repeatedly reminded you, is a standard component of European irrationalism and political romanticism.

It is therefore particularly disturbing to me that Gellner,[29] the anti-relativist par excellence, should state: 'in Islam, it is all different'[30] – which once again reminds me of an anti-Jesuit polemic of 1880, by a forgotten novelist, Jules Durantin, who wrote: 'Everything progresses, except the Company of Jesus'.[31] Gellner liberates himself from the burden of proof – but equally, and most saliently, he liberates himself from the discipline of his trade: sociologist, anthropologist, and theorist of history. He proceeds to state and re-state an entire interpretation of Muslim histories and of present-day Islam, which he reduces to an invariant model that supposedly emanates from his rustic observatory in the Atlas Mountains (whose schematism is breathtakingly peremptory), along with empirical objections, which he simply ignores. Briefly stated, this notorious 'pendulum-swing' theory of Islam postulates two forms of religiosity, the enthusiastic-rural and the puritanical-urban, in a primordial conflict and cyclical alternance which fundamentally constitutes Muslim history – so fundamentally, indeed, that the present condition of the Muslims can be conceived in no other terms, and which can have no outcome other than the triumph of urban puritanism. Correlative with this religious characterization of a history reduced to religious culture is the proposition that no modernism is inconceivable for Muslims in terms other than those of the Muslim puritanical doctrine and its corollaries.

Gellner's Moroccan village is an ethnological fragment he construed in terms of an ethnological theory, which he reads into the work of David Hume and Ibn Khaldun (whom Gellner needed to read in the poor standard English translation), who in turn based his own theories on a particular reading of the history of North African Muslim dynasties – Ibn Khaldun is less a guide to the interpretation of North African history than a Maghribi phenomenon interpretable historically. Yet this is a theoretical genealogy which appears largely fictitious when one looks at the actual origins of this theory in French colonialist historiography of North Africa, which had a substantial input from the German deterministic social geography of Ratzel, and which is best exemplified in the work of Emile-Félix Gautier and Robert Montagne[32] – the latter is much praised by Gellner overall. And if it were assumed – and this would be a very decidedly dubious assumption – that this model were applicable to certain moments of North African history, the fact is that it is still utterly foreign to, say, Ottoman history, and he seems simply and implicitly to regard the 500 years of Ottoman statehood over central Muslim lands to have been anomalous and uncharacteristic. Gellner never says this explicitly, but it arises from the logic of excision and abridgment he deploys in the various versions and redactions of his theory.

What this procedure displays, in fact, is a certain will to conceptual arbitrariness – arbitrariness with regard to facts of history and society, one which construes central facts as anomalous, and partial or local phenomena as normative; a conceptual arbitrariness which allows for a lack of discipline, flourishing under the title of exceptionalism. There is a definite objective correlation between this arbitrariness and its historical conditions of possibility in the world outside the university, for this intellectual unaccountability is matched only by the presumption of unaccountability built into an article published by Gellner in *The New Republic* which opens with the following statement: 'Muslims are a nuisance. As a matter of fact, they always were a nuisance'.[33] I shudder to think what would have happened to the author and to the *New Republic* had he said the same about Afro-Americans or Jews, for instance. But what is particularly salient in this statement is that it is simply a preface to reducing to a unity (in Islamic exceptionalism) of Moroccan corsairs off the coast of Newfoundland in the eighteenth century, Khomeini, and the Organization of Petroleum Exporting Countries. Clearly, the will to conceptual arbitrariness is correlative with the will to a certain form of combat which is bound by no rules. Societies, countries, territories, histories – all are reduced to a specific aspect that makes them manageable for purposes of confrontation or containment. The connection with, and anticipation of, the theses of Samuel Huntington is manifest; both repeat commonplace prejudices with equal banality.

What this will to violence, no longer symbolic since September 11 (this will to reduce complexity to simplicity, will wantonly to ignore reality, will to conceptual indiscipline, will to contradict both history and ethnography[34]) leads to in scholarship is precisely what I started with: the over-Islamization of Muslims, their endowment with a super-human capacity for perpetual piety, the reduction of their history and their present life to a play and recovery of religious motifs, and hence a denial of their actual history and present. It would be wrong to suppose that Gellner's statements and theories always amount to no more than vulgar Islamophobia or to some immediately political position. Yet they are, like Gellner's last theories about the impossibility of secularization for Muslim lands – the very secularization that is so evident in the fundamental thrust of modern Arab history[35] – based on an imperious will to denial, during the time of global post-Fordism when outsiders are barbarized in terms of a discourse of cultural incapacity: incapacity for economic, social, political, and cognitive development, cultural incapacity predisposing peoples to violence, overpopulation, factionalism, and even to famine.[36]

## Notes

1. For a clear statement of the radical position, see William E. Shepard, *Sayyid Qutb and Islamic Activism*, Leiden 1996; Gilles Kepel, *The Prophet and the Pharaoh*, transl. Jon Rothschild, London 1985.

2. Paul Valéry, 'Orientem Versus', *History and Politics*, New York 1962 (*Bollingen Series*, XLV.10), pp. 380–1.

3. We also have now an 'Islamic archaeology': Timothy Insoll, *The Archaeology of Islam*, Oxford 1999, proposes that there are 'Islamic' archaeological traces which find their unifying principle in the Muslim religion as a total and ineradicable 'way of life'. That the empirical evidence sketched in the book (on the domestic environment, dress, war, visual imagery and much else) indicates conclusions that are almost wholly and directly in contradiction to the basic proposition of the book, does not dent the spirited enthusiasm with which this proposition is repeated.

4. See Chapter 1.

5. I explore various facets of the relation between Islamism and universal irrationalism in politics throughout the course of this book.

6. Cf. Sascha Lehnarzt, 'Auch Muslime müssen müssen', *Frankfurter Allgemeine Zeitung*, 23 December 2001, p. 53.

7. Cf. Christopher Norris, *Uncritical Theory: Postmodernism, Intellectuals and the Gulf War*, London 1992.

8. Much uninformed writing has been devoted to this historically very complex notion by Islamist as well as by western authors. See the exemplary historical account of Mahmud al-Rahmuni, *al-Jihad. Min al-Hijra ila'-d-da`wa ila'd-dawla* [*Jihad: Emigration, Proselytism, State*], Beirut 2002.

9. Karl Mannheim, *Ideology and Utopia*, London 1966, pp. 215, 225 ff.

10. Cf. Richard D. Sonn, *Anarchism and Cultural Politics in Fin-de-Siècle France*, Lincoln and London 1989, pp. 263 ff.; Mark Juergenmeister, ed., *Violence*

*and the Sacred in the Modern World*, London 1992, pp. 106 ff. and passim.

11. Franklin L. Ford, 'Reflections on Political Murder: Europe in the Nineteenth and Twentieth Centuries', in Wolfgang Mommsen and Gerhard Hirschfeld eds, *Social Protest, Violence and Terror in Nineteenth- and Twentieth-Century Europe*, London 1982, pp. 182 and passim.

12. Cf. Sonn, *Anarchism and Cultural Politics*, p. 299.

13. Georg Wilhelm Friedrich Hegel, *Phänomenologie des Geistes*, eds Hans-Friedrich Wessels and Heinrich Clairmont, Hamburg 1988, pp. 387 ff., 130 ff. (English translation by A. V. Miller, *Phenomenology of the Spirit*, Oxford 1977, §§ 585-6, 184 ff.)

14. For instance, the memoir of a former member of one such group: Khaled al-Birri, *al-Dunya ajmal min al-janna* [*The World is Preferable Paradise*], Beirut 2001.

15. Cf. Roger Caillois, *L'homme et le sacré*, Paris 1950, pp. 223, 231 ff.

16. For instance, Roger Caillois, 'Guerre et sacré', *L'homme et le sacré*, Appendix III; Juergenmeister, ed., *Violence and the Sacred*, passim

17. See Brigitte Hamann, *Hitler's Vienna. A Dictator's Apprenticeship*, transl. Thomas Thornton, New York and Oxford 1999 pp. 206 ff., 236 ff.

18. E. B. Tylor, *The Origins of Culture*, Gloucester, MA 1970, p. 16.

19. Interview with Amos Oz in *Davar*, 17 December 1982. English translation is available at: http://www.counterpunch.org/pipermail/counterpunch-list/2001-September/01

20. Ibid.

21. For an exemplary analysis of a comparable phenomenon, see Aijaz Ahmad, 'Fascism and National Culture: Reading Gramsci in the Days of *Hindutva*', *Lineages of the Present: Ideology and Politics in Contemporary South Asia*, London 2000, ch. 5

22. Antonio Negri and Michael Hardt, *Empire*, Cambridge, MA pp. 13ff.

23. On the character of religious radicalism in Saudi Arabia, see Ali E. Hillal Dessouki, *Islamic Resurgence in the Arab World*, New York 1982, ch. 9; see also Chapter 8 of this book; and Mahmud A. Fakhash, *The Future of Islam in the Middle East*, Westport and London 1997, ch. 5. The best study of this and other aspects of Saudi Arabia remains Waddah Sharara, *Al-Ahl wa'l-ghanima: Muqawwimat as-siyasa fi'l-mamlaka al-ʿArabiya al-Suʿudiya* [*Clansmen and Booty: The Pillars of Politics in the Kingdom of Saudi Arabia*], Beirut 1981.

24. Cf. Serif Mardin, 1989, p. 118. A similar development took place in modern Buddhism and Judaism, and in other religions as well; see Aran, 1986, p. 122 and passim; and Swearer, 1991, pp. 649ff.

25. On this theme, see Aziz Al-Azmeh, 'The Middle East and Islam: a Ventriloqual Terrorism', in *Third World Affairs 1988*, London 1988, pp. 23–34.

26. Claude Lévi-Strauss, *The Savage Mind*, London 1966, ch. 5, passim.

27. See particularly Geoffrey Cubitt, *The Jesuit Myth: Conspiracy Theory and Politics in Nineteenth-Century France,* Oxford 1993, ch. 5, pp. 192–3 and passim.

28. This is perhaps most poignantly apparent in the cultural determinism of Margaret Mead, which has had a truly great impact in structuring cultural anthropology – a cultural determinism empirically built on an 'aberrant' construction of the object of her field-work in Samoa, a construction based upon the credulous

acceptance as serious of a prank played upon her by local adolescent girls, which 'produced such a spectacular result in centres of higher learning throughout the western world'. This 'wonderfully comic' matter is traced in detail in Derek Freeman, *Margaret Mead and the Heretic*, Harmondsworth 1996, pp. xiii, 107 and passim.

29. Note that I refer to Gellner specifically because he captures, with particular eloquence and limpidity, an increasingly firmer demotic mood, and expresses clearly and explicitly matters that others prefer to state more guardedly, and carries them with authority and with considerable ideological density outside the field of area studies and into general circulation.

30. Ernest Gellner, *Muslim Society*, Cambridge 1981, p. 62.

31. Quoted in Cubitt, *The Jesuit Myth* , p. 193.

32. On this constellation of topics, see Aziz Al-Azmeh, *Ibn Khaldun in Modern Scholarship*, London 1981, ch. 5.

33. Ernest Gellner, 'Mohammed and Modernity', in *The New Republic*, 5 December 1983, p. 22.

34. For ethnography, see particularly Martha Mundy, *Domestic Government*, I.B. Tauris, London 1995, especially pp. 52–54

35. Aziz Al-`Azma, *Al-`Ilmaniyya min manzur mukhtalif* [*Secularism from a New Perspective* ], Beirut 1992

36. See Chapter 2.

# Index